The Tyranny of Work

The Tyranny of Work

ALIENATION AND THE LABOUR PROCESS

Second Edition

James W. Rinehart
University of Western Ontario

with the assistance of Seymour Faber

Harcourt Brace Jovanovich, Canada
Toronto   Orlando   San Diego   London   Sydney

Canadian Cataloguing in Publication Data
Rinehart, James W., 1933-
    The tyranny of work : alienation and the
labour process

First ed. published: Don Mills, Ont. : Longman
Canada, 1975.
Bibliography: p.
Includes index.
ISBN 0-7747-3067-6

1. Work.   2. Labor and laboring classes.   3. Labor
and laboring classes—Canada.   I. Title.

HD4904.R55 1986   331   C86-095016-6

Edited by MICHAEL FEINDEL
Cover design by IVAN HOLMES DESIGN

The publishers wish to thank the following persons and organizations for permission to reproduce copyright material. Any errors or omissions brought to our attention will be corrected in future printings.

Extracts from *Working: People Talk About What They Do All Day and How They Feel About What They Do* by Studs Terkel, copyright © 1972, 1974 by Studs Terkel; reprinted by permission of Pantheon Books, a Division of Random House, Inc. Extracts from *Labor and Monopoly Capital: The Degradation of Work in the Twentieth Century* by Harry Braverman, copyright © 1974 by Harry Braverman and published by Monthly Review Press; reprinted by permission of Monthly Review Press. Extracts from "Autoworkers on the Firing Line," by Don Wells in *On the Job: Confronting the Labour Process in Canada*, edited by Craig Heron and Robert Storey, copyright © 1978 by McGill-Queen's University Press; reprinted by permission of McGill-Queen's University Press. Extracts from "Counterplanning on the Shop Floor" by Bill Watson from *Radical America*, Volume 5, Number 3, May–June 1971, copyright © 1971 by *Radical America*; reprinted by permission of *Radical America*.

Printed in Canada

1 2 3 4 5   91 90 89 88 87

Contents

Preface to the Second Edition

In the more than ten years since *The Tyranny of Work* first appeared the field of labour studies has grown enormously, thanks in no small part to Harry Braverman's now classic *Labor and Monopoly Capital*. Braverman's book amplified ideas and generated insights on the labour process that had lain dormant in the writings of Karl Marx. Despite certain analytic flaws, particularly the refusal to examine the consciousness and activity of workers, the popularity of *Labor and Monopoly Capital* transcended disciplinary lines and national boundaries. While Braverman's work left its imprint on Canadian labour studies, significant contributions to this area issued from a group of young and talented scholars whose approach to theory and research was more historically grounded than Braverman's analysis. Operating within a political economy perspective and representing several disciplines, these scholars began to construct Canadian labour studies upon a foundation whose key elements included the examination of political and economic developments, workers' activities, class struggles, and transformations of the labour process. This approach has matured rapidly, as evidenced by an impressive stock of theses, monographs, and collections of articles, as well as by the excellent materials published since 1976 in the journal *Labour/Le Travail*.

Prior to the completion of the first edition of *The Tyranny of Work*, only an abbreviated version of Braverman's book published in the *Monthly Review* was available, and the birth of *Labour/Le Travail* had not yet been celebrated. Over the past ten years or so, social, economic, and political developments and the outpouring of labour studies research meant that a second edition of *Tyranny* would necessarily entail much more than a cosmetic modification of the original. The scope and richness of these developments dictated selectivity—and I make no claim to having incorporated all the relevant materials.

Still, most chapters were altered substantially. While the new materials enabled me to provide a more detailed and nuanced description and analysis of activities, events, and trends, they contained no compelling logical or evidential bases for a major restructuring of the text's conceptual framework. Alienation is at least as pervasive today as it was a decade ago, and the constellation of sources of alienated labour—market forces, the capitalist division of labour, and narrowly held ownership and control of the means and ends of production—if anything have become more potent determinants of the organization and content of work.

Labour studies surged forward at the tail end of an era of progressive ideas and movements. Hopes for a better future were dashed by the onset of the world economic crisis in the mid-1970s and by the rise of neo-conservative ideologies, political forces, and governments. It is hard to be optimistic today. The goals of a democratically planned economy and worker-managed enterprises may seem more remote now than in the past, but the idea is no less compelling. I continue to believe that alienation is not inherent to the human condition, that human beings are not eternally doomed to toil under conditions of wage labour, and that ordinary people have the capacity and the desire to govern their own lives—on and off the job. These ideals inform the text of both editions of *The Tyranny of Work*.

The events of the past twelve years as well as the ideas of friends, colleagues, and students—too numerous to mention by name—have influenced this new edition. So too has the bi-annual Conference on Workers and Their Communities. Founded in the early 1970s to bring together labour-oriented people from trade unions, political organizations, and universities to share experiences and ideas, the Conference symbolizes the growth and vitality of Canadian labour studies and has been a continuing source of personal inspiration and knowledge. Finally, I would like to thank Keith Thompson of Harcourt Brace Jovanovich, Canada for convincing me to undertake the revisions for a second edition. I am also indebted to Chris Huxley for reading the revised manuscript and for offering at every point sound, constructive criticisms and advice.

Preface

Work is an enormously complex activity. To even begin to understand its complexities requires the use of theories or models, which always isolate and amplify some aspects of reality at the expense of others. I have chosen to examine the institution of work from the perspective of a theory of alienated labour. The central focus of this theory is power; the problem of alienated labour is inextricably bound to the issue of who determines the way work is organized and the purposes for which work is undertaken.

Conventional approaches to the study of work either completely ignore alienation, relegate it to the remote past, or locate it in an atypical segment of today's labour force. In contrast, a major theme of this book is that alienation is a *statistically normal* condition in modern society. This is not to suggest that some jobs are not better than others or that work is completely devoid of gratifications. Clearly, variations in the content and milieux of work do exist in contemporary society. At the same time, there is this striking sameness to work: The overwhelming majority of people—both those who wear blue collars and office personnel—do not exercise control over the process and purposes of their labour. It is this fact which must be grasped to comprehend work and its discontents. And it is this fact which establishes work as a major social problem, for the way work is structured is wasteful of human talent and impervious to human needs.

If only a handful of writers recognizes or admits that work adversely affects large numbers of people, fewer still believe that anything can be done to correct the problem. Troubles in the realm of labour are ordinarily viewed either as being inherent to the human condition or as an inevitable consequence of high technology. One of my objectives is to expose the fragile edifice of data and logic upon which such pessimistic beliefs are based. Unfortunately, many of that small group of academicians who reject the notion that discontents with work are an ineluctable feature of modern life lodge their faith in "top-down" solutions. In this book I have tried to show the weaknesses and dangers of schemes to reduce worker dissatisfaction that are formulated by an "intellectual" elite and addressed to the managerial elite. Alienation can only be overcome through the efforts of ordinary people to humanize and control the workplace and the community. That ordinary people have the ability and the desire to govern their own lives is a central tenet of this book, and one whose validity I have tried to demonstrate.

Acknowledgements are due to friends and colleagues who helped me write this book. First, I want to thank Seymour Faber. My initial interest in the sociology of work was stimulated by Seymour, and my orientation to the field was shaped by our discussions, which have spanned nearly a decade. Together we planned the contours of this book. And during the research and writing stages we engaged in a continuous dialogue over the substance of the manuscript. For critically evaluating sections of the manuscript I am indebted to Craig McKie, Joan Stelling, Peter Archibald, Richard Hamilton, Glenn Goodwin, Laura Hollingsworth, Lane Millet, and John Gartrell. For furnishing me with an insight into the complexity of history, particularly that of pre-industrial society, I am grateful to Donald Avery, Richard Alcorn, and José Igartua. I want to thank Peter Warrian for providing guidelines and sources for the study of the development of industrial capitalism in Canada. I am especially indebted to Bryan Palmer, who carefully read portions of the manuscript, offered valuable suggestions for revising them, and pointed out sources I otherwise would have overlooked. Thanks are also due to Judi Smith, who did minor editing and typed the manuscript. Finally, I want to thank Carol Rinehart for managing our household and for simply persevering during the period of time it took to write this book. While all of these people contributed materially to the manuscript, responsibility for its final form is my own.

1 Work as a Social Problem

Sooner or later, if we want a decent society—by which I don't mean a society glutted with commodities or one maintained in precarious equilibrium by overbuying and forced premature obsolescence—we are going to have to come face to face with the problem of work.
HARVEY SWADOS

WORK AS A CENTRAL HUMAN ACTIVITY

Work has always been a central human activity and one which differentiates mankind from all other forms of life. Only humans can take raw materials from the environment, transform them, and in the process change their own conditions of existence. By changing the world they live in through labour, human beings at the same time alter their own nature, for the lives of people are influenced both by what they produce and how they produce. As we develop the means to cope with and control the physical environment in order to satisfy basic needs, we simultaneously produce the very conditions that create new needs and aspirations, as well as new ideas, traditions, and institutions.

Work has always had a profound impact on the lives of those who perform it. How could it be otherwise? Today adults ordinarily spend at least one-third of their waking hours on the job. What people do during these hours often penetrates to the very core of their personalities. Work can offer a sense of accomplishment or meaninglessness; it can be a source of pride or shame. And an activity which consumes such a large portion of time cannot help but spill over into non-work spheres of life. How people work affects the way in which they spend their time away from work, for it places constraints on the enjoyment of "free time" and conditions the overall mode of adjustment to life.

IDENTIFYING WORK AS A SOCIAL PROBLEM

We know that work is a central human activity, but is it also a social problem? Whenever large numbers of people are adversely affected by a social condition we can speak of the objective existence of a social problem, that is, the undesirable condition exists independent of the recognition of it as problematic.[1] It is one of the main objectives of this book to reveal the manner in which the nature and organization of work have adversely affected Canadian people both in the modern era and the pre-industrial period. But there is another important dimension to social problems. The manifold consequences of any social problem, particularly those that prod individuals to rebel or to seek reforms, are only fully operative when an objectively undesirable situation comes to be perceived as such and regarded as amenable to change. In the brief discussion that follows, we examine in broad terms variations in the extent to which work has been perceived as a problematic condition and the socio-historical circumstances that influenced this recognition among groups of people differentially located in the class structure of this society.

Since its inception in the latter part of the nineteenth century, industrial capitalism and the organization of work associated with it have generated continuing protests from working people. Initially, grievances centred around the excesses of the new industrial order—child labour, low wages, long hours, harsh discipline, and physically debilitating and dangerous conditions. Ultimately, individuals advantageously located in the class structure were compelled to recognize the legitimacy of workers' complaints, and some of the most blatant excesses of the industrial system were corrected through legislation.

As the twentieth century progressed, workers continued to press for changes in their terms and conditions of employment. Government and employers just as persistently sought to contain or suppress expressions of discontent, while academicians

1. A conceptual analysis of the term "social problems" is contained in Richard L. and Anne-Marie Henshel, *Perspectives on Social Problems*, Second Edition, Don Mills: Academic Press, 1983.

virtually ignored them.[2]   Officially, work was no longer regarded as genuinely problematic, since the conditions under
which it was carried out had been improved by legislative
action. If problems were recognized at all, they were seen as
deriving from workers and their responses to work rather than
from the nature of work itself. "Defective" traits such as
laziness, low intelligence, or lack of respect for authority were
attributed to those who protested against their conditions of
employment.[3] There was also a complementary belief: protests
were explained away by reference to agitators (often of foreign
extraction) who played on the emotions of "irrational" workers
to *artificially* create crises.

Work resurfaced as a critical and officially recognized social
problem during the Great Depression. Naturally, the major
concerns during this period were jobs and economic security.
With the economic recovery brought on by World War II and
the enactment of welfare state programs—such as unemployment compensation, health care insurance, and old age pen-
sions—and legislation guaranteeing labour the right to collective bargaining, the average Canadian was now protected from
the *immediate* threat of being unable to provide for his or her
family. Work again was seen by many as non-problematic.

2. The silence of academics on this issue has been pointed out by Stuart
Jamieson: "One is led to suspect that there has been a sort of 'conspiracy of
silence' about the whole subject of labour unrest and industrial conflict,
particularly of the more violent kind, in this country. Perhaps it would be
more realistic to say that Canadian historians and other social scientists have
had a mistaken or misguided image of Canadians as a people, and have
consciously or unconsciously contributed to perpetuating that misleading
image." See his *Times of Trouble: Labour Unrest and Industrial Conflict in
Canada, 1900–66,* Ottawa: Information Canada, 1971, p. 7. This long-standing
silence was shattered in the mid-1970s by young Canadian labour historians.
A good sample of their scholarship is now available in the journal *Labour/Le
Travail* (entitled *Labour/Le Travailleur* prior to 1984).
3. The practice of deflecting responsibility for social problems from socio-
economic institutions and organizations onto individuals who suffer from the
undesirable condition has been called by William Ryan "blaming the victim."
Such beliefs have been used to "explain" a wide range of social problems. It is
notable that victim-blaming (a) is most prevalent among persons not directly
affected by the adverse condition, (b) serves as a justification for maintaining
the status quo, and (c) eventuates in policies and programs geared to changing
individuals to fit the status quo rather than the reverse. See Ryan's *Blaming
the Victim,* New York: Vintage Books, 1972.

During the two decades following the depression the public was exposed to repeated pronouncements of the arrival of the affluent society in which the majority of people purportedly had attained—or at least were on the threshold of achieving— the comfortable trappings of the middle class. Moreover, a virtual explosion of white-collar jobs and the prospect of an automated society, which was scheduled to accelerate demand for highly trained scientists, technicians, and professionals, combined to obscure official awareness of problems generated by the nature of work. What these changes seemed to imply was the eventual elimination of the most unpleasant, mindless, and insecure jobs.

Only in the 1960s did it become abundantly clear that the "Just Society" was not about to materialize, and we were once again alerted to the full dimension of the problems of work. Poverty was "re-discovered." And the unemployment rate in Canada, which since the mid-1950s had been consistently higher than that of any other Western nation, served as a constant reminder that economic maintenance remained problematic for many people. Work stoppages intensified in the 1960s, culminating in a series of strikes which rocked the nation in 1965–66. The labour situation prompted the federal government to launch a comprehensive study of industrial relations in this country.[4] Other manifestations of labour unrest became particularly obvious during the sixties. Working to rule, tardiness, absenteeism, labour turnover, insubordination, and product sabotage reached epidemic proportions in some sections of the economy.

Unrest among working people continued to be a source of official apprehension in the 1970s. In 1973 provincial and federal cabinet ministers agreed to support a broad investigation seeking to uncover the causes of illegal work stoppages as well as the sources of job dissatisfaction. Senator David Croll, who directed the Senate's massive investigation of poverty in Canada, called for another special senate study—this time of the work ethic. Noting that Canadians are increasingly reluc-

---

4. This massive investigation entailed 72 separate studies. The results are summarized in *Canadian Industrial Relations: The Report of the Task Force on Labour Relations*, Ottawa: The Queen's Printer, 1969.

tant to take just any job, Croll warned that a technologically advanced society "makes work as a means to any end other than putting food on the table and paying the bills, most uninviting."[5] These official responses to labour unrest were accompanied by a growing number of accounts on the topic in the popular media and in reports of social scientists. *Canadian Forum, Fortune, Time, Canadian Business,* and *Newsweek* all featured articles probing the scope and sources of unrest among manual labourers.[6] But the problem of labour unrest was not restricted to blue-collar workers. *Fortune* magazine published an article with the revealing title, "The Fraying White Collar." *Weekend* magazine ran a feature on "white-collar factories" in Canada. The latter article examined the deteriorating market situation and working conditions of white-collar employees. The circumstances of working women became the focus of numerous books and government documents, including the 1970 Royal Commission Report on the Status of Women in Canada.

The world recession, which took hold in Canada around 1975, deepened as the years passed, and in the mid-1980s the economy showed only modest signs of recovery. Business leaders regarded inflation as the most insidious aspect of the recession and argued that increased government spending and higher workers' wages were the root of the problem. Attempting to restore the basis for highly profitable investment, the government raised interest rates, enacted wage-restraint measures, restricted collective bargaining, and slashed expenditures on social programs.[7] Among the predictable outcomes of this policy were a decline in real wages and soaring unemployment which, by 1985, affected nearly one and a half million Canadians. The seriousness of the situation prompted Catholic

5. Cited in the Toronto *Globe and Mail*, March 13, 1974.
6. Several books on labour unrest were also published at the time, including Harold L. Sheppard and Neal Herrick's *Where Have All the Robots Gone?*, New York: Free Press, 1972.
7. *Cf.* John Calvert, *Government Limited: The Corporate Takeover of the Public Sector in Canada*, Ottawa: Canadian Centre for Policy Alternatives, 1984; Leo Panitch and Donald Swartz, "Towards Permanent Exceptionalism: Coercion and Consensus in Canadian Industrial Relations," *Labour/Le Travail*, 13, 1984, pp. 133–157.

bishops to issue a stinging indictment of our economic system and of government nostrums that deliberately sacrificed jobs for corporate profits.[8]

Job insecurity discouraged workers from any dramatic non-organizational expression of their discontents, which were now manifested in more subtle ways, like simple indifference to work. And although unions were forced by economic circumstances to adopt a more defensive approach, they still represented a force to contend with for management. These continuing problems led, particularly in the mid-1970s, to the emergence of various groups (including management consultants, personnel departments in large firms, university bodies, and government centres) that promoted reforms to improve working conditions. These "Quality of Work Life" initiatives were ostensibly oriented to making work a more satisfying experience. Yet underlying these reformist efforts was an attempt to restore corporate competitiveness and profitability: only by overcoming workers' resistance and union opposition could management expect to increase productivity.

Over the past several decades, the work situation of women, in and out of the home, has been another focal point of resentment and pressure for change. Throughout this century, more and more females have sought paid jobs, and by 1980 the majority of women in Canada were active in the labour force. Their presence is most evident in subordinate office jobs and in "women's jobs," such as elementary school teaching, nursing, and restaurant work, which entail functions similar to those that women have performed in the home. However, a growing number of women today are not content to limit themselves to their traditionally defined roles as housewives and workplace subordinates. Nor are they satisfied to accept "women's jobs," wage discrimination, and the lack of opportunities for advancement.[9]

---

8. Canadian Conference of Catholic Bishops, *Ethical Reflections on the Economic Crisis*, Episcopal Commission for Social Affairs, January, 1983.
9. Pat Armstrong and Hugh Armstrong, *The Double Ghetto: Canadian Women and Their Segregated Work*, Toronto: McClelland and Stewart, 1984; Bonnie Fox, *Hidden in the Household: Women's Domestic Labour Under Capitalism*, Toronto: The Women's Press, 1980; Meg Luxton, *More Than a Labour of Love*, Toronto: Women's Press, 1980; Paul Phillips and Erin Phillips, *Women and*

WORK: ITS FUNCTIONS AND MEANINGS

To understand the problematic aspects of work we must initially seek to establish its personal and social ramifications.[10] The most obvious function of work is an economic one. Throughout history, labour has been intimately linked with the provision of goods and services (and income) essential to the maintenance of human life. Today, one's occupation determines the extent to which life will be consumed by a struggle for maintenance. The availability of work and the differential economic rewards attached to occupations establish differential life chances and opportunities—to receive a decent education, to be healthy, to enjoy leisure activities, and in general to maintain oneself and one's family in a manner commensurate with acceptable community standards of living. Today, a substantial number of individuals are leaning towards an *instrumental* orientation to work. They feel that the basic reason for working is to maintain themselves and their families in order to do the things they "really enjoy." Life for these people begins when work ends.

While work in contemporary society retains its function and meaning of sustaining life, it has a significance which goes far beyond survival and the size of one's paycheque. How else are we to comprehend research which repeatedly demonstrates the tragic consequences of being without work? Unemployment erodes personal relationships and creates feelings of disorienta-

---

Work: Inequality in the Labour Market, Toronto: James Lorimer, 1983.
10. There is no consensus on the definition of work. Nels Anderson defines it as "continuous employment in the production of goods and services for remuneration." See his *Dimensions of Work,* New York: David McKay Company, 1964, p. 11. We, on the other hand, believe it is misleading to insist that only activities resulting in wages or salaries constitute work: we view work as any activity that entails the provision of goods and services for others. Despite our broad usage, this book concentrates on paid labour. As a consequence, we do not discuss the critically important areas of women's unpaid labour in the household or their role in the reproduction of labour power. (We recognize, however, that unpaid labour can sometimes merge into paid work, as in the case of women who contribute directly to household revenues by taking in children, boarders, and laundry.)

tion, despair, and worthlessness.[11] And if money were the only concern of individuals, there would be no explanation for the 35 000 persons in Toronto who worked at jobs that paid less than what they would earn if they quit and went on welfare.[12] Nor can the imputation of purely economic motivations account for the results of a major American survey which revealed that 80 percent of respondents, when asked if they would continue to work if they inherited enough money to live comfortably without working, claimed they would keep working. This finding might suggest that we have inflated the problematic aspects of work; if work is so bad why are people attached to it? On the contrary, when asked to elaborate on their answers, most respondents to the survey said they worked either to "keep occupied" or, what boils down to the same thing, to keep from becoming bored or idle.[13] Work as an activity, it seems, is preferable to no activity at all.

The persistent demand for work, any work, is only weakly explained by the contemporary grip of the Protestant work ethic. The Protestant ethic linked sacred and secular worlds by regarding success at work as an indication of salvation and avoidance of work as a sign of damnation. Max Weber, who wrote the classic statement on the subject, argued that the Protestant ethic facilitated the development of capitalism in the Western world. But even at the time of publication of the essay in 1904, Weber observed that the religious ethic was giving way to more secular justifications of work.[14] Today work is connected to a secular version of the Protestant ethic. Only persons who hold jobs are believed to be morally fit and deserving of an

11. This point has been amply documented. See E. Wight Bakke, *The Unemployed Worker*, New Haven: Yale University Press, 1940; L.M. Grayson and Michael Bliss, eds., *The Wretched of Canada*, Toronto: University of Toronto Press, 1971; David Dwyer, "Plant Shutdown: An Examination of the Human Consequences," M.A. Thesis, University of Western Ontario, 1984; J. Paul Grayson, *Corporate Strategies and Plant Closures: The SKF Experience*, Toronto: Our Times, 1986.
12. This figure was cited in 1971 by John Anderson, Metropolitan Toronto's Welfare Commissioner, to the Senate Committee on Poverty.
13. Nancy C. Morse and R.S. Weiss, "The Function and Meaning of Work and the Job," *American Sociological Review*, 20, 1955, pp. 191–198.
14. Max Weber, *The Protestant Ethic and the Spirit of Capitalism*, New York: Charles Scribner's Sons, 1930.

adequate income. This morality is captured in the derogatory labels ("welfare bum") applied to people who do not work. Individuals who hold steady jobs are evaluated, and often evaluate themselves, as better than those who do not work.[15]

Among persons who do have jobs, self-esteem is differentially distributed along the occupational spectrum. Traditionally, honour has been accorded to those who work in offices and wear white collars; the higher one's position in the office hierarchy, the more prestige accompanies it. Manual labour comes off a poor second in comparison. That these judgments often are shared by manual workers themselves has been documented by Sennett and Cobb.[16] Through intensive interviews, the authors uncovered a tragic sense of failure and self-degradation among working-class people. The depth of such feelings was shown by parents' efforts to ensure that their children would become *unlike* themselves. Working-class adults, Sennett and Cobb declare, "don't ask the child to take the parents' lives as a model but as a warning." Given these facts, it is not surprising to learn that people seek jobs with which they can identify and from which they can derive a favourable self-image. "What workers want most, as more than 100 studies in the past 20 years show, is to become masters of their immediate environment and to feel that their work and themselves are important—the twin ingredients of self-esteem."[17]

Another important dimension of work revolves around its social purposes. People derive satisfaction from being involved in work that demonstrably contributes to human well-being. In this case, gratification is based on the products and services of labour rather than on the labour process and the conditions under which it is undertaken. Such a concern is most evident immediately following successful popular revolutions. In his

15. See Angela Wei Djao, "The Welfare State and Its Ideology," in John Fry, ed., *Economy, Class and Social Reality: Issues in Contemporary Canadian Society*, Toronto: Butterworths, 1979, pp. 300–315.
16. Richard Sennett and Jonathan Cobb, *The Hidden Injuries of Class*, New York: Knopf, 1973.
17. U.S. Department of Health, Education, & Welfare, *Work in America: Report of a Special Task Force to the Secretary of Health, Education, & Welfare*, Cambridge: MIT Press, 1973, p. 19.

interviews with post-revolution Cuban workers, for example, Zeitlin found that they stressed the importance of participating in the construction of a new society in which materials were produced for the good of the community rather than for personal profit. One Cuban worker explained his new-found commitment in this way: "Before, I worked for another individual or for a company. Now I work for the people, that is, to provide hospitals, houses, et cetera, and whatever else the country needs most."[18] Identification with work that has a clear social purpose is not just generated in moments of revolutionary enthusiasm. This concern is an ordinary expression of ordinary people. For instance, a city fireman says:

> *I worked in a bank. You know, it's just paper. It's not real. Nine to five and it's shit. You're lookin' at numbers. But I can look back and say, "I helped put out a fire. I helped save somebody." It shows something I did on this earth.*[19]

Up to this point the discussion has dealt with *extrinsic* work rewards, that is, gratifications which are attached to but not an integral part of the work process itself. But work can also be an *intrinsically* gratifying activity. People often express a desire for jobs that are challenging, meaningful, and conducive to self-development and self-fulfillment. The industrial psychologist, J.A.C. Brown, has observed that most people would argue that one of the most basic satisfactions to be gained from work is the feeling of pride and achievement at having accomplished something.[20] There appears to be a growing tendency for people to expect jobs to be intrinsically worthwhile. "An increasing number of workers want more autonomy in tackling their tasks, greater opportunity for increasing their skills, rewards that are directly connected to the intrinsic aspects of work, and

18. Maurice Zeitlin, *Revolutionary Politics and the Cuban Working Class*, New York: Harper Torchbooks, 1970, p. 207.
19. Studs Terkel, *Working*, New York: Pantheon Books, 1974, p. 589.
20. J.A.C. Brown, *The Social Psychology of Industry*, Harmondsworth: Penguin Books, 1954, p. 205.

greater participation in the design of work and the formulation of tasks."[21]

It is apparent that people attach both economic and intrinsic significance to work. These are not necessarily contradictory orientations. The purely economic orientation to work is a practical and rational response to the way work is structured in contemporary society.[22] When work offers few gratifications, it is reasonable to expect that people will seek fulfillment and pleasure in other spheres of life. But "free time" and leisure also seem to fall short of providing meaningful satisfactions. People, therefore, are drawn back to work, any work, in order to "kill time." Moreover, emphasizing monetary rewards and seeking fulfillment off the job are not inconsistent with the presence of intense aspirations for a job that is personally absorbing and worthwhile. The instrumental response is practical—a reaction to what is; the other is a yearning for what work could be.

Most jobs as they are presently structured do not satisfy many of the needs and aspirations of the individuals who hold them. The central question is: What has happened to make an "important, necessary, and potentially pleasurable social activity which is capable of satisfying both material and psychological human needs into a source of strife, resentment, and boredom"?[23] Our main interest is to answer this question by seeking the root causes of discontent with work. Stated in more general terms, the problem of work is inextricably related to the issues of freedom and alienation. In the chapters which follow we define and discuss the concept of alienation and trace the historical conditions responsible for the intensification of alienated labour in Canadian society.

21. *Work in America, op. cit.,* p. 13.
22. For evidence on this point see Malcolm H. MacKinnon, "The Industrial Worker and the Job: Alienated or Instrumentalized?", in Katherina Lundy and Barbara Warme, eds., *Working in the Canadian Context*, Toronto: Butterworths, 1981, pp. 255–275.
23. J.A.C. Brown, *op. cit.,* p. 189.

2 Alienation and its Sources

Work and its discontents can be best understood when placed within a theoretical framework centring around the concept of alienation. The development of this term can be attributed to Karl Marx, who used it to describe and interpret the organization of work that emerged with industrial capitalism. His most comprehensive discussion of alienated labour was set forth in the *Economic and Philosophic Manuscripts of 1844*.[1]

According to Marx, there are four aspects of alienated labour. First, this condition entails an estrangement of working people from the products of their labour. The product—the purpose for which it is created, how it is disposed of, its content, quality, and quantity—is not determined by those whose labour is responsible for its manufacture. Under industrial capitalism, workers are obliged to surrender their power to determine the product of labour via a wage contract which in effect gives this power over to employers, that is, the capitalist class. The ends of capitalist production are not defined by the needs and interests of ordinary people but by employers' needs to generate profits and expand capital.[2]

Because the products of labour are determined by employers rather than by workers, it is employers who reap most of the

1. Moscow: Foreign Languages Publishing House, 1961.
2. This is not to say that some needs are not met; but when commodities do satisfy some portion of peoples' wants, this is a by-product of the system rather than its principal objective.

benefits of productive activity. Even when working people experience absolute gains in their standard of living, their position, relative to that of capitalists, deteriorates. Marx wrote: "It follows therefore that in proportion as capital accumulates, the lot of the labourer, be *his payments high or low,* must grow worse."[3] Because products are under the control of owners of the means of production, increases in labour output such as those resulting from scientific advances, technological innovations, and refinements in the social organization of the workplace, accrue to the benefit of the propertied class. "The increase in the quantity of objects," Marx observed, "is accompanied by an *extension* of the realm of alien powers to which man is subjected."[4] Intensified productivity, then, extends and deepens the alienated position of workers in the system of production; it simultaneously stretches out the class system by increasing the political and economic gulf which separates workers and capitalists.[5]

If working people are estranged from the products of labour, they must also be alienated from the work process itself, that is, from their own labour activity. As Marx wrote, "the external character of labour for the workers appears in the fact that it is not his own but someone else's, that it does not belong to him, but to another."[6] Just as workers must give up their power to control the product of their toil, they also cede their ability to determine the intensity and duration of work, to define the manner in which work is organized, divided, and allocated, and to determine the tools and machines used in the production

3. Karl Marx, *Capital,* Vol. I, London: Lawrence and Wishart, 1974, p. 604. (Italics added.)
4. Cited in Istvan Mészáros, *Marx's Theory of Alienation,* New York: Harper Torchbooks, 1972, p. 156.
5. The magnitude of the disparity in wealth and power of working people and capitalists is staggering. A rough estimate of the discrepancy could be obtained by comparing the net holdings of the working class with those of the capitalist class, which in the case of the latter must include not only their personal net worth but the factories, utilities, financial institutions, military establishments, etc., that they control and that are used to further their interests. *Cf.* Martin Nicolaus, "The Unknown Marx," in Carl Oglesby, ed., *The New Left Reader,* New York: Grove Press, 1969, pp. 84–110.
6. *Economic and Philosophic Manuscripts of 1844, op. cit.,* pp. 72–73.

process. Furthermore, it is the employer who decides whether or not work will be performed at all.

From the fact that working people are estranged from the process and product of labour, Marx deduced two more aspects of alienation. The first one, self-estrangement, is tied to his conception of the meaning and purpose of work, which he viewed as *the* medium for self-expression and self-development. Work, Marx said, was the activity in which people can most clearly manifest their unique qualities as human beings. Properly organized, work brings out and reflects distinctively human attributes, that is, those which differentiate humans from all other species. It is through labour that humans should be able to shape themselves and the society in which they live in accordance with their own needs, interests, and values. Under alienating circumstances, however, work becomes not an endeavour which embodies and personifies life, not a source of personal and social gratification, but simply a means for physical survival. Marx argues that working people come to feel most contented in those activities that they share with all other living species—in procreation, drinking, and eating—in a word, in the satisfaction of physiological needs, while in their peculiarly human activity—work—people feel debased. Accordingly, work takes on an instrumental meaning: it is regarded simply as a means to an end. Individuals, then, are estranged from themselves; they are alienated from their own humanity.

The final type of alienation deals with the relationship of individuals to one another. Marx believed that people who occupy dominant and subordinate positions at the workplace are alienated from each other. Their relationship is an antagonistic one and is based purely on pecuniary considerations. This asymmetry of workplace relationships creates the foundation for a class structure that entails sharp differences in power, privilege, and life chances, and that inhibits social intercourse across class lines. Marcuse argues that "the system of capitalism relates men to each other through the commodities they exchange. The social standing of individuals, their standard of living, the satisfaction of their needs, their freedom, and their power are all determined by the value of their commodities."[7] Alienation obviously characterizes the relationship between classes, but it also penetrates the interaction of people in the same class. Capitalists are compelled to drive out their competitors, and workers must competitively sell their labour power— their skills, talents, and energies—in order to survive.[8] This necessity leads to or exacerbates divisions within the working class, most notably along the lines of sex, age, and ethnicity.

Marx's most succinct statement on the meaning of alienation is contained in his essay, "Wage Labour and Capital." The elegance and power of the passage make it worth quoting at length.

> But the exercise of labour power, labour, is the worker's own life-activity, the manifestation of his own life. And this life-activity he sells to another person in order to secure the necessary means of subsistence. Thus his life-activity is for him only a means to enable him to exist. He works in order to live. He does not even reckon labour as part of his life, it is rather a sacrifice of his life. It is a commodity which he has made over to another. Hence, also the product of his activity is not the object of his activity. What he produces for himself is not the silk that he weaves, not the gold that he draws from the mine, not the palace that he builds. What he produces for himself is wages, and silk, gold, palace, resolve themselves for him into a definite quantity of the means of subsistence, perhaps into a cotton jacket, some copper coins and a lodging in a cellar. And the worker, who for twelve hours weaves, spins, drills, turns, builds, shovels, breaks stones,

---

7. Herbert Marcuse, *Reason and Revolution*, Boston: Beacon Press, 1968, p. 279.
8. "Labour power" refers to the human capacity for labour and consists of the mental and physical capabilities we exercise in the production of useful goods and services. The term "labour process," which appears throughout this book, is defined as the process "by which raw materials are transformed by human labour, acting on the objects with tools and machinery: first into products for use and, under capitalism, into commodities to be exchanged on the market." See Paul Thompson, *The Nature of Work: An Introduction to Debates on the Labour Process*, London: Macmillan, 1983, p. xv.

*carries loads, etc.—does he consider this twelve hours'
weaving, spinning, drilling, turning, building, shovelling,
stone breaking as a manifestation of his life, as life? On the
contrary, life begins for him where this activity ceases, at
table, in the public house, in bed. The twelve hours'
labour, on the other hand, has no meaning for him as
weaving, spinning, drilling, etc., but as earnings, which
bring him to the table, to the public house, into bed. If the
silk worm were to spin in order to continue its existence as
a caterpillar, it would be a complete wage-worker.*[9]

Since Marx's time, the concept of alienation has been broadened to apply to a bewildering array of disadvantaged groups,
deviant behaviours, and aberrant mental states. After examining the literature on the subject one writer concluded that the
term "has been used in such a variety of ways that it comes
close to being a shorthand expression for all the socially based
psychological maladies of modern man."[10] Despite this me-
lange, there are two ideas that are common to most usages of
the concept. Alienation always entails a notion of human
estrangement—from persons, objects, values, or from oneself.
Second, the source of alienation is seen as residing in the social
structure rather than in individual personalities; its causes are
social rather than psychological. Our usage of alienation retains the notions of estrangement and social causation. At the
same time, we follow Marx in viewing alienation as characteristic of a certain kind of organization of work, one whose source
lies primarily in the special set of socio-economic circumstances that accompanied the development of industrial capitalism.

When we speak of alienation in this book we are referring to
a condition in which individuals have little or no control over
(a) the purposes and products of the labour process, (b) the
overall organization of the workplace, and (c) the immediate

9. *Karl Marx and Frederick Engels: Selected Works*, Moscow: Progress Publishers, 1970, p. 74.
10. William A. Faunce, *Problems of an Industrial Society*, Second Edition, New
York: McGraw Hill, 1981, p. 134.

work process itself.[11] Defined this way, alienation is objective or structural in the sense that it is built into human relationships at the workplace and exists independent of how individuals perceive and evaluate their jobs. Alienation, then, can be viewed broadly as a condition of objective powerlessness.[12] As long as alienation is conceptualized purely as a structural phenomenon, observers of different ideological persuasions would probably agree that some work settings are more alienating than others. The consensus would disappear if these same observers were asked to assess the extent to which workers in objectively alienating situations *feel* and *experience* alienation.

Structural alienation means that work is not organized in accordance with the needs and interests, talents and abilities of working people. However, a complex set of psychological, cultural, and social forces influence the degree to which individuals *recognize* the sources of alienation, *adapt* to alienating work, and *express*—verbally and behaviourally—their disenchantment with work. Obviously, not all working people are conscious of their alienated position in work organizations in the sense that they are able to locate and articulate the socio-economic factors responsible for it. But all workers in objectively powerless circumstances do possess an *alienated consciousness* in that they directly experience and are acutely aware of the *effects* of structural alienation, such as repetitive and insecure jobs, insufficient wages, and arbitrary work rules. The test of the existence of alienated mental states is to be found not so much in the ability of individuals to articulate the causes of alienation, but primarily in their verbal and behav-

11. Alienation from the purposes and products of labour involves the question of whether the basic aim of production is profit or the satisfaction of human needs, and as a related question, what will be produced and for whom. Alienation from the organization of production entails issues like the allocation of jobs, employment policy, work rules, organization of the flow of work, the purchase of machinery, etc. The referent of the final dimension is the worker's specific job. Relevant considerations here are the pace of work, freedom of movement about the workplace, the choice of work techniques, etc.

12. While unequal power is at the root of alienation, for the most part power is neither sought nor maintained for its own sake. Under capitalism, for example, power enables those who hold it to extract economic surpluses from workers and to monopolize wealth and privilege.

ioural reactions to work. One of the objectives of this book is to assess how and the extent to which structural alienation penetrates the consciousness of working people.[13]

SOURCES OF ALIENATION

We can single out three major sources of alienated labour—concentration of the means of production in the hands of a small but dominant class, markets in land, labour, and commodities, and an elaborate division of labour. While the precise manner in which each of these factors contributes to alienation will be related in the subsequent chapter, a brief explanation of each is required at this point.

The alienating impact of elite ownership of the means of production is direct and obvious. If relatively few individuals control the productive apparatus, they will operate it to their own advantage. The majority of people, who will be obliged to work for the few, will be excluded from determining the products and the labour process.[14] The relationship between wage labour and capital is also an *exploitative* one, in so far as employers extract unpaid labour from working people. A major source of business profits is the appropriation by employers of

13. We believe that behavioural responses to work are more valid indicators of subjective alienation than verbal statements, although we do not entirely discount the latter. We are particularly suspicious of social scientists' efforts to measure alienation via fixed-alternative questions that ask people to state how satisfied they are with their jobs on a scale ranging from "very satisfied" to "very dissatisfied." It is quite likely that "satisfied" responses simply mean that individuals are satisfied *relative to job opportunities available to them*. Given the realistic range of jobs open to a worker, his or her present job may be the best of a bad lot. For an incisive critique of this technique see Robert L. Kahn, "The Meaning of Work: Interpretation and Proposals for Measurement," in Angus Campbell and Philip E. Converse, eds., *The Human Meaning of Social Change*, New York: Russell Sage Foundation, 1972, pp. 159–203. Also see James W. Rinehart, "Contradictions of Work-Related Attitudes and Behaviour: An Interpretation," *Canadian Review of Sociology and Anthropology*, 13, 1978, pp. 1–15; W. Peter Archibald, *Social Psychology as Political Economy*, Toronto: McGraw-Hill Ryerson, 1978.
14. In Western societies the basis of elite control of the means of production is private property, which confers on owners the legal right to use property as they see fit. In the Soviet Union and Eastern Europe, the means and ends of production are controlled by the upper echelons of the Communist Party. *Cf.* Milovan Djilas, *The New Class*, New York: Frederick A. Praeger, 1957.

surplus value, which is the difference between the value of commodities and services produced or provided by workers and the wage cost of maintaining these workers. Workers are required to remain at work beyond the point when they have produced an amount equal to their wages. During these unpaid hours a surplus (surplus value) is produced. Employers appropriate this surplus and reinvest a portion of it in the business in order to further expand their profits. This relationship of alienation and exploitation establishes the basis for permanent antagonisms between wage labour and capital. In their drive to generate profits and expand capital, employers strive to keep wages low, introduce labour-replacing machinery, and speed up, routinize, and control work. For their part, workers seek job security, adequate wages, the reduction of work time, and control over the labour process.[15]

The term "market" refers to an economic arrangement in which the distribution and use of land, the production of goods and services, and the income and security of individuals are regulated by money and prices, operating through supply and demand and subject to the relative power of buyers and sellers, employers and employees, and creditors and debtors.[16] A market society places land, labour, and commodity production under the domain of prices. Prices and profits become the ultimate determinants of the means and ends of production, and people are compelled to make decisions based on calculations of pecuniary gain. Business firms must take whatever steps are necessary to accumulate capital or to simply stay afloat. Consequently, human considerations are secondary to those of profitability. From the point of view of the employer workers represent merely another cost of production and are evaluated as commodities like any other object that is bought and sold.

The division of labour also exerts an alienating impact on work. While there are a number of different types of the division of labour, the most important ones are specialization

15. Karl Marx, *Capital, op. cit.*, pp. 173–221.
16. As Karl Polanyi notes, markets were never more than incidental to the economies of pre-capitalist societies. See his *The Great Transformation*, Boston: Beacon Press, 1957.

and the separation of mental and manual labour, or more accurately stated, the separation of the conception of work from its performance. Specialization is a twofold process which entails a fragmentation of work into minute tasks and the permanent assignment of these tasks to specific individuals. Performed under such conditions, work becomes repetitive and mindless and narrowly circumscribes the development of human capacities. Although the separation of the conception and performance of work is only one type of specialization, we discuss it separately because it is the most salient form of labour division in terms of its consequences for alienation. In this case, certain individuals are responsible for the organization, conceptualization, and design of work, while others are assigned to the role of carrying out the tasks.

The structure and consequences of the three sources of alienation can be analyzed separately, but what must be stressed is their interdependence. With the rise of industrial capitalism each one stimulated the development of the other two. While markets and the division of labour antedated the industrial revolution, industrial capitalists intensified the fragmentation of work and stimulated the expansion of domestic and international markets. In turn, the greater productivity and profits made possible by the extended division of labour and the growth of consumer demand, in conjunction with mergers and the bankruptcy of non-competitive firms, contributed to the concentration of the means of production in fewer and fewer hands.

TECHNOLOGY AND INDUSTRIALISM

All too often the three factors discussed above are ignored, and alienated labour in modern society, if recognized at all, is regarded either as a permanent feature of the human condition or as the inevitable price we pay for the benefits of industrial technology. One way of evaluating the first thesis—that alienation transcends socio-historical boundaries—is to review the anthropological materials on the subject of work. Even a cursory perusal of these data reveals situations that are completely different from our own. In peasant and primitive societies work is an integral and not unpleasant aspect of existence. Work is fused with the totality of activities carried out by the community; it is embedded in and permeated by family and community relationships and obligations. Instead of being viewed as an onerous necessity by those who perform it, work is often regarded as indistinguishable from play, sociability, and leisure.[17]

It may come as a surprise to some readers that technology, mechanization, or industrialism have not been included among the causes of alienated labour. Many scholars who acknowledge the presence of serious discontents with work in modern societies attribute the problem to sophisticated technology, which allegedly requires centralization of knowledge and authority and a detailed division of labour. We reject, for example, the position of writers such as Clark Kerr, who views a given level of technology as bearing organizational imperatives that operate independent of the social, economic, and political milieux in which technology is embedded.[18] This position of technological determinism cannot be sustained. At a given level of technological development, wide variations in alienation still exist in relation to the different ways in which production is socially organized. Alienation is *created* not by the existing state of technology and productive capacity but, as Edwards and his associates realize, by "the power relations in society which, for example, dictate the ends of productive effort, the use to which technology is to be put, and the very criteria by which some technologies are methodically developed and others left dormant and undeveloped."[19] The primary causes of alienation, then, reside in the social relations of production and

---

17. *Cf.* George Dalton, ed., *Tribal and Peasant Economies,* Garden City: The Natural History Press, 1967; Marshall Sahlins, *Stone Age Economics,* New York: Aldine-Atherton, 1972. For further discussion of this point see Chapter 6.
18. *Cf.* Clark Kerr, John T. Dunlop, Frederick Harbison, and Charles A. Myers, *Industrialism and Industrial Man,* Cambridge: Harvard University Press, 1960.
19. Richard C. Edwards, Michael Reich, and Thomas E. Weisskopf, eds., *The Capitalist System,* Englewood Cliffs: Prentice-Hall, 1972, p. 3. One illustration of the independence of alienated labour and technology is the transformation of Canadian Eskimo carving. In traditional Inuit society objects were carved

particularly in relations of domination and subordination which give to the few the ability to direct and shape production to their own ends.[20]

Under capitalism, the development and selection of technology are guided not only by the goals of productivity and profitability, but also by employers' and managers' determination to minimize workers' control over the labour process.[21] Braverman states: "The capacity of humans to control the labour process through machinery is seized upon by management from the beginning of capitalism as the *prime means whereby production may be controlled not by the direct*

---

for decoration, use in games, religious purposes, or self-amusement. However, over a long period of time the nature and functions of Eskimo carving were transformed through contact with white society. The change was accelerated around 1949 when the Canadian government began to encourage the development of a "carving industry" in order to provide a new income source for the Inuit. The result was a form of art which differed markedly from that which had prevailed in the remote past. The size, media, motif, and style of the carvings were shaped by government representatives so that the objects would appeal to the standards of taste of white society. From the point of view of our discussion of technology and alienation it is instructive to find out what happened to the modern Eskimo carver. In one study, 20 Inuit artists were interviewed. "With the exception of a seventeen year old boy who had made only three things in his life, and didn't mind it at all, all the others stated that they didn't like it, or that they hated carving. They went ahead at it in the realization that if they wanted money this was one of the few methods at hand for earning it. In this sense it happens to be a necessary occupation, but to the majority carving had become boring and mechanical." This study as well as a fascinating account of the development of Eskimo carving is contained in Charles A. Martijn, "Canadian Eskimo Carving in Historical Perspective," *Anthropos*, 59, 1964, pp. 546–596. The above quote is taken from page 570 of this article. We are grateful to Don Barr for bringing this case to our attention. For further discussion of technology, see Chapter 6.

20. The ideological implications of attributing alienation to technology per se or industrialism should be obvious. This common practice obscures and distorts the role of class relationships in creating and perpetuating alienation. It portrays technology as the villain and humans as helpless prisoners of the machine. Lewis Mumford writes: "It was because of certain traits of private capitalism that the machine—which was a neutral agent—has often served, and in fact has sometimes been, a malicious element in society, careless of human life, indifferent to human interest. The machine has suffered for the sins of capitalism; capitalism has often taken credit for the virtues of the machine." See *Technics and Civilization*, New York: Harcourt, Brace, 1934, p. 27.

21. *Cf.* David F. Noble, *Forces of Production: A Social History of Industrial Automation*, New York: Alfred A. Knopf, 1984.

producer but by the owners and representatives of capital. Thus, in addition to its technical function of increasing the productivity of labour—which would be a mark of machinery under any social system—machinery also has in the capitalist system the function of divesting the mass of workers of their control over their own labour."[22]

That the social relations of production are the primary cause of alienation does not mean that technology has no effect on workers. Some forms of technology are certainly more onerous to workers than others. The point we wish to stress is that technology's role in contributing to alienated labour is a derivative and secondary one.

22. Harry Braverman, *Labor and Monopoly Capital: The Degradation of Work in the Twentieth Century,* New York: Monthly Review Press, 1974, p. 193.

3   Alienation and the Development of Industrial Capitalism in Canada

Over the past one hundred years or so Western societies have undergone massive social changes that have fundamentally altered the way people work. While the three sources of alienation delineated in Chapter 2, when taken together, are almost synonymous with what we mean by the term industrial capitalism, they have followed unique developmental paths in different societies. Consequently, to understand how these factors have affected work in Canada requires an examination of Canadian history. The sections which follow trace the rise and development of industrial capitalism in Canada and its impact on work patterns. Special emphasis is placed on the manner in which changes in ownership, markets, and the division of labour have contributed to the intensification of alienation.

THE PRE-INDUSTRIAL SETTING

Prior to 1840 there were but few signs of the future industrial society. As a colony first of France and later of Great Britain, Canada was built up around the exploitation and export of natural resources. This economic emphasis persisted long into the nineteenth century. Although the dominant industries were trade in lumber, timber, and grain (the fur business was in a state of decline), the lives of the majority of nineteenth century Canadians were relatively untouched by the international trade in staples. The majority of the populace was engaged in agrarian pursuits; the family farm was the unit of production upon which a sizable proportion of inhabitants depended for a livelihood. The nexus of economic activity was the small rural village, which was virtually a self-contained economic unit. As late as the 1860s, Harris and Warkenton observe, pre-industrial methods of production and distribution made rural areas self-sufficient in most of the necessities of household and farm.[1]

The average farmer was only marginally linked to markets in agricultural produce. Wheat was grown as a cash crop, but between 1815 and 1850 it proved to be a highly unreliable source of income. Market ties were also attenuated by the fact that most farmers were unable to generate much of a surplus for sale.[2] Many household essentials were produced domestically. Farm families prepared their own soap, candles, and sugar, turned out clothing on handlooms, and fashioned their own ploughs and harrows.[3] Needs that could not be provided by domestic production were supplied by local artisans and tradesmen. The rural economy also had saw, grist, and fulling mills, breweries and distilleries, and small village workshops or *manufactories* where artisans, working with hand tools rather than machines, set their talents to the production of needed goods.[4] The economy of the period was rounded out by itinerant peddlers and craftsmen such as tailors and shoemakers. Barter was the prevalent mode of exchange in this local economy; articles produced or processed in village shops and mills typically were exchanged for payment in kind rather than for money.

The stability and harmony often attributed to rural life in

1. R. Cole Harris and John Warkenton, *Canada Before Confederation: A Study of Historical Geography,* Toronto: Oxford University Press, 1974.
2. *Cf.* Gary Teeple, "Land, Labour, and Capital in Pre-Confederation Canada," in Gary Teeple, ed., *Capitalism and the National Question in Canada,* Toronto: University of Toronto Press, 1972, pp. 43–66. There were variations in wheat production by region. Farmers in the Maritimes and the Western Interior and the habitants of Quebec's seigneuries commonly produced almost no surpluses. In contrast, the Eastern Townships of Quebec and Southern Ontario were much more prosperous. See Harris and Warkenton, *op.cit.*
3. *Cf.* J. Spelt, *The Urban Development in South-Central Ontario,* Assen: Koninkeyke Van Gorcum, 1955; Stanley B. Ryerson, *Unequal Union,* Toronto: Progress Books, 1973.
4. These enterprises were small, usually employing fewer than five people, and they catered to individuals in a limited geographic area. Most production was in response to personal orders from local inhabitants.

pre-industrial communities were upset in Canada by the presence of capitalist institutions. Pre-industrial capitalist formations created insecurity, dependency, and impoverishment in what was essentially a *petit bourgeois* society of small, independent producers.[5] One major source of instability was the pattern of land ownership. Land was concentrated in the hands of a few persons who amassed fortunes through market speculation.[6] As a result of land monopolies and land markets, large numbers of nineteenth century immigrants, who arrived in Canada virtually penniless, were prevented from purchasing land and establishing their independence. A second cause of instability was the political and economic dominance of a mercantile capitalist class. As the nineteenth century progressed, more and more farmers who relied on the adverse terms of credit advanced by merchants were reduced to indebtedness. Many were ultimately forced to sell their land. The hegemony of large land owners and mercantile capitalists drove or kept many individuals from ownership of the means of production. By the 1840s thousands of landless people were forced into dependent employment as farm labourers or workers on the construction of roads, canals, and railways. That many individuals were unsuccessful in the pursuit of land or jobs is evidenced by the high rate of transiency within Canada and by the large scale emigrations to the United States.[7]

5. This *petit bourgeois* label serves to broadly differentiate pre-industrial Canada from feudalism and capitalism. Canadian society of the period can be described this way despite the presence of a seigneurial system in Lower Canada. For evidence that the seigneurial system was closer to one of independent ownership than to feudal land tenure see Pierre Deffontaines, "The 'Rang' Pattern of Rural Settlement in French Canada," in Marcel Rioux and Yves Martin, eds., *French Canadian Society*, Vol. I, Toronto: McClelland and Stewart, 1970, pp. 3–19; Morden H. Long, *A History of the Canadian People*, Vol. I, Toronto: The Ryerson Press, 1942; R.C. Harris, *The Seigneurial System in Early Canada*, Madison: University of Wisconsin Press, 1966; J. Wallot, "Le Regime Seigneurial et Son Abolition Au Canada," *Canadian Historical Review*, 50, 1969, pp. 367–393.

6. *Cf.* Gustavus Myers, *A History of Canadian Wealth*, Toronto: James Lewis and Samuel, 1972, and Teeple, *op. cit.*

7. *Cf.* Teeple, *op. cit.*; Leo A. Johnson, "Land Policy, Population Growth and Social Structure in the Home District, 1793–1851," *Ontario History*, 63, 1971, pp. 41-60; David Gagnan and Herbert Mays, "Historical Demography and Canadian Social History: Families and Land in Peel County, Ontario," *Canadian Historical Review*, 14, 1973, pp. 27–47.

Despite the fact that capitalist institutions affected the lives of Canadians in the pre-industrial era, priorities of work and life were not ordered strictly in terms of economic criteria. Prices and profits were not the sole or decisive determinants of the means and ends of productive activity. The cultivation of the soil and the production of goods and services were guided by considerations of what was useful as well as by what could be exchanged on a profitable basis. Certainly, cultural factors influenced individuals' orientations to work and the market. Upper Canadians, with backgrounds predominantly in the British Isles, had been exposed in their native lands to the Protestant ethic and its positive enjoinment of hard work, frugality, and commercial success. Because of their exposure to these religious tenets, it is probably true that the relaxed and sporadic work patterns characteristic of other pre-industrial peoples found no strict parallel in Upper Canada.[8] Nevertheless, the structure of the pre-industrial economy dictated a rather casual adherence to the principle of economic rationality and the maximization of pecuniary gains. Local markets, lack of agricultural surpluses, domestic production, a barter system, and workshop and artisanal production geared to personal orders—all combined to form a matrix which inhibited the development of "economic man."

The undeveloped state of the market was accompanied by a rudimentary division of labour that was manifest in the limited number of occupational specialties and in the diversity of tasks performed by individual workers. The distinction between persons who worked with their hands and those who worked with their minds was not a sharp one. Moreover, work often allowed for a relatively broad use of talents and skills and required initiative and responsibility from the worker. Certainly, there were differences in the functions and duties of shop owners and clerks, craftsmen and apprentices, farm owners and farm workers. But in comparison to the intense specialization that accompanied the rise of industrial technol-

8. French Canadians were much less concerned with material success and were content to simply "get by." In this respect the attitudes and life styles of habitants were similar to those of most pre-industrial people.

ogy, the pre-industrial division of labour was much less detailed.

The early farm family could be described as a multi-faceted production unit whose members were not permanently saddled with performing a single task or a delimited set of operations. In addition to the diverse skills required by agricultural production, people became proficient at a large number of different kinds of work. Typifying the diversified worker was the French Canadian farmer of that time who, writes Deffontaines, "was a remarkable and resourceful jack-of-all-trades who managed to make the most of what he needed."[9] Speaking of Upper Canadians of the period de T. Glazebrook says, "Men and women needed to be Jacks and Jills of all trades, and even those unaccustomed to manual tasks—whether carpentry and stone-masonry or cooking and sewing—found that minimum skills must be developed quickly."[10]

Artisans too were free from the constraints imposed by a complex division of labour. As late as Confederation, "blacksmiths, coopers, wheelwrights, tinsmiths, and many other artisans practised their trades much as they had been practised for centuries. . . ."[11] They established their own production goals and patterns of labour. The finished product initially took shape in the minds of artisans, and it was they who were responsible for executing the operations necessary to complete the project. In discussing the nineteenth century craftsman, Rocher says, "this is a stage where the division of labour still does not exist and where the maker or manufacturer carries out himself the entire labour for the object from which he derives his name."[12] Of course, the growing number of crafts-

9. Deffontaines, *op. cit.*, p. 15.
10. G.P. de T. Glazebrook, *Life in Ontario,* Toronto: University of Toronto Press, 1968, p. 37.
11. Harris and Warkenton, *op. cit.* p. 322. For discussions of work styles in pre-industrial societies see E.P. Thompson, "Time, Work-Discipline, and Industrial Capitalism," *Past and Present,* December 1967, pp. 56–97; Keith Thomas, "Work and Leisure in Pre-Industrial Society," *Past and Present,* December 1964, pp. 50–62; Herbert G. Gutman, "Work, Culture, and Society in Industrializing America, 1815–1919," *American Historical Review,* 78, 1973, pp. 531–587.
12. Guy Rocher, "Research on Occupations and Social Stratification," in Rioux and Martin *op. cit.,* p. 239.

men who worked for wages in manufactories had less control over the labour process than their independent counterparts. Employers began to subdivide the labour process and assign specialized jobs to individual workers. Nevertheless, specialization in these transitional production units rarely advanced beyond a primitive stage, because handicraft technology did not lend itself to a detailed division of labour.

Our final concern is with pre-industrial patterns of control of the means of production and their impact on the labour process. As we mentioned above, from an early date the political economy of Canada was ruled by a loose coalition of political office holders, merchant traders, and large land owners. The broad economic contours of the nation were shaped by its colonial status and by the activities of this mercantile ruling class. Native peoples and settlers alike were forced to accommodate themselves in one way or another to these forces. Nevertheless, the continued hegemony of the mercantile class derived mostly from activities connected with the staples trade, land speculation, and control over the credit market, rather than from appropriation of a surplus (and capital) through ownership of the means of production and regulation of the labour process.

This was a society of small producers. Independent artisans set the pace of work in accordance with their own inclinations. Farmers too could control the flow of work, subject, of course, to such exigencies as climate and seasons. Because of their independent status and the undeveloped market, such persons were likely to be task-oriented rather than time-oriented. Labour was not geared to the clock. There was a certain irregularity and lack of precise scheduling of work. Activities were carried out with an eye to accomplishing what was an absolute necessity, and people often alternated between toiling steadily for several days and enjoying extended periods of idleness and leisure.

A casual approach to work is found in the fusion of work, sociability, and play characteristic of the activities of many nineteenth century farm families. During this period, Lower writes, people worked together, played together, lived together.[13] One prevalent pattern of labour was the "bee"—a gathering of neighbours who collectively assisted with necessary chores. Bees were occasions for entertainment and sociability as well as plain hard work. Guillet gives the following description of bees in Upper Canada: "Besides large quantities of food and drink, it was customary to provide a dance or a 'hoe-down' as the main amusement, while those who chose not to dance engaged in sports, games, and conversation."[14] A tradition of co-operation also permeated the lives of habitants in Lower Canada. Deffontaines says that work bees, whether they were for moving, wood cutting, land clearing, wool spinning or husking, were frequently organized for mutual aid.[15]

While these attitudes to work were probably widespread among the pre-industrial populace, the likelihood of putting them into practice was partly related to whether or not one was an *employee.* Recall that alongside the independent producers there was a growing number of individuals who were becoming subject to the dictates of employers. Control of the work process fell in these instances to small employers rather than to a powerful class of industrial capitalists and their managerial representatives. In manufactories the power of owners was constrained by their dependence on the skills and knowledge of craft workers. In all types of enterprises the cash nexus between employers and employees was overlaid by a paternalism that bound the two emergent classes together. "As a prevailing ethos that defined relations of superordination and

13. Arthur R.M. Lower, *Canadians in the Making*, Toronto: Longman Canada, 1958, p. 261.
14. Edwin C. Guillet, *Pioneer Days in Upper Canada*, Toronto: University of Toronto Press, 1964, p. 120.
15. Deffontaines, *op cit.*, p. 14. Some idea of the importance of this institution can be gained from a partial enumeration of tasks around which bees were formed. There were bees for quilting; home, mill, and barn building; ploughing; hay cutting; fence making; paring; butchering; preserving; and linen spinning. In some sections of North America the term "frolic" was used interchangeably with the word "bee," a substitution indicative of the admixture of work, sociability, and play. Harris and Warkenton, *op. cit.*, argue that Lower Canadian bees were expressions of co-operative relationships, whereas in Upper Canada bees were occasions to let off steam. The different motivations and emphases do not detract from the main point being made.

subordination in an age of commercial capital and nascent industrialism, paternalism grew out of the necessity to justify exploitation and mediate inherently irreconcilable interests."[16] Because employer–employee relations were relatively personal and non-contractual, employees were not hired, evaluated, and dismissed in accordance with strict criteria of cost. Under such circumstances, the nature of work and the conditions under which it was performed probably varied widely.

The main argument of the above discussion is this: The undeveloped state of the division of labour, the virtual absence of advanced markets in commodities and labour, and the relatively widespread ownership of the means of production meant that a greater proportion of people in pre-industrial Canada exercised control over the means and ends of production than is the case in modern society. The way people worked and the way they defined work were quite different from what now prevails. The consequence of this set of circumstances was that there was less alienation from work than there is in Canadian society today.[17]

THE SETTING AT MID-CENTURY

After 1840 the self-contained rural economy was gradually transformed into a more sophisticated system of production and exchange. By mid-century the basis for the emergence of industrial capitalism had been laid by the construction of railways and canals. These transportation arteries stimulated the growth of cities and linked the scattered rural villages, integrating them into a national market.

By 1850 there were over 3000 manufactories in Upper Canada, and in the next two decades the number of skilled tradesmen—carpenters, bricklayers, coopers, iron-founders,

16. Bryan D. Palmer, *Working Class Experience: The Rise and Reconstitution of Canadian Labour, 1800–1980,* Toronto: Butterworth, 1983, p. 14.
17. To say that alienated labour in early Canada was less prevalent than today is not to idealize that era. On the contrary, we have pointed out that many persons were engaged in a grim struggle for subsistence. However, it should be remembered that alienation refers to the way work is controlled and organized. It does not deal, except indirectly and in relative terms, with standards of living.

and tailors—grew rapidly throughout the country. The economic crisis of the late 1850s eroded the dominant position of merchant capitalists and simultaneously hastened the decline of small-scale craft producers, who often depended on merchants' credit.[18] At the same time a new trend was emerging: steam-powered shops increased twofold, and mechanization was introduced into the iron, wool, and wood industries. That the new society was growing up in the midst of the old one was clear in a city like Hamilton where small stores, offices, artisan shops, and manufactories were still very much in evidence. In such enterprises, relationships between employers and employees were often personal, and their duties and functions did not differ greatly. Production was still largely shaped by direct orders from customers.[19] Appearing alongside these pre-industrial institutions were larger, more capital-intensive enterprises. "Before the end of the fifties, Hamilton, besides its locomotives and railroad cars and foundry products, was turning out ready-made clothing, tobacco products, and sewing machines. The expansion was geared to investment in labour-saving machinery, involving growth of the cities at the expense of village handicraft."[20] Between 1851 and 1871, the number of machinists in Hamilton increased by 800 percent. During this same period the percentage of the city's labour force working in firms employing ten or more persons rose from 24% to 83%.[21]

But overall, the process of change was slow and uneven. At the time of Confederation, Canada remained a basically rural nation (50 percent of the labour force was engaged in agricul-

18. Bryan D. Palmer, *A Culture in Conflict: Skilled Workers and Industrial Capitalism in Hamilton, Ontario, 1860–1914*, Montreal: McGill–Queen's University Press, 1979.
19. *Cf.* Michael Katz, "The People of a Canadian City: 1851–2," *Canadian Historical Review*, 53, 1972, pp. 402–426.
20. H.C. Pentland, "The Development of a Capitalistic Labour Market in Canada," *Canadian Journal of Economics and Political Science*, 25, 1959, p. 469. The same uneven development in Toronto has been described by Gregory S. Kealey in *Toronto Workers Respond to Industrial Capitalism, 1867–1892*, Toronto: University of Toronto Press, 1980.
21. Palmer, *op. cit.*, pp. 16, 17.

tural pursuits).[22] The future shape of the Canadian economy was most clearly visible in the presence of factories located in metropolises like Hamilton and Toronto, and particularly Montreal, which, by the 1870s, accounted for approximately three-quarters of all production in the nation.[23] A set of forces were actively at work in these urban centres rendering craft skills redundant by the substitution of factories for the craftsman's shop and the small manufactory. We can regard the decades of the fifties and sixties, then, as the prelude to the industrial revolution in Canada. And while the take-off point for industrialization had not yet arrived, this period was important, for during it the village economy was slowly being eroded. Ryerson emphasizes the significance of the gradual dissolution of the local economy:

> The "division of labour" between owner and non-owner, between industrialist and factory hand, became possible only with the break-up of the old, self-sufficient, "natural economy" and with the spread of trade, the universalizing of commodity production to embrace labour power itself as a marketable item.[24]

THE EMERGENCE OF INDUSTRIAL CAPITALISM

Although the date is an arbitrary one, 1870 can be considered as the year when large scale production first began to dominate productive activity in Canada. Between 1870 and 1890, stimulated by a protective tariff, investment in machines increased,

---

22. Agricultural production was also being transformed under the impact of enlarged markets. Pentland argues that farmers did not turn potential surpluses into real surpluses until there was someone to purchase them. He maintains that "with the solution to the market problem in the forties and fifties the farmer became fully capitalistic and acquisitive. Increasing emphasis fell on improvement and mechanization, hard work and the dignity of labour, thrift and temperance." See *op. cit.*, p. 462. These passages not only illustrate the extension of market forces to agriculture, they also support our earlier claim that prior to around 1840 Upper Canadian farmers, despite having been exposed to the capitalistic tenets of the Protestant ethic, did not regulate production in accordance with purely market objectives.
23. Palmer, *Working Class Experience, op. cit.*, p. 63.
24. Ryerson, *op. cit.* p. 36.

and more and larger factories emerged. In 1870 there were about 38 000 manufacturing units in Canada. By 1890 the figure had swollen to 70 000. And during these two decades the number of firms with a capital of $50 000 or more nearly doubled. Manufacturing output increased rapidly, especially in agricultural equipment, furniture, foundry products, tobacco, wood products, and textiles.[25] While the major cities of Ontario and Quebec were the locus of this growth, the Maritime provinces also enjoyed substantial industrial development.[26]

The Factory System

Canadian industry arose in a competitive, market-oriented context under the aegis of capitalist ownership. Since the driving force of a capitalist economic system is the necessity to generate profits and accumulate capital, workers are treated as "costs" and it is to the competitive advantage of employers to keep costs at a minimum. Employers also seek to exercise maximum control over workers, for when workers regulate the labour process their activities reflect their own interests and inclinations, not those of employers. Before the factory system came to dominate production, Canadian skilled workers customarily regulated modes of wage payment, the methods, pace, scheduling, and allocation of work, and the recruitment and training of workers. Employers regarded these craft regulations as inimical to their drive for profits and sought to transfer power from the shop floor to the front office. To cheapen and subordinate labour, employers specialized and rationalized the work process, installing machines that replaced workers and reduced the need for skilled labour, and constructing a hierarchy of authority ranging from top executives to supervisors. These measures were used in varying degrees in all spheres of production, but the organization that epitomized the new order was the factory.

A factory is a large scale production unit that uses machinery and a central source of power, such as steam or electricity.

25. Michael Cross and Gregory Kealey, eds., *Canada's Age of Industry 1849-1896*, Toronto: McClelland and Stewart, 1982, p. 11.
26. T.W. Acheson, "The National Policy and the Industrialization of the Maritimes," in Cross and Kealey, *ibid.*, pp. 62-94.

Power-driven machinery offered multiple advantages to the capitalist. It reduced the production time per unit as well as the "value" of commodities. Machines with fixed motion paths or those whose speed could be regulated by management, intensified the pace of work and eroded workers' capacity to govern the labour process. In contrast to handicraft technology, machines generally required less skilled, more easily replaceable, and hence cheaper workers. As a result, the number of unskilled and semiskilled workers—including women and children—grew rapidly. In fact, capitalist employers often preferred to hire women because they were viewed as docile, quick, sober, and above all, cheap.[27] An early twentieth century article in *Canadian Machinery* extolled the virtues of the machine, which

> can work the whole twenty-four hours without stopping, knows no distinctions between Sundays, holidays and any ordinary day, requires as its only lubricant a little oil, being in fact abstinent in all other matters, has no near relatives dying at awkward moments, has no athletic propensities, belongs to no labour organization, knows nothing about limitation of output, never thinks of wasting its owner's time in conversation with its fellow machines. Wars, rumours of war and baseball scores, have no interest for it and its only ambition in life is to do the best possible work in the greatest possible quantity.[28]

While employers were keenly aware of these benefits, skill degradation via mechanization was a lengthy and uneven process. Some machines generated a demand for skilled workers, and some traditional crafts managed to escape the degrading impact of the new technology. For example, the slowness of technological innovation in the metal-working industry enabled Canadian iron moulders to retain a considerable degree of control over the work process and conditions of employment

27. Susan Trofimenkoff, "One Hundred and Two Muffled Voices: Canada's Industrial Women in the 1880's," in Cross and Kealey, *op. cit.,* pp. 212–229.
28. Cited in Craig Heron, "The Crisis of the Craftsman: Hamilton's Metal Workers in the Early Twentieth Century," *Labour/Le Travailleur,* 6, Autumn, 1980, p. 23.

until the 1920s. Printers also held on to craft prerogatives despite the introduction of the linotype machine, because their organizational strength compelled employers to use skilled workers to operate the new equipment. But the experience of coopers was more common: their inability to regulate the introduction of machine tenders led to the virtual extinction of the coopers' craft by the 1880s.[29]

While we correctly associate the factory with machines and a central source of power, another of its prominent features involves techniques of human co-ordination, supervision, and discipline used by employers to shape the work process to their own ends.[30] A nineteenth century chronicler of the factory system in England, Andrew Ure, recognized this fact, attributing the success of the factory to human rather than technical factors. Writing of Richard Arkwright, who was recognized as the first successful English industrialist, Ure says:

> *The main difficulty (faced by Arkwright) did not, to my apprehension, lie so much in the invention of a proper self-acting mechanism for drawing out and twisting cotton into a continuous thread, as in . . . training human beings to renounce their desultory habits of work, and to identify themselves with the unvarying regularity of the complex automaton. To devise and administer a successful code of factory discipline, suited to the necessities of factory diligence, was the Herculean enterprise, the noble achievement of Arkwright.*[31]

29. *Ibid.*; Gregory Kealey, "The 'Honest Workingman' and Workers' Control: The Experiences of Toronto Skilled Workers, 1860–1892," *Labour/Le Travailleur*, 1, 1976, pp. 32–68.
30. In a much-cited article, Stephen Marglin argues that it was just such techniques of human control that established the productive superiority of the factory system over more randomly organized work systems. "The key to the success of the factory," Marglin writes, "as well as its inspiration, was the substitution of capitalist for workers' control of the production process: discipline and supervision could and did reduce costs without being technologically superior." See "What Do Bosses Do? The Origins and Functions of Hierarchy in Capitalist Production," *Review of Radical Political Economics*, 6, Summer, 1974, p. 84.
31. Andrew Ure, *The Philosophy of Manufacturers*, London: Charles Knight, 1835, p. 15.

Paul Mantoux, in his classic work on the industrial revolution in England, provides a lucid description of conditions of early factory life, and one which could be applied equally well to the Canadian factory system over a century later.

Hard and fast rules replaced the freedom of the small workshops. Work started, meals were eaten and work stopped at fixed hours, notified by the ringing of a bell. Within the factory each had his allotted place and his strictly defined and invariable duty. Everyone had to work steadily and without stopping, under the vigilant eye of a foreman who secured obedience by means of fines or dismissals, and sometimes by more brutal forms of coercion.[32]

Wherever it has occurred, the change from pre-industrial to industrial modes of work has been harsh, and the Canadian experience was no exception. We emphasized conditions of work in the factory because it was the prototypical organization of industrial capitalism. Labourers in construction camps and wage earners in the extractive industries—fishermen, loggers, and miners—were also exposed to miserable working and living conditions. Women, as well as being paid far less than men, experienced working environments as domestics, seamstresses, and laundresses that were at least equally oppressive. So intolerable were these "feminine" jobs that many women working at them preferred employment in factories. In some cases, for example, in the textiles and garment industries, the work forces were predominantly female.[33]

---

32. Paul Mantoux, *The Industrial Revolution in the Eighteenth Century,* London: Jonathon Cape, 1961, p. 375. How closely this resembles the depiction by the economic historian, David Landes: Factory work was done "at a pace set by tireless, inanimate equipment, as part of a large team that had to begin, pause, and stop in unison—all under the close eye of overseers, enforcing assiduity by moral, pecuniary, occasionally even physical means of compulsion. The factory was a new kind of prison; the clock a new kind of jailor." See his *The Unbound Prometheus,* Cambridge: University Press, 1969, p. 43.
33. *Cf.,* D. Suzanne Cross, "The Neglected Majority: The Changing Role of Women in 19th Century Montreal," in Susan Mann Trofimenkoff and Alison

In both the primary and secondary sectors of the Canadian economy workers were driven to toil diligently by a series of punitive measures, which were later supplemented by the more refined techniques of persuasion, manipulation, and economic incentives. Among the early measures were oppressive work rules forbidding talking, leaving one's work station, lateness, absenteeism, laxness, and spoilage. Rules were enforced through fines, dismissals, and physical coercion.

Spurred by unrest among the nascent working class, factory acts were repeatedly introduced at sessions of the Canadian Federal Parliament during the 1880s—though none were passed. In the latter years of the decade the federal government launched an investigation of working conditions faced by factory workers, longshoremen, miners, and construction hands. The inquiry documented the exploitation and brutality of the new system—child labour, long hours, appalling working conditions, authoritarian discipline, and low wages.[34]

The testimony of those interviewed and the summary reports of the commissioners unmasked the full meaning of the industrial revolution in Canada. The chairman of the commission bemoaned the growth of the profit motive, which drove the new employers to hire and exploit women and children. Another member of the committee, criticized in labour circles for his anti-labour sentiments, could conclude from the hearings that:

> *Many children of tender age, some of them not more than nine years old, were employed in cotton, glass, tobacco and cigar factories . . . Some of them worked from six o'clock in the morning till six in the evening, with less*

Prentice, eds., *The Neglected Majority: Essays in Canadian Women's History*, Toronto: McClelland and Stewart, 1977, pp. 66–86; Leo Johnson, "The Political Economy of Ontario Women in the Nineteenth Century," in Janice Acton, Penny Goldsmith, and Bonnie Shepard, eds., *Women at Work: Ontario, 1850–1930*, Toronto: Canadian Women's Educational Press, 1974, pp. 13–31; Wayne Roberts, *Honest Womenhood: Feminism, Femininity and Class Consciousness Among Toronto Working Women, 1893 to 1914*, Toronto: New Hogtown Press, 1976.

34. The commissioners questioned 1800 witnesses, whose testimony filled five volumes. Excerpts from the report may be found in Greg Kealey, *Canada Investigates Industrialism*, Toronto: University of Toronto Press, 1973.

than an hour for dinner, others worked from seven in the evening till six in the morning.[35]

He then added:

> *The darkest pages in the testimony . . . are those recording the beating and imprisonment of children employed in factories. Your Commissioners earnestly hope that these barbarous practices may be removed, and such treatment made a penal offence, so that Canadians may no longer rest under the reproach that the lash and the dungeon are accompaniments of manufacturing industry in the Dominion.*[36]

Reactions to the Industrial System

We have seen how the new industrial order intensified structural alienation among Canadian workers. But was there a subjective counterpart to this structural powerlessness? And if working people were in fact psychologically estranged from their work, how can this be demonstrated?

Initial information on the extent to which structural alienation penetrated the consciousness of Canadian working people can be inferred from the known disparity of work styles typical of pre-industrial and industrial societies and the major adjustments in work habits and culture necessitated by the latter. Wherever it has arisen, industrial capitalism and its work requirements have clashed with pre-industrial cultural values and practices. E.P. Thompson informs us that "the transition to mature industrial society entailed a severe restructuring of working habits—new disciplines, new incentives, and a new human nature upon which these incentives could bite effectively."[37]

As in England and other societies that experienced an industrial revolution, early Canadian capitalists had to call on people from non-industrial backgrounds to form their work forces. The bankruptcy of small farms and the shrinkage of

35. *Ibid.*, p. 22.
36. *Ibid.*, p. 14.
37. Thompson, *op. cit.*, p. 57.

land available for settlement forced individuals with agricultural interests and work habits to search for jobs in industry. It takes no special imaginative powers to understand why these "men and women fresh from Canadian farms and Old World fields did not adjust easily to the new discipline of machines and factories."[38] Tradesmen accustomed to the more irregular pace of work typical of small manufactories (which were being forced to close because of their inability to compete with larger, mechanized units) and independent artisans were also obliged to join the ranks of the industrial proletariat. With the exception of Irish labourers who worked as navvies in the construction of Canadian canals and railways, all the others who made up the new working class had been accustomed to patterns of work and life far different from what they were exposed to in industrial settings.[39] Given the dramatic disruption of work patterns induced by the emergence of industrial capitalism, a solid *prima facie* case can be advanced for the presence of widespread and intense feelings of alienation among the early Canadian working class.

More direct evidence of alienated mental states can be inferred from behavioural expressions of discontent among Canadian workers. The most obvious of these were the formation of trade unions, strikes, picketing, demonstrations, and other easily recorded manifestations of unrest. These easily identified expressions of restiveness can be construed as efforts to reduce or overcome alienation by striking at its

38. Kealey, *op. cit.*, p. xxi.
39. How much skilled tradesmen had to modify their traditionally irregular work patterns depended both on their cohesion and organization as a group and on the degree to which their skills were in demand. A scarcity of skills would force the industrialist to think twice before imposing a strict regimen of toil on the skilled tradesmen. Moreover, by their very complexity, skilled jobs entailed a degree of worker discretion and control not easily penetrated by employers. One could reasonably estimate that the degree of control over work exercised by skilled Canadian industrial workers fell somewhere between that of artisans in small manufactories and unskilled factory hands. For a discussion of work among skilled tradesmen of this era see Kealey, *Toronto Workers Respond to Industrial Capitalism, 1867–1892, op. cit.*, and Palmer, *A Culture in Conflict, op. cit.*

sources. Workers organized in various ways to challenge the power of employers to dictate the terms and conditions of work. Their efforts were also directed at regulating market forces, upon which wages as well as the right to work depended. Equally revealing of subjectively experienced alienation are activities that ordinarily elude public recognition. These largely unrecorded behaviours involve, in part, the *ad hoc* devices workers employ to resist on a day-to-day basis the organization of work.[40] These behaviours range from individual acts of sabotage to various forms of insubordination and subversion, operating through the medium of cohesive groups of workers. Such actions can be interpreted not only as angry reactions to work but also as attempts to humanize work and to establish control over the production process.

Driven by the need to earn a living, the early proletariat adjusted in various ways to the industrial system. Some simply endured the hardships and deprivations. Others embarked on a lifelong series of job hunts, moving from town to town in search of a living wage and more tolerable working conditions. But the majority of workers never passively surrendered to the exploitative and alienating nature of industrial life. We can only piece together a vague, albeit revealing, picture of the *ad hoc* resistance among working people of this era. Testimony given to the 1889 Royal Commission affords glimpses of workers' daily unwillingness to put up with industrial injustice and the strategies they used to protest against it. Expressions of discontent included spontaneous walkouts, work stoppages in the plant, restriction of output, industrial sabotage, insubordination, and simple refusals to show up at work on holidays and the day after payday.

This picture of alienation can be supplemented by examining the more overt and obvious forms of unrest. The advance of industrial capitalism during the years 1870 to 1890 was accompanied by an upsurge of formally organized activities. As early

40. On the neglect of this aspect of the history of the Canadian working class see the introduction to Russell G. Hann, Gregory S. Kealey, Linda Kealey, Peter Warrian, *Primary Sources in Canadian Working Class History, 1860-1930*, Kitchener: Dumont Press, 1973.

as the 1860s the Knights of St. Crispin combined to prevent the mechanization of shoe factories. The Knights were not opposed to machines as such. "The workers welcomed technological improvements; what they reacted violently against was the way in which the capitalist used these improvements to lower wages and further rationalize the work place."[41] By the early 1870s there were some 120 local and international unions in Canada. Work stoppages became more frequent—the most prominent walkouts being staged by moulders, cigarmakers, coopers, and shoemakers.[42] During the seventies labour militancy, centred around beleaguered craft workers, arose on more than a local basis, rallying around the demand for a nine-hour day. In 1872 labourers formed the Workingman's Political Party. Canada's first labour-oriented newspaper was published during this era, and the inaugural convention of the first national Canadian union, the Canadian Labour Union, was held. The growing alienation induced by the economy brought forth an early solution from the new unionists. At its fourth annual meeting in 1876 the Canadian Labour Union adopted a resolution calling for the co-operative ownership of industry. This was not an isolated demand:

> *As early as the eighteen seventies, Canadian working people were clearly searching for egalitarian alternatives to industrial capitalist society; they were thinking in terms of collective community control of the economy and its development; and they were ready to take direct political action to further such ideas.*[43]

The more than 430 strikes and lockouts of the 1880s was double the labour–capital confrontations that had occurred in the previous decade. While these actions often were undertaken for higher wages, many were protests against oppressive

41. *Ibid.*, p. 15. Also see Don D. Lescohier, *The Knights of St. Crispin, 1867–1874*, Madison: Bulletin of the University of Wisconsin, 1910.
42. Palmer, *Working Class Experience, op. cit.*, p. 74.
43. Steven Langdon, "The Emergence of the Canadian Working Class Movement, 1845–75," *Journal of Canadian Studies*, 8, 1973, p. 22.

working conditions or struggles over control of the labour process (especially among the skilled).[44] In the 1880s the Knights of Labour, a union movement whose membership was drawn from all grades of labour and branches of industry, unified and galvanized North American workers. Local assemblies of Knights could be found across Canada, but their stronghold was Ontario where, in 1881, nearly twenty percent of manufacturing workers were members. The Knights were interested in more than seeking improvements in wages and working conditions and defending themselves against the excesses of employers. They sought comprehensive reforms and called for a society constructed on the basis of producer and distributor co-operatives. In more than one instance the Knights did initiate co-operative ventures. They established knitting and trunk factories, a candy works, and grocery stores. In 1886 they operated a free bus service in Toronto. The Knights of Labour reached their peak in the late 1880s, giving way to the craft-oriented Trades and Labour Congress, which began in 1886. The demise of the Knights of Labour was due to a complex of factors. The Knights' program of uniting all workers in pursuit of societal transformation was a prophetic vision. However, the tactics of the Knights—their focus on local politics and their policy of opposing strikes (even though that policy was regularly violated) and favouring co-operation with employers and the arbitration of disputes—had been forged out of past experiences in an era of community politics and small-scale production that was being eclipsed by the centralization of political power, by the emergence of monopoly capitalism, and by the increasingly powerful opposition of employers determined to weaken or destroy unions. These emergent circumstances created cleavages among workers. Feeling their interests were best served by distancing themselves from the rest of the working class, skilled workers turned for protection to the exclusionist and pragmatic "bread and butter" unionism represented by the Trades and Labour Congress, whose affiliates were mainly branches of the conservative American

44. Palmer, *Working Class Experience, op. cit.*

Federation of Labor. The working-class unity witnessed in the 1880s would not resurface until the strike wave of 1919.[45]

THE CONCENTRATION OF PRODUCTION: 1890–1920

If the 1870s and 1880s witnessed the rise of the factory system, the period 1890 to 1920 was one of concentration of the means of production. The 70 000 manufacturing units of 1890 dwindled to 22 000 by 1920, a reduction which indicated more rather than less industrial activity.[46] Through the formation of joint-stock companies (business organizations set up to amass large sums of capital), mergers (between 1900 and 1914, 73 mergers absorbed 345 firms), and internal growth, the manufacturing industry was becoming more concentrated, centralized, and bureaucratized.[47] This trend was also evident in the extractive industries, particularly in British Columbia and Nova Scotia.[48]

As industrial units grew in size, business activity became more complicated, and the work process was further specialized and rationalized. This created a demand for administrators, managers, and clerks. In 1901 approximately 15 percent of the work force was employed in white-collar occupations. By 1921 one of every four members of the Canadian labour force

45. See Douglas R. Kennedy, *The Knights of Labor in Canada*, London: University of Western Ontario, 1956; Gregory S. Kealey and Bryan D. Palmer, *Dreaming of What Might Be: The Knights of Labor in Ontario*, New York: Cambridge University Press, 1982.

46. M.C. Urquhart and K.A.H. Buckley, eds., *Historical Statistics of Canada*, Toronto: Macmillan Company of Canada, 1965, p. 463. Also see G.W. Bertram, "Economic Growth in Canadian Industry, 1870–1915: The Staple Model," in W.T. Easterbrook and M.H. Watkins, eds., *Approaches to Canadian Economic History*, Toronto: McClelland and Stewart, 1967, pp. 74–98.

47. Charles Lipton, *The Trade Union Movement of Canada 1827–1959*, Montreal: Canadian Social Publications, 1968. Increasing concentration is also evidenced by the fact that in 1890 the average number of persons employed in manufacturing enterprises was five, compared to an average of 25.8 in 1920. See Urquhart and Buckley, *op. cit.*

48. For a good account of industrial development and workers' reactions to it in Cape Breton see *The People's History of Cape Breton*, Halifax: Opportunities for Youth, 1971.

wore a white collar, a proportion that would hold fairly constant until the middle of the century. The rationalization of production also stimulated the need for unskilled labourers. Old skills were now rapidly being built into machines and factory work was increasingly subdivided and simplified. By 1920 the factory system had virtually eliminated the manufactories and handicraft production.[49]

Factory owners were not alone in their need for unskilled workers. The mechanization of the mining industry and the growth of railway construction also created demands for fresh labour supplies. Employers, unable to satisfy their labour needs domestically, looked for help outside Canada. Immigrants, especially those unfamiliar with the English language, were regarded as eminently suitable recruits. Many Canadian businessmen "wanted hardy, malleable labourers whose salary requests would be 'reasonable', who were not unionized, and who could not use the English-Canadian press to focus public attention on their grievances."[50] Responding to the call of employers, the government initiated an "open-door" immigration policy. Between 1900 and 1920, huge waves of immigrants reached Canadian shores.

Immigrants were employed by factories, mines, and construction camps to take on the heaviest, dirtiest, cheapest, and most dangerous jobs.[51] Their presence also created a surplus of low-skilled labourers, which enabled employers to hold wages down and to impose strict discipline on those fortunate enough to have jobs. But new Canadians, counted on to serve as a cheap, docile labour force, were not as enamoured of their circumstances as employers would have liked. Once they became accustomed to their conditions of work and life, immigrants enthusiastically supported unions, published radical foreign-

49. Industrial expansion and the mechanization of agriculture also led to a decline in farm employment from 46 percent in 1890 to 33 percent in 1920.
50. Donald Avery, "Canadian Immigration Policy and the 'Foreign' Navvy, 1896–1914," Canadian Historical Association, *Historical Papers*, 1972, p. 138.
51. For a first hand account of railway construction work in the early twentieth century see Edmund W. Bradwin, *The Bunkhouse Man*, Toronto: University of Toronto Press, 1973.

language newspapers, and built their own militant organizations.[52]

Scientific Management and Mass Production

Despite the reduced importance of handicraft production, industry still depended on skilled workers. Skilled workers, many of whom were members of craft unions affiliated with the Trades and Labour Congress, fiercely resisted the rationalization of production, which they correctly perceived as an assault on their skills and a challenge to the control they had traditionally exercised over the labour process and conditions of employment. The manufacturers' drive to restructure production and hence to deskill, cheapen, and subordinate labour was facilitated by two new developments introduced in the twentieth century: scientific management and mass production techniques. The application of the principles of scientific management (Taylorism) to the work process and the advent of assembly line production (Fordism) were to have a profound impact on the organization of work.

The leading proponent of scientific management was Frederick Winslow Taylor. Taylor's objectives were to boost productivity, to transfer control over the labour process from workers to managers, and to cheapen labour. Workers, he insisted, were all too prone to mix work and play, to consciously restrict output, and to work far below their capacity. This tendency to "soldier" could be overcome by the application of scientific methods to the work process. Taylor believed the same techniques that had been used so successfully by scientists in the study of physical objects could be applied to the measurement, analysis, and control of human beings at work.[53]

At the first stage of the "scientific" reorganization of the labour process, management personnel systematically observed workers' activities. This enabled management to pene-

52. Donald Avery, *"Dangerous Foreigners": European Immigrant Workers and Labour Radicalism in Canada: 1896–1932,* Toronto: McClelland and Stewart, 1979.

53. Taylorism's impact on work in Canada is discussed in Craig Heron and Bryan Palmer, "Through the Prism of the Strike: Contours and Context of Industrial Unrest in Southern Ontario, 1901–1914," *Canadian Historical Review,* 8, 1977, pp. 423–458.

trate "trade secrets" that allowed workers, especially the skilled, to govern the pace and methods of work and thus maintain a comfortable margin of independence. Taylor urged managers to assume the burden of gathering together all the traditional knowledge which in the past had been possessed by the workmen and then of classifying, tabulating, and employing this knowledge "scientifically" to establish rules, laws, and formulae applicable to the production process.[54] Having appropriated these trade secrets, management could systematically rationalize production by specifying stricter job descriptions and by increasing the regulation of work pace and procedures. "All possible brain work," Taylor urged in *Shop Management*, "should be removed from the shop and centred in the planning or laying-out department. . . ."[55] Plans specifying the job to be done and the means to be used in carrying it out were now to be formulated by management and relayed, preferably in writing, to workers.

> *Perhaps the most prominent single element in modern scientific management is the task idea. The work of every workman is fully planned out by the management at least one day in advance, and each man receives in most cases complete written instructions, describing in detail the task which he is to accomplish, as well as the means to be used in doing the work. . . . This task specifies not only what is to be done but how it is to be done and the exact time allowed for doing it.*[56]

Scientific management had two intended effects on the division of labour. The first effect was the simplification and compartmentalization of tasks. Taylor recommended "a narrowing down of functions involved in a job, an extension of the division of labour, a trimming off of all variant, non-repetitive

54. Frederick Winslow Taylor, *Scientific Management,* New York: Harper and Brothers, 1947, p. 40. This volume contains Taylor's *Testimony Before the Special House Committee* and two books, *The Principles of Scientific Management* and *Shop Management*.
55. *Ibid.,* pp. 98–99.
56. Frederick Winslow Taylor, *The Principles of Scientific Management,* New York: Harper and Brothers, 1919, p. 39.

tasks."[57] For example, a man working on a lathe traditionally was responsible for sharpening his cutting tool, determining the correct speed of the lathe and the angle of cut. This same machinist obtained materials from the storeroom and moved work from one place to another in the shop when the production process demanded it. Taylor insisted that each of these tasks constituted a job in itself; the work of the machinist would now be subdivided and assigned to several workers.[58] In his 1915 report to the U.S. Commission on Industrial Relations, Robert Hoxie concluded that scientific management "gathers up and transfers to management the traditional craft knowledge and transmits this again to the workers only piecemeal as it is needed in the performance of a particular job or task. It tends, in practice, to confine each worker to a particular task or small cycle of tasks. It thus narrows his outlook and skill and the experience and training which are necessary to do the work. He is, therefore, more easily displaced."[59] As for the second effect, managers' appropriation of shop floor knowledge, their regulation of work, and the increased specialization of labour all combined to sharpen the distinction between the planning of work and its execution, thus broadening the gulf between mental and manual labour. Under Taylorism workers were paid to work, not to think.

Having broken down jobs into their constituent parts, Taylor sent men out with stop watches to determine the speed at which jobs ought to be performed. Once standard speeds had been ascertained, management was in a position to exact from workers a certain quantity of work in a given period of time. Time study also established the basis for piece and bonus systems of wage payment, which make some portion of wages dependent on the number of items produced during a given period of time. Taylor believed that the "exact knowledge" furnished by these time studies would ensure that work speed

57. Hugh G.T. Aitken, *Taylorism at Watertown Arsenal*, Cambridge: Harvard University Press, 1960, p. 23.
58. *Ibid.*
59. Robert Franklin Hoxie, *Scientific Management and Labor*, New York: Augustus M. Kelley Publishers, 1966, p. 104. Hoxie's report was based on an investigation of 35 shops where scientific management had been implemented and on interviews with prominent disciples of Taylor and trade unionists.

and wages would no longer be open to dispute. The objectivity of the stop watch, however, was more fictitious than real. The Hoxie Report uncovered seventeen sources of bias in time study and concluded that this practice was "the special sport of individual judgment and opinion, subject to all the possibilities of diversity, inaccuracy and injustice that arise from human ignorance and prejudice."[60] Aitken concurs: Time study is a "ritual whose function it was to validate by reference to the apparently objective authority of the clock a subjective estimate of the time a job should take."[61] But even if one could precisely measure how fast individuals *can* work and *do* work, it is not possible to scientifically determine how fast a person *ought* to work. The answer to this question is a matter of values and preferences, not science.

Taylor claimed there was no inherent conflict between capital and labour; greater productivity, he argued, meant higher profits as well as higher wages. Still, Taylor was skeptical enough of his own rhetoric to devise ways of overcoming the anticipated worker resistance to his methods (in labour circles scientific management was known as "speed-up").[62] He recommended that wages should be tied to output through the implementation of incentive systems and proposed a multiplication of foremen and gang bosses, whose job it would be to make sure that the detailed orders sent down from the office were followed to the letter.

By transferring job knowledge from workers to management and by breaking up craft work into discrete, simplified, and standardized task units, scientific management undermined

---

60. *Ibid.,* p. 40.
61. Aitken, *op. cit.,* p. 26. "Scientific management," Braverman asserts, "enters the workplace not as the representative of science, but as the representative of management masquerading in the trappings of science." Harry Braverman, *Labor and Monopoly Capital,* New York: Monthly Review Press, 197, p. 86.
62. For all his attempts at logical consistency, precision, and clarity of principles, Taylor's managerial bias always surfaced. For example, despite his insistence that both employers and workers would benefit from the application of his principles, Taylor was able to write that the full benefits of scientific management "will not have been realized until almost all of the machines in the shop are run by men who are of smaller calibre and attainments, and who are therefore cheaper than those required under the old system." See *Scientific Management, op. cit.,* p. 105.

skilled workers' capacity to govern the labour process. But Taylorism was not limited to skilled work; its principles were applied to semiskilled and unskilled labour as well. The broad applicability of Taylor's principles is illustrated by the classic case of pig-iron handling. "This work is so crude and elementary in its nature that the writer firmly believes that it would be possible to train an intelligent gorilla so as to become a more efficient pig-iron handler than any man can be."[63] Taylor selected a certain Schmidt and informed him that he would earn more money if his output increased. Taylor succeeded in getting Schmidt to increase his daily output of moving pigs of iron from 12½ tons (at 92 pounds a pig) to 47 tons. The success formula was a simple one: "When he [the foreman] tells you to pick up a pig and walk, you pick it up and you walk, and when he tells you to sit down and rest, you sit down. You do that right straight through the day. And what's more, no back talk."[64]

Discipline, obedience, and management control were the keys to the "successful" application of the principles of scientific management. For Taylor, a good worker is a co-operative worker; a co-operative worker is one who willingly obeys orders. He writes:

> *For success, then, let me give one simple piece of advice beyond all others. Every day, year in and year out, each man should ask himself, over and over again, two questions. First, 'What is the name of the man I am working for?' and having answered this definitely, then, 'What does this man want me to do right now?'*[65]

Scientific management found its mechanical counterpart in mass production, and particularly in the assembly line. Henry Ford, who introduced the assembly line in 1914, wrote that this

63. *Ibid.,* p. 40.
64. *Ibid.,* p. 46.
65. Cited in *Work in America*, Cambridge: The MIT Press, 1973, p. 50. The changes engineered by Taylor and his associates provide a clear illustration of the manner in which *social* forces are responsible for structural alienation. Scientific management dealt exclusively with the social organization of the workplace. Its impact on the production process was independent of technology. The fact that Taylor's ideas were applied to highly skilled work in

new form of production was predicated on three basic notions: "(a) the planned, orderly, and continuous progression of the commodity through the shop; (b) the delivery of work instead of leaving it to the workman's initiative to find it; (c) an analysis of operations into their constituent parts."[66] Mass production, as Ford pointed out, embodied the principles of accuracy, economy, continuity, speed, and repetition. On the line, work was minutely subdivided and work techniques predetermined; the intelligence behind the operations was moved from the shop floor to the design room.

Although the assembly line was more productive than earlier modes of manufacture, employers had other reasons for favouring it. The assembly line drastically reduced the need for skilled workers, and employers were free to exploit the much larger unskilled labour market comprising more malleable (because they were easier to fire and replace), cheaper, often immigrant, workers. Since managers controlled the speed of the line, they, not workers, determined the pace of production. In the assembly line, management believed it had found, at last, the final solution to the problem of "soldiering."

Scientific management and the assembly line were complementary developments. Both extended the division of labour, thereby increasing the repetitiveness and monotony of work. And both techniques, by creating a system of highly specific, interdependent, and easily measured segments of work, had the consequence of further increasing the need for managerial co-ordination and regulation of the work process. This effect, while intentional, is inherent in any extension of the division of labour. Bell states:

> In a simple division of labour, for example, the worker had a large measure of control over his own working conditions, i.e., the set-up and make-ready, the cleaning and repairing of machines, obtaining his own materials, and so

---

machine shops as well as to unskilled labour like shovelling, inspecting ball bearings, and lifting pig irons further illustrates this point.
66. Henry Ford, "Mass Production," in Charles R. Walker, ed., *Technology, Industry and Man,* New York: McGraw-Hill, 1968, p. 51.

*on. Under a complex division of labour, these tasks pass
out of his control and he must rely on management to see
that they are properly done. This dependence extends
along the entire process of production. As a result, modern industry has had to devise an entire new managerial
superstructure which organizes and directs production.*[67]

The New Paternalism

In the early 1900s some companies began to adopt reformist
measures that appeared to contradict the callous, balance-
sheet ethos of big business. These measures, which came to be
known as industrial betterment or welfare work, fell into three
categories: improved working conditions, including proper ventilation and lighting, the provision of lunchrooms and lockers,
and medical care; recreational facilities ranging from libraries
to athletic fields; economic benefits, like profit-sharing, options
on the purchase of company stocks, insurance, and pension
plans. By the 1920s welfare work in corporations was well
established in Canada, particularly among the larger firms.[68]

Philanthropic attitudes may have motivated some businessmen to institute reforms, but the more usual rationale was the
desire to transform resistant workers into loyal and co-operative workers. Personal ties between employers and employees
had been severed by the sheer size and complexity of the
twentieth century firm. Responsibility for the day-to-day operations of the large firm gradually passed from owners, who were
becoming more distant and imperious, to a cadre of management personel. In workers' experience, the foremen came to
represent corporate power: they hired, pushed, evaluated, promoted or demoted, and dismissed workers as they saw fit. Often

---

67. Daniel Bell, *Work and its Discontents*, New York: League for Industrial
Democracy 1970, p. 10. It should be noted that Taylorism exerted its influence
on the organization of work and the worker's immediate job. It had no impact
at all on alienation from the purposes and products of the labour process.
68. A 1928 study conducted by the Ontario Department of Labour showed well
over one-half of the 300 sampled firms had pension plans. One-third offered
group insurance, one-quarter had bonus schemes, and 15 percent allowed
employees to buy stock. See Tom Traves, "Security Without Regulation," in
Michael Cross and Gregory Kealey, eds., *The Consolidation of Capitalism,
1896–1929,* Toronto: McClelland and Stewart, 1983, p. 35.

arbitrary in their judgments and relying heavily on intimidation to exact compliance from subordinates, foremen further soured the already bitter relationship between capital and labour.[69] All that remained to link the two parties was the cash nexus, which in itself was insufficient to ensure a loyal and co-operative work force. Industrialists believed corporate welfare measures might reduce absenteeism and turnover and immunize workers to the appeal of unions. *Industrial Canada*, an organ of the Canadian Manufacturers Association, looked on welfare work "as the surest safeguard against the more aggressive and most objectionable demands of socialists and labour agitators."[70] Moreover, shop floor resistance to management authority and to the rationalization of production might be replaced by the worker's pride in peak work performance and by an appreciation of management's interest in controlling work and reducing labour costs. Finally, strikes might be avoided. As the *Canadian Manufacturer* dreamily proclaimed, welfare work "would introduce a millenium where strikes, lock-outs, labour disputes and unpleasant relations between employer and employee would be known no more."[71]

While some wage earners gained from corporate welfare programs, the intended transformation of workers' consciousness and behaviour was for the most part never achieved. Workers in welfare firms continued to find unions attractive, shop floor resistance persisted, and strikes were commonplace. Although the generally meagre level of benefits offered by welfare firms had something to do with this outcome—only a few companies had what might be considered generous programs—the failure could be attributed largely to the inability of industrial betterment programs to eliminate the basic sources of labour unrest. What the worker experienced on the shop floor day after day went unchanged; reformist measures did not compensate for long hours of toil, inadequate wages, routinized

69. For discussions of the role of foremen during this era see Richard Edwards, *Contested Terrain*, New York: Basic Books, 1979 and Daniel Nelson, *Managers and Workers*, Madison: University of Wisconsin Press, 1975.
70. Cited in Michael Bliss, *A Living Profit*, Toronto: McClelland and Stewart, 1974, p. 70.
71. Cited in *Ibid.*, p. 89.

and regimented work, tyrannical bosses, and job insecurity. It was evident that welfare work was never conceived by employers as an alternative to their efforts to rationalize production and subordinate labour. Rather, it was a means of *adapting* workers to alienating and exploitative conditions. As such, welfare work was simply another weapon in the already impressive arsenal of the employer.

Class Struggle

Employers' concerted drive to restructure production threatened the skills and prerogatives of craft workers. Moreover, all grades of labour were required to adjust to increasingly routinized, regimented, and subordinate modes of work activity. Employers were also bent on crushing unions, because union rules and solidarity impeded the reorganization of the labour process. The predictable outcome was heightened class struggle. In this contest the principal weapon of workers was the strike. Between 1900 and 1914, 421 strikes and lockouts occurred in ten Southern Ontario cities. About one-half of these disputes focussed on union recognition and issues such as oppressive supervision and the implementation of efficiency schemes.[72] During the same time span, other major strikes were undertaken by coal miners and railway workers in the West and by mill hands in the Quebec cotton industry.[73] Over 1300 Canadian strikes were recorded by the Department of Labour between 1901 and 1911, making this an era of "unprecedented tensions."[74]

Less dramatic varieties of discontent were often not reported by the mainstream press. One interesting event was recorded in

72. Heron and Palmer, *op. cit.*
73. Palmer, *Working Class Experience.*
74. Paul Craven, *An Impartial Umpire: Industrial Relations and the Canadian State 1900-1911,* Toronto: University of Toronto Press, 1980, p. 113. The Industrial Workers of the World attracted adherents across Canada during these years, but it was Western miners, loggers, farm hands, and construction workers who found this union most appealing. The IWW concentrated on organizing workers irrespective of their trade or skill level and viewed the general strike as a means of supplanting capitalism with a worker-controlled system of production. See Ross McCormack, "The Industrial Workers of the World in Canada: 1905-1914," Canadian Historical Association, *Papers,* 1975, pp. 167-190.

the *Industrial Banner.* To alleviate the high unemployment prevailing during the depressed years of 1908 and 1909, the Trades and Labour Council of London, Ontario, set up a toy factory. Among the "rules" posted on the walls of the new workshop was one which acknowledged workers' distaste for factory discipline:

> *The committee of management believes that the promulgation of a set of cast-iron rules, with restrictive provisions is unnecessary, feeling assured the employees will heartily co-operate and recognize that the largest possible measure of liberty is not incompatible with the operation of an efficient system from which the best results shall accrue.*[75]

Employers had at their disposal an array of tactics aimed at avoiding or eliminating unions, breaking strikes, and crushing shop floor resistance. Employers encouraged immigration of craft workers from the British Isles. This flooding of the skilled labour market weakened unions, contributed to the defeat of strikes, and drove down the price of labour. On a more insidious level, strikebreaking "became something of an art, involving intricate infiltrations of plants and factories by spies, detectives, and 'spotters', as well as massive influxes of often notorious 'blacklegs'."[76] The employers' anti-union campaign also featured a disregard of union rules governing the training and use of apprentices, victimization of trade unionists and their sympathizers, an open-shop campaign, and the use of legislated injunctions to limit picketing. In many instances of industrial conflict, employers did not hesitate to call on special teams of private police to supplement beleaguered regular police forces. When these tactics failed, more extreme steps were taken to defeat workers. On numerous occasions, Jamieson informs us, "local or provincial authorities read the Riot Act or proclaimed Martial Law, banned public assemblies and

75. Quoted in Bryan D. Palmer, "Industrial Capitalism and the Emergence of a Local Proletariat: The Case of London, Ontario," unpublished paper, University of Western Ontario, 1973.
76. Heron and Palmer, *op. cit.,* p. 447.

brought in militia or regular units of the armed forces."[77] Between 1900 and 1913 no less than eleven strikes across the nation were confronted by regular military forces.[78]

The escalation of class struggle prompted the Canadian state to adopt a more interventionist role in industrial relations. The architect of state policy at the time was William Lyon McKenzie King. The Department of Labour was established in 1900, and King was installed as the first Deputy Minister of Labour and, following his election to Parliament in 1908, the first full-time Minister of Labour. King defined industrial conflict as a disease, albeit a curable one. He strove to create an industrial relations system marked by co-operation, peace, and continuous production. King's most lasting contribution to labour relations was the Industrial Disputes and Investigation Act (IDIA), which he drafted in 1907. The Act prohibited strikes and lockouts pending the completion of an investigation of the contested issues in each case and attempts at conciliation by a board consisting of representatives of labour, employers, and the government. If the dispute was still unresolved, the law required 30 days notice before a strike or lockout could be legally staged. Failure to comply with the Act resulted in penalties including jail sentences. The IDIA also enshrined the notion that disputes endangering the "public interest" should be limited by state action. While King viewed the state as a neutral party to labour–capital conflict—an "impartial umpire" as he regarded it—the state's efforts to ensure continued production reinforced capital and weakened labour. By requiring a cooling-off period prior to a walkout, unions lost, at least temporarily, their major bargaining leverage—the strike. Of the 101 disputes processed by the IDIA between 1907 and 1911, 90 were resolved before strike action was taken. While the major weapon of workers was blunted, the IDIA contained no prohibi-

---

77. Jamieson, *op. cit.,* p. 72.
78. For accounts of working class life in Montreal and Toronto during these years see Terry Copp, *The Anatomy of Poverty: The Condition of the Working Class in Montreal 1897–1929,* Toronto: McClelland and Stewart, 1974; and Greg Kealey, *Working Class Toronto at the Turn of the Century,* Toronto: New Hogtown Press, 1973.

tions of employers' anti-union tactics, such as the use of scab labour, injunctions, victimization of unionists, or yellow dog contracts.[79] As a result of the Act, striking workers found themselves confronted with a more or less united opposition of both employer and state.

During the recession of 1914-15 unionization and strikes declined, but between 1915 and 1919 union membership nearly tripled and strike activity increased each year, peaking in 1919. Two spectacular events in the workers' movement occurred in these years—the formation of the One Big Union and the Winnipeg General Strike. The One Big Union organized workers along industrial rather than craft lines—a response reflecting the breakdown of craftsmanship and the burgeoning demand for unskilled labour. The militant and avowedly anti-capitalist stance of the OBU was evident in the preamble to its constitution.

> *The O.B.U. . . . seeks to organize the wage worker not according to craft but according to industry; according to class and class needs; and calls upon all workers irrespective of nationality, sex, or craft to organize into a workers' organization, so that they may be enabled to more successfully carry on the every day fight over wages, hours of work, etc. and prepare themselves for the day when production for profit shall be replaced by the production for use.*[80]

There were far more strikes—over 320—in 1919 than in any previous year. The largest and most dramatic walkout occurred in Winnipeg, where workers across the city walked off their jobs to support demands by building-trades workers for higher

79. Craven, *op. cit.*, and Reginald Whitaker, "The Liberal Corporatist Ideas of Mackenzie King," *Labour/Le Travailleur*, 2, 1977, p. 137-169. Yellow dog contracts required as a condition of employment that workers vow not to involve themselves in any manner with trade unions.

80. Quoted in Harold A. Logan, *Trade Unions in Canada,* Toronto: MacMillan, 1948, p. 313. Also see Peter Warrian, "The Challenge of the One Big Union Movement in Canada 1919-1921," M.A. Thesis, University of Waterloo, 1971.

wages and metal-trades workers for union recognition.[81] The city came to a virtual standstill as normal commercial functions and municipal services were curtailed or closed down. While the general strike was not conceived of as a revolutionary tactic, it posed a dual challenge to the authorities. First, the prerogative of employers to exercise sole control over the conditions of employment came under attack. A major precipitant of the strike had been the demand for the right to bargain collectively through organizations workers *themselves* had formed. Second, for the duration of the strike workers decided what establishments would function and what services would be provided. As Bercuson notes, this transfer of decision-making power from elites to workers constitutes a *de facto* challenge to "constituted authority"; in a general strike, he remarks, "the existing order is undermined, whether by accident or design and whether on a purely local level or a more national one."[82]

LABOUR DECLINE AND THE DEPRESSION

Industrial development during the 1920s coincided closely with the investment of American capital in the Canadian economy, which increased rapidly between 1914 and 1930. Rapid growth and concentration of production were particularly evident in American-owned firms—in the extractive industries, automobile manufacturing, electrical appliances and supplies, and paper and pulp production.[83] A second great wave of mergers took place between 1925 and 1930 (90 companies merged in the peak year of 1928) and left substantial sections of the Canadian economy operating under monopoly or oligop-

81. The Winnipeg workers were supported by sympathy strikes in at least 30 cities and towns in Ontario, Manitoba, Alberta, British Columbia, and Saskatchewan. See Gregory Kealey, "1919: The Canadian Labour Revolt," *Labour/ Le Travail,* 13, Spring, 1984, pp. 11–44.
82. David Bercuson, "The Winnipeg General Strike," in Irving Abella, ed., *On Strike,* Toronto: James Lewis and Samuel, 1974, p. 29. The general strike, which lasted nearly six weeks, was finally broken when the federal government, using all the repressive measures available to do it, intervened in support of the employers.
83. *Foreign Direct Investment in Canada,* Ottawa: Information Canada, 1972.

oly conditions.[84] As the fortunes of large capitalist enterprises rose, the labour movement foundered. The 1920s was "a decade of anti-union violence, strikebreaking, wage reductions and industrial paternalism."[85] With the exception of many bitter struggles in the coal fields, labour militancy dissipated during this decade. The strikes that did occur were commonly undertaken for defensive purposes—to oppose wage cuts or to preserve the right to unionize. By the end of the decade, union membership had suffered a sharp decline.[86]

A new strain of corporate paternalism appeared just after World War I. Known variously as works councils, joint councils, employee representation, or company unions, these labour–management bodies were promoted by government officials and corporate moguls who, by the end of the war, had "accepted the apparently undeniable fact that large-scale enterprise and capitalist social relations created a profound sense of alienation from work and from the prevailing social system among the industrial working class."[87] Massey-Harris, International Harvester, Bell Telephone, and Imperial Oil formed joint councils in 1919. These pioneering efforts in Canada were soon followed by seventeen other large companies. At the end of 1920 it was estimated that between 145 000 and 200 000 employees (roughly 40 to 50 percent of the number of unionized workers) were employed by companies with joint councils.[88] Although the joint council movement faded in the second half of the decade, in 1928 one-fifth of the 300 firms sampled by the Ontario Department of Labour were operating with labour–management bodies.[89]

Joint councils in Canada were modelled after the so-called

84. Traves, *op. cit.*, p. 30.
85. Palmer, *Working Class Experience*, p. 189.
86. Shop floor resistance in union and non-union plants continued throughout this period of labour quiescence. See, for example, Stanley Mathewson, *Restriction of Output Among Unorganized Workers*, Carbondale: Southern Illinois University Press, 1969.
87. Traves, *op. cit.*, p. 40.
88. See Graham Lowe, "The Rise of Modern Management in Canada," *Canadian Dimension*, 14, 3, December, 1979, pp. 32–38; Bruce Scott, " 'A Place in the Sun': The Industrial Council at Massey-Harris, 1919-1929," *Labour/Le Travailleur*, 1, 1976, pp. 158–192.
89. Traves, *op. cit.*

Rockefeller Plan devised by Mackenzie King (while in the employ of John D. Rockefeller) and instituted at the Colorado Fuel and Iron Company in 1914, one year after the infamous Ludlow Massacre.[90] The Plan provided for elected worker representatives and an equal number of management personnel to sit on committees or larger forums to discuss grievances, recreation, health and safety, wages (in some instances), and matters pertaining to production efficiency. Ostensibly adopted by employers to establish a measure of industrial democracy, the councils did nothing to redress the blatant imbalance of power at the workplace. The councils could not veto management decisions, council resolutions needed the support of management to be implemented, and management reserved the right to make decisions (on any matter) without consulting the councils.[91] Employee representation plans did not seriously challenge management's authority. While the plans were implemented to promote a co-operative work force, their primary purpose was to deter unionization.[92] The evidence supporting this conclusion is unequivocal. Joint councils were formed mainly in periods of turbulent industrial relations, but when labour unrest subsided, as it did after the early years of the 1920s, corporate interest in "democracy" flagged. As industrial unionism gathered steam in the 1930s, companies once again began adopting joint council programs. Studies of individual firms showed that employee representation plans were most likely to be implemented when a strike was in progress or recently ended and when the union was gaining ground in the plant. The anti-unionism of an employee representation plan

90. In the Ludlow (Colorado) massacre, government troops and hired gunmen killed eleven children and two women related to miners who were striking for union recognition in 1913.
91. Scott, *op. cit.,* found that the industrial council of Massey-Harris's Toronto plant operated as a "device through which the management announced its decisions and policies, hoping thereby to legitimize those actions in the eyes of the workers."
92. *Cf.* Irving Bernstein, *The Lean Years,* Boston: Houghton–Mifflin, 1960. The United States Bureau of Labor Statistics found that two-thirds of the 126 employee representation plans it investigated were adopted to head off trade unions. See U.S. Department of Labor, *Characteristics of Company Unions 1935,* Bulletin no. 634, June, 1937.

instituted at Hamilton's Stelco plant in 1936 was made explicit by the plant manager in a memo to employees:

> *It is not necessary for an employee to join a union to receive a fair hearing or fair treatment. The works council was organized to provide a medium of approach permitting the discussion of any problem that may arise. The company feels that in joining a union the employees will be acting against their own best interests. . . . In the interests of their own peace and comfort the employee representation plan offers better opportunities for the management and the employees to confer with one another than does the intervention of any outside parties whose interest is chiefly in the furtherance of their union and not in the welfare and comfort of the employees and their families.*[93]

It is difficult to offer anything but a tentative assessment of how successful the joint council movement was in attaining corporate objectives. Employee representation plans undoubtedly defused labour unrest and delayed the establishment of unions in some firms. More often, however, these programs were too patently a device of capital, too obviously a means of circumventing genuine unions to be entirely effective in this regard. Though workers were able to use the councils to achieve some of their ends, managers often burdened councils' agendas with trivial matters, leaving most workers disillusioned with the process. In the end, employee representation plans proved no match for the great surge of industrial unionism of the late thirties and early forties. Ironically, this unionizing drive was often advanced by workers who had developed leadership and organizational skills as worker representatives on joint councils.[94]

93. Robert Storey, "Unionism, Politics and Culture: Steel Workers and the Hamilton Working Class 1935-1948," Ph.D. Thesis, University of Toronto, 1981, p. 201.

94. Cf. *Ibid.;* Bernstein, *op. cit.;* Scott, *op. cit.;* John Schacht, "Toward Industrial Unionism: Bell Telephone Workers and Company Unions, 1919-1937," *Labor History*, 16, 1, 1975, pp. 5-36; Stuart Brandes, *American Welfare Capitalism 1880-1940,* Chicago: University of Chicago Press, 1976.

During the depression years of the 1930s, industry stagnated, hundreds of thousands of Canadians were without jobs, and those who did work were subject to intense discipline from employers who could easily find replacements among the huge army of the unemployed. Overall union membership continued to shrink under the lacklustre leadership of the Trades and Labour Congress. However, militant unions did surface during the thirties, led by the Communist-dominated Workers' Unity League. Ignoring craft jurisdictions, the WUL organized the unemployed as well as workers in industries that had been previously ignored or regarded as too difficult to canvass. The depression brought on militant strikes (many to prevent wage cuts), such as those at Stratford and Estevan, and intensified the struggle for jobs and unemployment insurance. This surge of unrest reached its height with the protest march, "On to Ottawa," until the protesters reached Regina, where the march was tragically interrupted by the RCMP.

Toward the end of the decade the economy picked up somewhat, and a new wave of union militancy, industrial unrest, and strikes reached a peak in 1937.[95] A landmark struggle took place in Oshawa in 1937. Reacting to an assembly line speed-up proposed by American efficiency experts, General Motors workers, represented by the Congress of Industrial Organizations (CIO), walked away from their jobs. While the demand to reduce work speed remained important throughout the strike, another issue assumed growing prominence—the recognition by employers of the CIO. The workers held out and won a contract, improved wages and hours of work, and limited union recognition. This strike, as Abella points out, marked the birth of industrial unionism in Canada. Workers in mass production industries had taken the first successful step toward organization along industrial rather than craft lines. Nevertheless, employer intransigence, state repression, and strong divisions within the labour movement temporarily retarded the forward march of the CIO.[96]

95. Jamieson, *op. cit.*, p. 268.
96. Irving Abella, "Oshawa 1937," in Abella, *op. cit.*, pp. 93–128; Wayne

WORLD WAR II AND ITS AFTERMATH

With the onset of World War II the Canadian economy had fully recovered. The wartime economy underwent further expansion and diversification, and ever more complex machinery was introduced in the industrial sphere. Labour shortages and the wartime emphasis on productivity intensified the drive toward industrial unionism which had stalled in 1937. Union membership nearly doubled during the war years. Walkouts in the early forties occurred with increasing frequency: In 1943 alone over one million worker-days were lost to strikes. Between 1946 and 1947 another strike wave, involving even greater numbers of workers than in 1943, spread across Canada. One of the more notable instances of conflict during this decade took place in Quebec in 1949, where the asbestos strike marked what many regarded as a turning point (to the left) in the history of the province.[97]

Workers discontent in the forties generally revolved around wages, work speeds, and above all, union recognition. In response to these struggles, the federal government in 1944 enacted PC 1003, an order of Privy Council that guaranteed automatic union recognition when a majority of workers voted for the union. The 1945 strike at the Ford Motor plant in Windsor was significant in that it led to an inquiry in which Mr. Justice Ivan Rand handed down a landmark decision. The Rand Formula provided for union security by allowing unions to automatically deduct dues (the dues "check-off") from all workers in a union shop. But the Formula restrained direct action by workers by removing their right to strike during the life of a contract, thus individualizing grievances and bottling

---

Roberts and John Bullen, "A Heritage of Hope and Struggle: Workers, Unions, and Politics in Canada, 1930–1982," in Michael S. Cross and Gregory S. Kealey, eds., *Modern Canada 1930–1980's,* Toronto: McClelland and Stewart, 1984, pp. 105–140.

97. The demands of asbestos workers were among the most progressive in Canadian labour history, for they entailed significant encroachments on management's rights. The union demanded approval of promotions, disciplinary action, incentive systems, job methods, and pay rates. It is not surprising that the owners resisted the strike so bitterly. See Fraser Isbester, "Asbestos 1949," in Abella, *op. cit.,* pp. 163–196.

them up in legal machinery. The provisions of PC 1003 were incorporated in the 1948 Industrial Relations and Disputes Investigation Act.[98]

The war opened up job opportunities for women which *might* have dismantled traditional conceptions of women's role in Canadian society and provided the cutting edge of a movement toward greater gender equality. The federal government undertook a vigorous campaign to recruit women into jobs in war industries vacated by men serving in the military. Special measures, such as income tax concessions and day-care centres in Ontario and Quebec, were established with great success. For the first time thousands of women moved out of the household and traditional female job enclaves into jobs and industries previously dominated by men. In 1939 roughly 630 000 women were in the labour force (about one-third of whom worked as domestic servants). By November, 1943, an estimated 1 200 000 women were employed at full-time jobs. In wartime women held jobs as machine operators, welders, electricians, crane operators, and painters in ship yards, steel mills, aircraft plants, and munitions factories. Yet these breakthroughs were never viewed by government officials or employers as more than a temporary measure. Agencies responsible for recruiting women changed their tune as soon as the war wound down and servicemen were demobilized. By 1945 women who had left the home or jobs in service industries for higher paying employment in war industries were being urged to return to their traditional pursuits. Tax concessions were withdrawn and nurseries closed. Government agencies began to redirect women into sex-segregated employment in restaurants, schools, hospitals, laundries, households, and the garment and textile industries. Toronto newspapers printed advertisements encouraging women to return to "their" jobs, and posters appeared urging women to trade the riveter for the dust mop. As Pierson says, "Women's obligation to work in wartime was the major theme [of recruitment campaigns], not women's right to

---

98. Roberts and Bullen, *op. cit.* This legislation pertained only to industries under federal jurisdiction. The provinces subsequently enacted similar laws.

work."[99] The demobilization of women and their return to the home and sex-segregated occupations was as "successful" as the recruitment efforts, and no legacy of equal opportunity remained. By 1946 the female labour force had dwindled to 650 000, only 20 000 more than were in paid employment in 1939.[100]

After the war, American capital continued to rapidly penetrate the Canadian economy, particularly in manufacturing and resource industries, until about 1970 when the percentage of foreign-owned firms began to decline somewhat.[101] Post-war concentration of economic activity also accelerated. In 1965 there were half a million business firms in Canada, yet as few as forty-four privately owned, large corporations were responsible for 44 percent of the value of assets held by all non-financial firms.[102] In 1958 firms with assets of $500 000 and over comprised only about 15 percent of all manufacturing concerns. However, these same large firms employed over three-quarters of all persons working in the manufacturing sector of the economy.[103] An accelerated pace of corporate mergers and acquisitions in the 1960s and 1970s left the economy more concentrated than at any other time in the past. High concentration is characteristic not only of the manufacturing sector but also of transportation and utilities, finance, trade, and mining ventures. Despite the presence of many small busi-

99. Ruth Roach Pierson, *"They're Still Women After All": The Second World War and Canadian Womanhood,* Toronto: McClelland and Stewart, 1986, p. 23.
100. The material on women during World War II is taken from *Ibid.* and Diana Lynn Rankin, "The Mobilization and Demobilization of Canadian Women in the Work Force During the Second World War," M.A. thesis, University of Western Ontario, 1986.
101. Jorge Niosi, *Canadian Multinationals,* Toronto: Garamond Press, 1985; William Carroll, "Dependency, Imperialism and the Capitalist Class in Canada," in Robert Brym, ed., *The Structure of the Canadian Capitalist Class,* Toronto: Garamond Press, 1985, pp. 21–52.
102. G. Rosenbluth, "Concentration and Monopoly in the Canadian Economy," in Michael Oliver, ed., *Social Purpose for Canada,* Toronto: University of Toronto Press, 1961, pp. 199–248. Also see John Porter, *The Vertical Mosaic,* Toronto: University of Toronto Press, 1965.
103. George W. Wilson, Scott Gordon, Stanislaw Judek, *Canada: An Appraisal of its Needs and Resources,* Toronto: University of Toronto Press, 1965.

nesses, the dominant force in the Canadian economy by the mid-1980s was the giant corporation.[104]

Growing economic concentration was accompanied by several trends—many already evident at the turn of the century—that virtually reshaped the economy in the 1940s. The scope of government functions expanded enormously and there was a marked acceleration of employment in the public (government) sector of the economy. In 1946 about nine percent of the labour force was employed by public institutions, compared with approximately twenty-five percent in 1965. Within the public sector the most notable advances occurred in jobs connected with health care, education, and government service.[105] Massive growth in the public sector and the increasing size and complexity of industrial and commercial enterprises resulted in a burgeoning demand for white-collar personnel. White-collar employees accounted for one-quarter of the labour force in 1941; by 1961 nearly forty percent were engaged in this type of work. Most sections of the white-collar work force have undergone substantial transformations in their conditions of work. Ironically, many of these jobs, which once were viewed as an escape from factory labour, have turned out to bear a strong resemblance to blue-collar work.

Overt labour unrest declined during the 1950s but resumed in the following decade, reaching a peak in 1966. The horizons of organized labour were broadened considerably during this decade by an infusion of "new" unionists. Led by the example of inside postal workers, who in the aftermath of their 1965 strike formed a genuine union (empowered to bargain collectively and to strike) and affiliated with the Canadian Labour Congress (CLC), 50 000 white-collar and public sector workers

104. Wallace Clement, *The Canadian Corporate Elite*, Toronto: McClelland and Stewart, 1975; Paul Phillips and Stephen Watson, "From Mobilization to Continentalism: The Canadian Economy in the Post-Depression Period," in Cross and Kealey, *Modern Canada 1930*–1980's, pp. 20–45.
105. Stephen Peitchinis, *Canadian Labour Economics*, Toronto: McGraw-Hill of Canada, 1970, pp. 83–85; Hugh Armstrong, "The Labour Force and State Workers in Canada," in Leo Panitch, ed., *The Canadian State: Political Economy and Political Power*, Toronto: University of Toronto Press, 1977, pp. 289–310.

joined CLC-affiliated unions between 1965 and 1968.[106] Strikes during the 1960s were located primarily in the industrial belt of Quebec and Ontario, and most notably involved workers employed in manufacturing, construction, postal work, and transportation and communications (railworkers and truckers).

The labour unrest of this period had several distinctive characteristics. First, there was an unprecedented tendency for rank and file workers to refuse to ratify agreements negotiated by union leaders and the company. These actions indicated not only that workers lacked faith in union leaders but also that the expectations, grievances, and militancy of ordinary workers were greater than those of union officials. A second feature of the mid-1960s era was the willingness of the labour movement to defy "law and order"; court orders were ignored and injunctions were violated. Third, an inordinately high proportion of work stoppages were accompanied by violence and illegality, including property damage, personal injury, and arrests and convictions. Finally, an unusually high number of strikes were illegal; in 1966 about one-third of all work stoppages were not sanctioned by law.[107] The depth of labour militancy during this era was captured in the following terse observation of the 1969 Task Force on Labour Relations: "One can find varying manifestations of each of these phenomena in past generations, but never in the same intense combination as in recent years."[108]

THE RECENT EXPERIENCE

Work stoppages skyrocketed again in the early 1970s. Quebec was the site of a dramatic confrontation between public employees and the provincial government which culminated in a general strike in 1972. In 1975 Canada outranked all other Western nations (including strike-prone Italy) in worker-days lost to strikes. Partly as a response to inflationary pressures, the

106. Roberts and Bullen, *op. cit.*
107. John Crispo and H.W. Arthurs, "Industrial Unrest in Canada: A Diagnosis of Recent Experience," *Industrial Relations*, 23, 1968, pp. 237–265; Jamieson, *op. cit.*
108. *Canadian Industrial Relations: The Report of the Task Force on Labour Relations*, Ottawa: The Queen's Printer, 1969, p. 99.

government imposed wage controls in 1975, thus curtailing strike activity. A year after the imposition of wage controls, one million workers took to the streets to protest the actions of the Anti-Inflation Board. As international competition intensified and the recession deepened in the late 1970s, the state searched desparately for ways to restore profit margins. Keynesian policies of stimulating investment and demand through wage maintenance and welfare programs were abandoned in favour of monetarist restraint measures.[109] Federal and provincial governments gave priority to controlling inflation over reducing unemployment, and they increasingly restricted the right to strike, especially among public service workers.[110] These actions generated massive opposition in the public sector. In 1983 British Columbia government employees and school teachers walked away from their jobs and hundreds of thousands of people across the province demonstrated to protest the Social Credit party's draconian attacks on labour and social rights and welfare-related services.[111] And in 1986 thousands of employees of the Newfoundland government, including administrative and clerical workers, engaged in an illegal strike for wage hikes and to protest anti-strike legislation.

The corporate world responded to the crisis by rationalizing their operations, relocating plants in non-union regions, and demanding concessions from employees. The bitter 1978 strike of Fleck workers (almost all of whom were women) signalled the renewed determination of employers to resist unionization and improvements in wages and working conditions. Reminiscent of nineteenth-century struggles between labour and capital, the massive show of police force evident during the strike was unprecedented in Ontario history. That employers' attacks on labour were as durable as the recession was demonstrated dramatically by events at the Gainers meat packing plant in

109. David A. Wolfe, "The Rise and Demise of the Keynesian Era in Canada: Economic Policy 1930–1982," in Cross and Kealey, *op. cit.*, pp. 46–78.
110. Leo Panitch and Donald Swartz, *From Consent to Coercion: The Assault on Trade Union Freedoms,* Toronto: Garamond Press, 1985.
111. For an incisive analysis of these events see Bryan D. Palmer, "The Rise and Fall of British Columbia's Solidarity," in Bryan D. Palmer, ed., *The Character of Class Struggle: Essays in Canadian Working-Class History, 1850–1985,* Toronto: McClelland and Stewart, 1986, pp. 176–200.

Edmonton, Alberta, which occurred nearly ten years after the Fleck strike. When the workers struck for higher wages, management immediately hired scab labour and announced their intention to break the union. The result was predictable: a massive police presence, disregard of court injunctions, picket line violence, and hundreds of arrests. In June of 1986, 8000 workers gathered outside the Alberta legislature (the largest labour demonstration in Alberta since the depression) demanding that the province's reactionary labour laws be rescinded. But as one major newspaper noted, "the real villain behind the province's current round of labour turmoil may, however, be a declining economy and a deep-seated anti-union atmosphere in the province, both of which have made bosses more aggressive in dealing with workers."[112]

Developments in computers and micro-electronics have enabled industrialists to step up the pace of automation, which now includes robots and numerically controlled machines. But the impact of microtechnology is being felt most profoundly in offices, banks, retail stores, and other workplaces in the service sector. Previously impervious to significant technologically-based productivity gains, service work is being dramatically restructured and a massive displacement of employees looms. Women are most threatened by this development, since they are concentrated in tertiary occupations. Efforts to organize these workers are seriously hampered by employers' fierce anti-union campaigns, as illustrated by recent struggles at K-Mart, Radio Shack, Eatons, and the Canadian Imperial Bank of Commerce.

Joblessness also has taken its toll. Throughout the 1980s the *official* unemployment rate has hovered around ten percent. The manufacturing sector has been particularly hard hit as hundreds of plants have closed down permanently or have relocated their operations. The spectre of job loss and the aura of restraint promoted by the state facilitate employers' demands for concessions on wages and fringe benefits, work rules, and employment and remunerative practices (particularly the hiring of part-time workers and instituting two-tier wage struc-

112. Toronto *Globe and Mail*, June 19, 1986.

tures). As the 1990s approach, it is clear that the advances in labour and social legislation won by working people in the post-World War II era are in danger of being destroyed by capital and the state.

THE TRANSFORMATION OF WORK AND SOCIETY: BROAD TRENDS

In a little over 100 years developments in the ownership of the means of production, the division of labour, and markets have combined to transform the nature and organization of work in Canadian society. From a rural society of small independent producers and shopkeepers in the middle of the nineteenth century, Canada has become a nation dominated by monopoly capital, giant enterprises, and government bureaucracies. Once numerically and politically dominant, the traditional *petite bourgeoisie* (self-employed persons in trade, business or the professions, like farmers, fishermen, independent artisans, or physicians) now constitutes about six percent of the Canadian labour force. If we add to the category of *petite bourgeoisie* small employers (about four percent) and major capitalists (no more than one percent), then approximately 89 percent of persons in the Canadian labour force are dependent employees who must sell their labour power for wages or salaries. This enormous growth of employment dependency has meant that the work of more and more individuals is defined and controlled by central authorities.[113]

As the *petit bourgeois* mode of production was being replaced by large corporate and government organizations, labour was increasingly fragmented, first on the shop floor and later in offices. While this trend was facilitated by the introduction of ever more sophisticated technology, the elaborate division of labour did not flow inevitably from technical and mechanical innovations and their requirements. The vertical and horizontal extension of the division of labour was initiated, stimulated, and institutionalized by the employing class, who

113. These calculations were derived from data presented in Carl J. Cuneo, "Has the Traditional Petite Bourgeoisie Persisted?", *The Canadian Journal of Sociology*, 9, Summer, 1984, pp. 269–301, and Social Change in Canada Project, Institute for Behavioural Research, York University, 1979.

stood to benefit materially from such changes. In the 1870s the casual rhythms of toil and the comparatively rudimentary division of labour characteristic of the pre-industrial period were shattered by the rise of the factory system in which work was specialized, timed, and closely supervised. The compartmentalization and regimentation of work entailed in the factory system were heightened in the early twentieth century by the application of the principles of scientific management and the introduction and spread of mass production techniques. By chopping up work into minute tasks and divorcing the conception of work from its execution, these two innovations not only made the labour process more repetitive, stultifying, and meaningless; they also were responsible for substantially reducing workers' control over the production process.

Hand in hand with the trends described above, markets in labour and commodities grew and matured. In the middle of the nineteenth century markets were still local and undeveloped and only of marginal importance to the lives of many Canadians. With the construction of major transportation arteries and the emergence of capitalist production units, trade and commerce spread, and the self-sufficiency of the small village was destroyed. Increasingly, Canadian people were compelled to order their lives in terms of economic criteria. Human labour was converted into a commodity that was bought and sold. The overriding objective of business firms—to generate profits and amass capital—was often achieved at the expense of the needs and interests of workers and the community.

The developments delineated above extended and deepened structural alienation. And the alienation spawned by the new industrial order penetrated the consciousness of workers. Since its inception, industrial capitalism has been met by fierce resistance on the part of Canadian working people. While this resistance varied widely in substance and effect, it can be seen as an attempt by workers to deal with the causes and consequences of their inability to govern the process and products of labour.

4 Post-Industrial Society and White-Collar Worlds

CHARACTERISTICS OF POST-INDUSTRIAL SOCIETY

Over the past several decades prominent social scientists have claimed that massive and qualitative changes have taken place in the central institutions of advanced capitalist nations. These changes are said to be so vast that concepts such as "industrial society" or "capitalist society" no longer capture the essence of the new social order. In their place, new terms have arisen, symbolic of the changing social realities—the service society, the knowledge society, technetronic, post-capitalist society, and most commonly, post-industrial society. At the root of this transformation are technological advances and the consequent shift from an economy based on the production of goods to one centred around the provision of services.

Most theorists of post-industrial society are optimistic about the direction in which social change is moving.[1] The typical shortcomings of industrial capitalism are allegedly in the process of being solved by evolutionary transformations in technology and the economy. As an ever-increasing proportion of the labour force is engaged in cleaner, more complex, and

1. This brief discussion of post-industrial society follows most closely the writings of Daniel Bell in his *The Coming of Post-Industrial Society*, New York: Basic Books, 1973. There are substantial disagreements among post-industrial theorists, many of which stem from different ideological positions. Contrast, for example, Bell's analysis, which can be described as politically reformist, with that of the neo-Marxist Alain Tourraine. See his *The Post-Industrial Society*, New York: Random House, 1971.

more desirable white-collar jobs, problems growing out of the nature and organization of work are becoming less of an issue. Manual jobs, the traditional source of dissatisfaction and conflict, are destined to disappear. Because of automation, surviving factory jobs will require more technical skills and broader spheres of worker discretion. The man–machine relationship, which was the crux of work relations in capitalist society, is being replaced by a new focus. People now deal with other people rather than with machines. These changes portend the virtual eradication of alienated labour and class struggle.

Technological changes, it is suggested, have put a premium on education. The labour market requires continuous educational upgrading of the populace to meet the demands of sophisticated technology and to plan and administer an increasingly complex society. Where the business firm and the factory were the central institutions of industrial society, the key institution of post-industrial society is the university (or some other form of "knowledge institute"). Therefore, professionals, scientists, and technicians are said to constitute a new dominant class. Their rise to power rests on the possession of knowledge and skills that are becoming increasingly necessary to the functioning of post-industrial society.

Since adherents of the post-industrial thesis believe we are in the initial phase of the new society, it is possible to use existing data to evaluate the validity of their position. The remainder of this chapter is devoted to this task. We should state at the outset that the bulk of the evidence does not support the sanguine forecasts of post-industrial theorists.

TRENDS IN THE LABOUR FORCE: JOBS AND EDUCATION

Post-industrial theorists quite correctly stress that the economies of advanced capitalist nations have undergone a major shift from resource extraction and goods-producing industries to service-producing industries. For example, employment in the service or tertiary sector of the Canadian economy rose from approximately 28 percent of the labour force in 1901 to

FIGURE I
Employment by Economic Sector, Canada 1911-1983

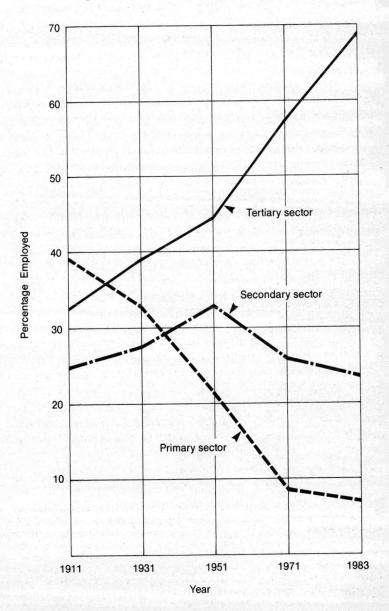

SOURCE: Adapted from Alton W.J. Craig, *The System of Industrial Relations in Canada*, Second Edition, Scarborough: Prentice-Hall of Canada, 1986, Table 2.5, p. 29.

nearly 70 percent in 1981 (see Figure I).[2] This massive expansion of the tertiary sector, however, does not in itself betoken improvement in the content and conditions of work. The first step toward evaluating the thesis of progressive job upgrading involves examining changes in the proportion of the populace employed in the major occupation groups.

As Table I indicates, white-collar occupations have grown enormously over this century. In 1901 about 15 percent of the Canadian labour force was employed in white-collar jobs. White-collar labour increased to approximately 25 percent by 1921, held constant at this point until 1941, and then grew rapidly between 1941 and 1961. By 1981, 52.2 percent of Canadian workers were engaged in white-collar occupations. The expansion of the tertiary sector and the white-collar stratum, however, was accompanied by only a marginal reduction of blue-collar employment, from a 1941 peak of 48.7 percent to 42.2 percent of the labour force in 1981. There has been a decline of employment in manufacturing from a high of 16.4 percent of the labour force in 1961 to 14.8 percent in 1981 (and to 13.8 percent in 1985), with further decline being a certainty. This shrinkage of blue-collar jobs has been partially offset by employment gains between 1961 and 1981 in construction and service occupations. Many jobs in these latter occupation groups require no special training or skill and hence make no contribution to the alleged trend toward job complexity. We can conclude, therefore, that the long term gains in white-collar employment have come not at the expense of blue-collar jobs, but rather through job losses in the agricultural sector, where employment fell sharply from 40.3 percent of the labour force in 1901 to 4.1 percent in 1981.

The expansion of white-collar occupations is said to have created a demand for highly educated people, yet evidence shows this belief to be erroneous. In 1981, over one-half of all

---

2. The tertiary or service sector is residually defined as those industries not involved in the production of items such as food, clothing, houses, cars, and other tangible goods. It is distinguished from the primary sector, comprising agriculture and resource extraction, and the secondary sector, which consists of manufacturing and construction.

TABLE I
Canadian Labour Force, Distributed By
Major Occupation Groups, 1901–1981

	1901	1921	1941	1961	1981
All occupations	100.0	100.0	100.0	100.0	100.0
White-collar	15.2	25.1	25.2	38.6	52.2
Proprietary and managerial	4.3	7.2	5.4	7.9	8.9
Professional and technical	4.6	5.5	6.7	10.0	15.5
Clerical	3.2	6.8	7.2	12.9	18.9
Sales	3.1	5.6	5.9	7.8	8.9
Blue-collar	44.5	42.0	48.7	48.6	42.2
Manufacturing and mechanical	15.9	11.4	16.0	16.4	14.8
Construction	4.7	4.7	4.7	5.3	6.6
Labourers	7.2	9.7	6.3	5.4	—
Transportation and communications	4.4	5.5	6.4	7.8	7.3
Service	8.2	7.1	10.5	10.8	12.0
Fishing, logging, mining	4.1	3.6	4.8	2.9	1.7
Agriculture	40.3	32.7	25.8	10.2	4.1
Occupation not stated or unclassified	—	.2	.3	2.6	1.3

SOURCE: Adapted from Noah M. Meltz, *Manpower in Canada 1931 to 1961*, Ottawa: Department of Manpower and Immigration, 1969, Table A.1; *1981 Census of Canada, Vol. I*, Cat. 92–917, Table 1, Ottawa: Statistics Canada, 1983. It should be noted that in 1971 some occupational classifications differed from previous years. The "labourer" category was dropped; the category "manufacturing and mechanical" was broken into the divisions of "processing," "machining," "product fabricating," "assembling," and "repairing."

white-collar workers were employed in clerical or sales positions; jobs that, for the most part, are neither complex nor challenging. In addition, by a conservative estimate, approximately 70 percent of the individuals designated by Statistics Canada as "professionals and technicians" are not in fact engaged in "knowledge work," i.e., in work that requires the training and knowledge or that affords the autonomy characteristic of true professional work.

Nevertheless, how are we to interpret the enormous expansion of educational facilities and the rising educational attainments of the population?[3] It would be misleading, albeit tempting, to conclude that work has become a more complex and demanding activity. But the education industry, while responsive to the labour market, is propelled by forces often independent of technology and the economy. For example, in the United States, of the overall increase in educational attainments among members of the labour force, only 15 percent can be attributed to broad changes in the occupational structure over the first seven decades of this century, that is, to a decline in low-skilled jobs and an increase in jobs with high-skill requirements. Nor is there evidence that the expansion of the education industry can be accounted for by a gradual upgrading of skill requirements of the same jobs. This means education has increased over and above advances in the complexity of work and that many people today are over-educated for the jobs they hold.[4] The situation is much the same in Canada. As

3. The 1960s was a decade of spectacular growth in education in Canada. School and university enrollments grew by about 50 percent and staff expanded by 70 percent. In the mid–1950s only six percent of the age group 18-24 was enrolled in Canadian universities. By 1968 the figure had swollen to 14 percent. Edward Harvey declares that this development was in part based on the mistaken belief that economic growth and progress are dependent upon a highly educated labour force. See his *Educational Systems and the Labour Market*, Don Mills: Longman Canada, 1974.
4. Randall Collins, "Functional and Conflict Theories of Educational Stratification," *American Sociological Review*, 36, 1971, pp. 1002–1019. Collins' findings are not unique. Researchers in the United States agree that educational attainments of the work force have outstripped educational requirements of the economy. See David Livingstone, "Job Skills and Schooling: A Class Analysis of Entry Requirements and Underemployment," in *Transitions to Work*, University of Manitoba: Institute for Social and Economic Research, 1985, p. 106.

Harvey and Blakely concluded from their research, the problem Canada faces is not an absence of good workers but a lack of good jobs.[5]

The "surplus" of educated individuals in the work force can be explained, at least in part, by the hiring practices of employers. A continuous over-supply of job-seekers allows employers to be highly selective in their recruitment practices, demanding educational credentials whether or not they are required for the job. This process is a self-fulfilling one insofar as individuals come to recognize that successful job hunting depends on acquiring educational credentials. It would be comforting to think that new technology will alleviate this imbalance, but recent advances in automation, micro-computers, and high tech industries indicate that this bleak trend is not about to change. While sophisticated technologies do create jobs that need to be performed by highly educated professionals, the majority of new jobs (including those in high tech industries) require little training or skill.[6]

WHITE-COLLAR WORLDS

While the evidence presented above reveals that the complexity and autonomy of white-collar jobs has been exaggerated, it is necessary to look more closely still at the nature of white-collar work. To identify someone simply as a white-collar worker reveals almost nothing about the precise character of his or her work: the level of education it requires, the complexity of the job, its income or status. To understand white-collar work—especially the discontent associated with it—it is necessary, first of all, to break down white-collar employees into sub-categories, even though these smaller units are themselves often too broad to permit solid generalizations.

White-Collar Masses: Office and Sales Clerks
In today's job market, clerical work differs substantially from what it was in the past. At the turn of the century, the clerk was

5. Edward B. Harvey and John Blakely, "Education, Social Mobility and the Challenge of Technological Change," in *Transitions to Work, Ibid.*, pp. 46–62.
6. This issue is discussed in more detail in Chapter 6.

usually employed in a small office where he (clerks were almost always male) was in close contact with company owners. Consequently, the clerk identified his interests with those of the company and, by extension, conceived of himself as middle class. Furthermore, because of the small number of company personnel and the limited amount of paperwork, the duties of the clerk were varied: "The traditional clerk performed as a sort of human integrated data-processing system, handling purchasing and inventory, correspondence, accounts receivable and payable, bookkeeping, the preparation of financial statements, accounting, banking and so on, and may have helped out in the shipping room or with counter transactions in his spare time."[7]

During the early decades of the twentieth century, when corporate capitalism was taking root, the industries of manufacturing, transportation and communications, finance, and trade came to be dominated by large corporations. These corporate entities expanded their clerical staffs to handle a mounting flow of paperwork. "The office became the managerial nerve centre through which voluminous information vital for controlling all aspects of business was compiled, processed, and stored."[8] Between 1891 and 1931, the proportion of the Canadian labour force engaged in clerical work rose by over 300 percent.

This "administrative revolution" entailed more than just growth: As offices got larger, managers increasingly specialized clerical duties, progressively subordinated clerical labour, and, in more and more cases, hired women to fill clerical positions. With the concentration of enterprises into fewer and larger businesses, their internal organization underwent marked changes. Business operations were broken down into departments which handled separate functions such as purchasing, sales, and accounting. For example, in 1904, the clerical duties

7. J.C. McDonald, *Impact and Implications of Office Automation*, Ottawa: Department of Labour, 1964, p. 4. In terms of authority, dress, pay, and tasks, Harry Braverman argues, the early clerk was more closely related to the employer than to the production worker. *Labor and Monopoly Capital*, New York: Monthly Review Press, 1974.
8. Graham S. Lowe, "Class, Job and Gender in the Canadian Office," *Labour/Le Travailleur*, 10, Autumn, 1982, p. 15.

of the British Columbia Telephone Company's commercial office were carried out with only two women on staff: "They kept the accounts of all Vancouver subscribers, making out service bills, taking cash payments, making up the directory, taking orders for new telephones, and serving those customers who wanted to make long-distance calls from the company office. By the late twenties these functions had to be delegated to special departments, each of which required a staff of a dozen people or more."[9] Within each department work was further subdivided. At one time, increased business simply entailed hiring another clerk to duplicate the tasks of the first one; now this "additive principle" was shelved in favour of assigning specialized duties to office workers.[10]

Orthodox organization theorists like William Leffingwell (author of *Scientific Office Management* [1917], a classic on the subject), and Lyndal Urwick and Luther Gulick (who applied the principles of Taylorism to the office workplace) reflected as well as stimulated the trend toward the subdivision of clerical labour and the centralization of office authority.[11] The introduction of office machines—first the typewriter, the dictation machine, and the adding machine, and later punch-card equipment—facilitated the further specialization of office work. For example, although the typewriter can be used as an adjunct to general clerical duties, management decided to create specialized positions around the machine itself (such as "loans typist" or "policy typist" in insurance companies).[12] Always alert to labour intensification, management also created central-

9. Elaine Bernard, *The Long Distance Feeling: A History of the Telecommunications Workers Union*, Vancouver: New Star Books, 1982, p. 68.
10. Mcdonald, *op. cit.*, p. 5.
11. *Cf.* Robert A. Dahl, "The Science of Public Administration: Three Problems," in J.E. Hodgetts and D.C. Corbett, eds., *Canadian Public Administration*, Toronto: Macmillan of Canada, 1960, pp. 24–31. Braverman, *op. cit.*, argues that offices can be rationalized more easily than factories because paperwork is simpler to rearrange and move from post to post and because a great deal of clerical work can be easily counted and mathematized.
12. Graham S. Lowe, "Mechanization, Feminization, and Managerial Control in the Early Twentieth-Century Canadian Office," in Craig Heron and Robert

ized typing pools where workers spent all day at their typewriters (in contrast to a departmental typist who might enjoy slack periods). Many stenographers, who were responsible for a variety of tasks, now saw their jobs broken down into full-time specialties such as dictaphone typist, clerk typist, filing clerk, and receptionist.[13] By 1920 the impact of rationalization on the large Canadian office was easily discernible, as was noted that year by a weekly business newspaper published in Toronto, the *Monetary Times*:

> *The construction of the modern office grows constantly more like the construction of the factory. Work has been standardized, long rows of desks of uniform design and equipment now occupy the offices of our large commercial and financial institutions. With the increasing division of labour each operation becomes more simple. The field in which each member of the staff operates is narrower.*[14]

The introduction of Hollerith punch-card equipment in the 1930s contributed further to the fragmentation of work; coding, key-punching, sorting, collating, and computing operations could each become the sole preserve of specialized clerks. As the rationalization process unfolded, it was women who were recruited to fill the emergent office specialties. In the 1890s men dominated the ranks of the clerical labour force (85 percent male); by 1931, nearly one-half of clerical jobs were occupied by women.

Storey, eds., *On the Job: Confronting the Labour Process in Canada*, Montreal: McGill–Queen's University Press, 1986, pp. 112–209. It is important to distinguish between office machines that are adjuncts to and facilitate one's duties—desk calculators, duplicating machines, etc., and machines that one is required to work at constantly. Only in the latter instance is there a parallel with machine operators in factories.

13. Lowe, "Class, Job and Gender in the Canadian Office," *op. cit.*

14. Cited in Graham S. Lowe, "The Administrative Revolution in the Canadian Office: An Overview," in Tom Traves, ed., *Essays in Canadian Business History*, Toronto: McClelland and Stewart, 1984, p. 114.

Office rationalization continued during and after World War II; jobs were increasingly fragmented, the use of office machines spread, and new forms of mechanization were introduced. More and more clerks, mainly women, were relegated to the status of full-time office-machine operators.[15] These changes were accompanied by three significant developments. First, offices were becoming more and more impersonal, and, as office staffs expanded, clerks could be more easily replaced. Their individuality was becoming submerged in routinized procedures and a sea of desks, paper, office machines, and filing cabinets. The big bosses were people clerks heard about, but never saw. As Gooding describes it, "the strong mutual loyalty that has traditionally bound white-collar workers and management is rapidly eroding. These workers—clerks, accountants, bookkeepers, secretaries—were once the elite at every plant, the educated people who worked alongside the bosses and were happily convinced that they made all the wheels go around. Now there are platoons of them instead of a privileged few, and instead of talking to the boss they generally communicate with a machine."[16] In such settings, personal recognition and work gratification are elusive goals.[17] Second, the rationalization of office work was associated with the hiring of more and more women to fill clerical positions. At the turn of this century, about one of every five clerks was a woman; in 1941 the ratio rose to one-half; by 1981, women constituted nearly eight of every ten clerical workers. Thus, women clerks have been the primary victims of the gradual degradation of clerical work. They have been exposed to working conditions not unlike those experienced by blue-collar wage earners. Opportunities for promotion are limited, and those who do

15. Lowe, "Mechanization, Feminization, and Managerial Control in the Early Twentieth-Century Canadian Office," *op. cit.*
16. Judson Gooding, "The Fraying White Collar," *Fortune*, 82, 1970, p. 78.
17. This depiction, of course, applies mainly to large offices. As Lockwood has noted, in some large organizations office personnel are located in sub-units where the average number of people in the work group is small and where relations with the supervisor may be personal and cordial. See David Lockwood, *The Blackcoated Worker*, London: Unwin, 1958.

move up ordinarily advance only one step up, to low-level supervisory positions. The swollen ranks of female clerks, however, have resulted in the creation of higher level supervisory positions for men. It is the male employee who is almost always selected to assume a position of genuine control.[18] Finally, clerical wages have suffered a long-term relative decline. Average clerical earnings were higher than (a) the average wages of production workers in manufacturing until 1931, and (b) the average earnings of the overall labour force until 1941. After these dates, clerical income slipped even more. By the 1970s, clerks' annual earnings were over $1000 less than all workers and more than $2000 less than blue-collar workers in manufacturing.[19]

Despite mechanization, office work remained a labour-intensive process whose level of productivity had not changed significantly since the introduction of punch-card equipment. However, developments in microtechnology in the early 1970s together with the sharply falling costs of new automatic equipment promise to revolutionize the office labour process. The microprocessor has been described as a computer on a "chip" smaller than a fingernail. On this chip are thousands of electrical circuits that carry out operations once requiring a large mainframe computer. Microprocessors can be applied to a wide variety of office tasks. Recall that the office is the site where information is compiled, processed, and stored. "Information originates in speech, typed or handwritten texts and accounts, diagrams or photographs. The new technology can deal with all these forms: word processors deal with text; data processors with accounts; electronic telephone systems with speech; and facsimile transmitters with images. The computer services all of them."[20] Although still in its infancy, microtechnology has already eliminated jobs in offices, banks, telephone

18. *Cf. Royal Commission on the Status of Women in Canada*, Ottawa: Information Canada, 1970, p. 92. For additional evidence see Patricia Marchak, "Women Workers and White Collar Unions," *The Canadian Review of Sociology and Anthropology*, 10, 1973, pp. 134–147.
19. Lowe, "Class, Job and Gender in the Canadian Office," *op. cit.*
20. "Automating the Office," *Canadian Dimension*, 15, December, 1981, p. 32.

companies, and other sites of white-collar employment.[21] Even more drastic job loss is likely to occur in the near future. European studies have estimated that by the end of this century thirty to forty percent of present office work could be carried out by computers.[22] And Menzies projects that unemployment rates among Canadian clerks will be two to six times higher in 1990 than they were in 1980.[23] The character of clerical work is also destined to change. The Canada Task Force on Microtechnology has cited evidence suggesting that employers who implement micro-electronic equipment are tempted to maximize the return from their investment by requiring more full-time machine operators and by instituting shift work. Some clerical positions are eliminated altogether by the new equipment, while others are restricted to feeding data into computers or to processing information. At the same time, specialists with advanced training or experience are needed to program computers and to analyze the output. The divide that already exists between routine clerical jobs (held by women) and professional, technical, and managerial personnel (usually males) will therefore grow even larger, and the clerical worker's chances for promotion will be that much more limited. Finally, the new equipment may generate a whole new set of health and safety hazards. Questions have been raised as to whether radiation emitted by micro-electronic equipment, especially word processors, contributes to eye problems, cataracts, birth defects and miscarriages, and cancer.[24]

It is often claimed that because the work of office employees (with the exception of office-machine operators and typists) is not quantifiable, it is difficult to impose on them the kind of output standards that are normally applied to factory workers. This claim requires qualification. First, the absence of quantifiable outputs by no means implies an absence of management's

21. *Cf.* Heather Menzies, *Women and the Chip: Case Studies of the Effects of Informatics on Employment in Canada*, Montreal: Institute for Research on Public Policy, 1981. Between 1980 and 1986 Canadian banks dropped 9000 employees from their payrolls. Toronto *Globe and Mail*, March 28, 1986.
22. "Automating the Office," *op. cit.*
23. Menzies, *op. cit.*
24. *Ibid.*; Labour Canada Task Force on Micro-Electronics and Employment, *In the Chips*, Ottawa: Labour Canada, 1982.

high expectations and strict supervision of clerical workers.[25] In the larger offices, periodic evaluations of workers' performance and a virtual army of low-level supervisors ensure that the pace and atmosphere of office work is neither leisurely nor relaxed. For example, a Toronto service representative for Bell Canada complains that "all forms ... are checked for accuracy and completeness by the Service Analyst, and from time to time my calls are monitored by supervisors. There is one supervisor for every five girls."[26] And Canadian banks use performance evaluations in conjunction with arbitrary supervision, personal favouritism, disregard for seniority in promotions, and petty harassment.[27] Second, the spheres of office work immune from output quantification are shrinking. The continued application of scientific management to the office labour process has made it easier for managers to measure and control the activities of clerical workers. In the true spirit of Taylorism, organizations like General Tire & Rubber Company, Stanford University, and General Electric contributed to a manual entitled *A Guide to Office Clerical Time Standards*. The manual provides time standards (measured in fractions of a minute) for virtually every conceivable office activity. For example, according to the manual, it should take a worker .33 minutes to get up from a chair, the same amount of time to sit down in a chair, and .009 minutes to turn in a swivel chair. These standards are subsumed under the general heading "chair activity." Examples of other timed activities are: opening and closing drawers, walking specific distances, typing (per character and per inch), cutting with a scissors, stapling, opening envelopes, and so on.[28] Apparently manuals like this one and their informing logic are being put to use in this

25. Stanley Aronowitz claims that there is approximately one supervisor for every three-and-one-half office workers in both government and private bureaucracies. See his *False Promises*, New York: McGraw–Hill, 1973.

26. Joan Newman Kuyek, *The Phone Book: Working at the Bell*, Kitchener: Between the Lines, 1979, p. 13.

27. These problems were seen as organizing foci of the now defunct Service, Office and Retail Workers Union. See Elizabeth Beckett, *Unions and Bank Workers: Will the Twain Ever Meet?* Ottawa: Labour Canada Women's Bureau, 1984.

28. Braverman, *op. cit.*

country. Wallace relates how a group of management consultants changed productivity standards in a large Canadian life insurance company: The criteria for time standards were derived from a manual which "contains detailed and accurate measurements of the methods and time required for virtually any clerical operation."[29] Wallace also points out: "Many of Canada's largest employers of office staff—insurance companies, banks, and trust companies—are embarking on major programs aimed at reducing the cost of processing their mountains of paper work."[30] A keystone of these programs is the formulation and application of precise work measurement standards.

The capacity to monitor clerical work performance is greatly enhanced by recent developments in micro-electronic equipment. New forms of automation can keep a record of the number of strokes on a word processor, the number of customers processed by reservation clerks, the number of phone calls handled by telephone operators, and so on.[31] At the telephone company, for instance, "the new computer systems automatically routed calls to operators. A call came on the line immediately after the last call was completed. The new computer-controlled operator systems removed what little control the operator still had over her pace of work, and could monitor operators to a fraction of a second."[32] In 1982 the Canada Task Force on Micro-Electronics and Employment concluded that monitoring is based on mistrust and lack of respect for basic human dignity and ultimately constitutes an infringement on the rights of individuals. The Task Force concluded emphati-

29. Joan Wallace, "Building Up Office Efficiency," *Canadian Business*, 43, 1970, p. 55.
30. *Ibid.*, p. 46.
31. *Cf.* Patricia McDermott, "The New Demeaning of Work," *Canadian Dimension*, 15, December, 1981, pp. 34–37.
32. Bernard, *op. cit.*, p. 155. A newspaper release noted: "From the moment she plugs into her terminal in the morning to the second she unplugs it at night, every telephone operator in Canada is monitored by a machine. ... Every airline passenger agent has an automated terminal that reports on the number and length of calls, mistakes and the length of time away from the phone and then compares it with company performance requirements." London *Free Press*, October 9, 1985.

cally: "We strongly recommend that this practice be prohibited by law."[33] So far this recommendation has been ignored.

Over one-half of all persons in the occupational category "sales" (see Table I, page 77) are sales clerks, the majority of them women. Sales clerks have also been affected by changes similar to those taking place in offices. Many small retail sales outlets have been replaced by giant department stores, supermarkets, and discount stores. In such settings, the sales relationship is a depersonalized one, and jobs auxiliary to sales are specialized and routinized. Many clerks have been relegated to performing check-out tasks, and growing numbers of the retail work force have been reduced to materials handlers who load, stock, and move goods. In supermarkets, for instance, "the demand for the all-around grocery clerk, fruit and vegetable dealer, dairyman, butcher and so forth has long ago been replaced by ... truck unloaders, shelf-stockers, check-out clerks, meat wrappers, and meat cutters; of these, only the last retain any semblance of skill, and none requires any knowledge of retail trade."[34] Although automation has not proceeded nearly as rapidly in retail sales as it has in offices, recent U.S. studies suggest that the potential for a dramatic restructuring of retail sales operations is great.[35] Micro-electronic equipment is already contributing to the further routinization of sales work, as exemplified by the use in supermarkets of the universal product code and electronic scanners at check-out counters. With these innovations all the cashier does is pass the groceries over the scanner, bag them, and take the customers' money. Moreover, electronic cash registers can monitor the exact number of customers and items that the cashiers process during each shift.[36] According to Menzies, cashiers reported feeling pressured to work faster because of the record the computer kept of their activities. These fears were not unfounded because, as Menzies remarks, "colleagues who fail to

33. Labour Canada Task Force on Micro-Electronics and Employment, *op. cit.*, p. 56.
34. Braverman, *op. cit.*, p. 371.
35. *Cf.* Menzies, *op. cit.*
36. McDermott, *op. cit.*

meet the store standard find their work hours reduced."[37] In addition, there are few or no opportunities for advancement in retail trade, and the wages and overall working rules and conditions are among the least desirable in the white-collar world.[38] Again, as was the case among office clerical staff, a high percentage of these low-level positions are filled by women. A study of thirty-eight department store chains revealed that 80 percent of the women employees (both full-time and part-time) occupied low-paid clerical positions or were cashiers, while about three-quarters of the men in the same organizations held more responsible and better-paid jobs.[39] The wages and fringe benefits of retail sales employees have deteriorated even more due to a growing tendency among employers to hire part-time help: over 40 percent of the jobs created in retail sales between 1975 and 1980 were filled by women working part-time.[40]

Although one might have expected otherwise, the deterioration of the market situation and of the working conditions of office and sales clerks has not been accompanied by a concomitant rise in unionization. Some areas of clerical labour have been unionized: almost all civil servants in the three levels of government, clerks in supermarkets, and office workers in companies with strong blue-collar unions. A large part of the private sector, however, has not been organized into unions.[41] One reason commonly advanced to explain this fact is that white-collar employees continue to cling to whatever gratifications they may derive from perceiving themselves as members of a rather special, if not privileged, stratum of workers. Some employees regard union membership as demeaning and threat-

37. Menzies, *op. cit.*, p. 54.
38. *Cf.* Pamela H. Sugiman, "The Sales Clerks: Worker Discontent and Obstacles to its Collective Expression," *Atlantis*, 8, 1982, pp. 13–33.
39. *Report of the Royal Commission on the Status of Women in Canada, op. cit.*
40. Julie White, *Women and Part-Time Work*, Ottawa: The Canadian Advisory Council on the Status of Women, 1983.
41. Approximately 38 percent of office workers in Canada are covered by collective agreements, the great majority of whom are in the public sector. Joseph B. Rose, "Growth Patterns of Public Sector Unions," in Mark Thompson and Gene Swimmer, eds., *Conflict or Compromise: The Future of Public Sector Industrial Relations*, Montreal: Institute for Research on Public Policy, 1984, pp. 83–119.

ening to their status; they feel unionization would render them even more indistinguishable from manual wage earners. A second explanation for the lack of unionization among clerical employees is derived from sexual stereotypes. Women, representing an overwhelming majority of office and sales clerks, are sometimes depicted as "docile" and "compliant," traits that are not the stuff union movements are made of. Women are also viewed as secondary wage earners less committed to paid employment than males and thus indifferent to the content and conditions of their work. Finally, because it is women who are chiefly responsible for household labour, they are believed not to have the time or interest to engage in union activities.

Both these explanations for the lack of unionization among clerical workers are problematic. Feelings of distinctiveness and an identification with management and middle-class status do not suffice to insulate white-collar people from joining unions because such feelings are essentially illusory. As Braverman observes:

> In the clerical routine of offices, the use of the brain is never entirely done away with—any more than it is entirely done away with in any form of manual work. The mental processes are rendered repetitious and routine, or they are reduced to so small a factor in the work process that the speed and dexterity with which the manual portion of the operation can be performed dominates the labour process as a whole. More than this cannot be said of any manual labour process, and once it is true of clerical labour, labour in that form is placed on an equal footing with the simpler forms of so-called blue-collar manual labour. For this reason, the traditional distinctions between 'manual' and 'white-collar' labour, which are so thoughtlessly and widely used in the literature on this subject, represent echoes of a past situation which has virtually ceased to have meaning in the modern world of work.[42]

42. Braverman, *op. cit.*, pp. 325–326.

Nor can femininity be accepted as an impediment to unionization. The dissemination of ideas originating in the women's movement among ever broader segments of the female population have countered traditional notions of gender-linked character traits and made women (and men) more conscious of sex discrimination and the superprofits companies derive from it. The unionization of female-dominated occupational groups like nurses and elementary school teachers challenges stereotypical images of the docile female worker. Moreover, the great majority of women (both married and single) who work outside the home do so out of economic need and, consequently, are no more indifferent than men to the content and conditions of work.[43]

The principal obstacle to organizing office and sales clerks is the intransigent anti-union attitudes and actions of private sector employers. Companies have increased wages and fringe benefits, improved working conditions, and instituted quality of work life programs in an attempt to persuade employees that unions are unnecessary. In a tougher vein, companies like Radio Shack, K-Mart, and Eatons have used an array of tactics to discourage union-organizing drives or to get existent unions decertified. In 1984–1985 workers who struck six Eaton stores in Ontario in search of a first contract were continually frustrated by the company's fierce opposition to collective bargaining and the company's ability to keep the stores open while the strike was in progress. The final settlement was a pyrrhic victory for the union; while the workers won a first contract, it contained no substantial improvements. At the Eaton's store in Brandon, Manitoba, employees unionized in 1985, after a long struggle, but the company reacted by threatening to lay off one-half of the store's employees, a move which led some individuals to seek union decertification to save their jobs.

The situation in banking is much the same. Only about one percent of the 165 000 bank employees are unionized. Between 1977 and 1985, 168 bank branches were unionized, but in 1986

43. Pat Armstrong and Hugh Armstrong, *The Double Ghetto: Canadian Women and Their Segregated Work*, Rev. ed., Toronto: McClelland and Stewart, 1984.

only sixty-seven branches remained with the union. The lack of unionization in banks has little to do with status pretensions or the fact that 90 percent of bank workers are women. Bank branches have small work forces and relatively high rates of personnel turnover. Turnover erodes cohesiveness, and the small size of units magnifies the cost to the union of organizing and servicing them. Moreover, small unionized branches, each of which constitutes an independent bargaining unit, lack leverage in negotiating contracts, and have been unable to win any significant concessions from management. But, as a Labour Canada report concludes, "the biggest barrier to women bank workers joining unions [is] fear."[44] Wilfred List reports: "In the nearly ten years that unions have struggled to gain and preserve a precarious foothold in the banking industry, it has become clear that the hostility of banks to union representation has been a greater obstacle than workers' reluctance to join a union."[45] The Canadian Labour Relations Board has found banks guilty of unfair labour practices, including strategic transfers of non-union personnel, firing union members, shutting down unionized branches, and freezing wages in unionized branches.[46] In 1986 a strike by Toronto data centre employees of the Canadian Imperial Bank of Commerce was resolved in favour of the workers, and a first contract was imposed by the Canadian Labour Relations Board. Unionists are hopeful that this settlement will open the door to more successful organizing campaigns.

Covert forms of on-the-job resistance among clerical workers have received little research attention. The dearth of examples of white-collar workers' resistance to management directives is perhaps more reflective of social scientists' neglect of this phenomenon than it is of an actual absence of resistance. Restriction of output and the establishment of norms which run counter to management expectations have been observed in department stores, government offices, insurance compa-

44. Beckett, *op. cit.*, p. 41.
45. Toronto *Globe and Mail*, April 28, 1986.
46. Beckett, *op. cit.*; Toronto *Globe and Mail*, June 29, 1981; Paul Phillips and Erin Phillips, *Women and Work: Inequality in the Labour Market*, Toronto: James Lorimer, 1983.

nies, and telephone companies.[47] These few examples suggest that the on-the-job struggles among clerks and sales workers are ordinarily expressed by individuals through subtle methods usually confined to ignoring or evading management directives rather than direct confrontations. At Bell Telephone, for instance, "the symptoms of dissatisfaction are usually internalized. They emerge in various forms—absenteeism, illness, tears, or just plain bitchiness."[48] Similarly, a Labour Canada study of bank workers concluded: "Because their jobs do not pay well and offer only marginal opportunity for advancement, a worker is much more likely to quit than fight, if the job becomes too unpleasant."[49] This is not to suggest that highly militant collective action is totally foreign to clerical employees. A notable case in point (apart from unionization and strikes) is the six-day occupation in 1981 of twenty installations of the privately-owned British Columbia Telephone Company. Having barred supervisors from the offices, employees took charge of handling calls, deciding shift schedules, job assignments, and work rules. As one worker said, "Imagine walking onto the floor, ignoring management completely, deciding amongst ourselves what work needs to be done. We are now the managers at B.C. Tel."[50] Because the operators were governing their own work, they were not subjected to rules obliging workers to put up a flag when they visited the washroom or prohibiting them from combing their hair while on the job. No one was monitored, and there were no reprimands for spending more than the allotted time on the phone with a customer.[51] When asked by a reporter

47. See George Lombard, *Behavior in a Selling Group*, Boston: Harvard University Press, 1955; Peter Blau, *The Dynamics of Bureaucracy*, Chicago: University of Chicago Press, 1955; Elinor Langer, "The Women of the Telephone Company," *New York Review of Books*, March 12, 1970; Maarten de Kadt, "Insurance: A Clerical Work Factory," in Andrew Zimbalist, ed., *Case Studies on the Labor Process*, New York: Monthly Review Press, 1979, pp. 242–256.
48. Kuyek, *op. cit.*, p. 78.
49. Beckett, *op. cit.*, p. 49.
50. Rosa Collette, "Operators Dial Direct Action," *Open Road*, 12, Spring/Summer, 1981, p. 8.
51. Bernard, *op. cit.*

what the occupation of the premises meant to her, one operator replied, "That we don't need management."[52]

Professionals and Technicians

The second largest sub-category of white-collar personnel is professionals and technicians, who constitute about 16 percent of the Canadian labour force. The growth of this category reflects the progressive applications of science and technology to the labour process. It is this educated stratum which proponents of the post-industrial thesis view as inheritors of the seats of power allegedly vacated by the propertied class. The basis of this "new class" power, Gouldner maintains, is knowledge and expertise—what he calls "cultural capital."[53] Knowledge workers' scheduled ascent to power is predicated on their functional importance to the effective co-ordination, operation, and growth of society's key institutions.

At the core of the term "professional" is the notion of autonomy and freedom from external controls; ideally, professionals, either individually or as a group, establish their own working rules. While it is true that some persons in the classic professions of law and medicine have, for the most part, retained this autonomy (about one-half of all Canadian lawyers and physicians are self-employed) most professional groups have never been free from external regulation and supervision. Today, less than 10 percent of professionally trained people work for themselves. The vast majority of professionals are dependent on bureaucratic organizations and, as part of the salariat, are subject to varying degrees of organizational constraint. It is fair to say that most professionals are alienated from their work in the sense that, as employees, they have no control over the goals, policies, and social purposes of their employing organizations. As Derber stresses:

> *Professionals, like other workers, now have "jobs" consisting of tasks within a complex division of labour planned and administered by top management. If they frequently*

52. Collette, *op. cit.*, p. 9.
53. See Alvin W. Gouldner, *The Future of Intellectuals and the Rise of the New Class*, New York: Continuum, 1979.

command privileged incomes, are often conspicuously exempted from such indignities as "punching in," and experience little direct supervision, they nevertheless are increasingly proletarianized in the sense that management or administration sets the terms of their employment, largely defines the nature of their tasks or projects and the clients they will serve, and ensures that they work according to predefined "standard operating procedures" consistent with the technology, productivity requirements, and policy interests of the enterprise.[54]

Derber further argues that this form of professional alienation "reduces the domain of freedom and creativity to problems of technique; it thus creates workers, no matter how skilled, who act as technicians or functionaries."[55] Even when professionals (especially lawyers and accountants) sit on the board of directors—the pinnacle of corporate power—they operate solely in an advisory capacity to those board members who hold real power.[56] When Daniel Bell ascribes immanent dominance to the professional stratum, he can do so because he fails to make a sharp distinction between persons who manage and those who are managed, between technocrats and technicians, and between owners of the means of production and professionals.[57]

In the private sector, for example, research and development activity is largely restricted to projects that will turn a profit. "By their own standards of policy," *Fortune* editor William Whyte says, "corporations make it plain that they wish to keep

54. Charles Derber, "Toward a New Theory of Professionals as Workers," in Charles Derber, ed., *Professionals as Workers: Mental Labor in Advanced Capitalism*, Boston: G.K. Hall, 1982, p. 194.
55. Charles Derber, "Ideological Proletarianization and Mental Labor," in *Ibid.*, p. 172.
56. Jorge Niosi, *The Economy of Canada: A Study of Ownership and Control*, Montreal: Black Rose Books, 1978.
57. John Kenneth Galbraith explicitly rejects the difference, lumping together under the rubric of "technostructure" both managers and their subordinates. He finds it impossible to locate any definite and centralized authority. Instead, power is seen as being lodged deeply in the technical, planning, and specialized staffs of large enterprises. See his *The New Industrial State*, New York: Signet Books, 1967.

their researchers' eyes focussed clearly on the cash register."[58]
Few scientists are free to select their own research problems;
few engineers work on projects they have chosen; and corporate lawyers pursue whatever cases are assigned to them.[59]
Illustrative of the subordination of professional and scientific
standards to profit is the case of an agricultural specialist
employed by a company that manufactures farm equipment.
The technician relates how he ran rigorous performance tests
on the firm's small and large tractors. His tests unequivocally
demonstrated the superiority of the larger tractor. When the
research report reached company executives, they called in the
technician and explained to him that the small tractor was their
top seller. "The report had therefore to be recalled at once and
every copy destroyed. No mention was made of the true and
worthwhile objective of our tests."[60] A similar case is related by
Tanzer. Scientists employed by a large multinational firm
discovered a technique of making fertilizer which could have
substantially increased the production of rice. The potential
importance of the discovery was obvious. Millions of people in
underdeveloped countries could benefit, many might be spared
from starvation. Yet, upon reporting their findings to management, the scientists were instructed to discontinue developing
the product along these lines and to re-orient their research to
the creation of a fertilizer that would make lawn grass greener
in the United States. "The reason was that calculations showed
the potential buying power of Americans desiring a more
verdant lawn was far greater than that of impoverished peas-
ants needing improved fertilizers."[61]

58. William H. Whyte, *The Organization Man*, New York: Doubleday Anchor
Books, 1957, p. 231.
59. *Cf. Ibid.*; William Kornhauser, *Scientists in Industry*, Berkeley: University
of California Press, 1962; Simon Marcson, *The Scientist in American Industry*,
New York: Princeton University Press, 1960; Peter F. Meiksins, "Science in the
Labor Process: Engineers as Workers," in Derber, *op. cit.*, pp. 121–140.
Employment in the state sector is analogous because this sector has been
"invaded" by operating criteria originating in profit-making enterprises. This
question is discussed more fully below.
60. Clint Forsyth, "The Technician," in Ronald Fraser, ed., *Work: Twenty
Personal Accounts*, Vol. I, Harmondsworth: Penguin Books, 1968, p. 229.
61. Michael Tanzer, *The Sick Society*, New York: Holt, Rinehart, and Winston,

Certain structured forms of accommodation between professionals and managers have been worked out in some organizations. One entails segregating professionals into their own departments and providing them with a measure of autonomy from bureaucratic authority. Another adjustment is the creation of the role of professional–administrator, a position that combines bureaucratic authority and professional know-how. Persons who occupy such positions are known as technocrats. While the technocratic role may mitigate problems of authority, it does not fully solve them. Nor can professionals–administrators be construed as an emergent knowledge-elite. When highly trained people move up the organizational hierarchy, their technical expertise becomes less and less important to the execution of their tasks. Administrative duties become so time-consuming that professional and technical skills often atrophy through disuse.[62] As sociologist Everett Hughes once ironically remarked, "The engineer who, at forty, can still use a slide rule or a logarithmic table, and make a true drawing, is a failure."[63] Thus, avoiding professional subordination entails sacrificing one's scientific training and knowledge for business

---

1968, p. 22. These cases illustrate how corporations can warp scientific and humanitarian ideals. But scientists and technicians are not always innocent victims of organizational pressures. Some have been willing participants in, or initiators of, corporate deception—even in situations where human lives are at stake. See, for example, Robert Heilbronner, ed., *In the Name of Profit*, New York: Doubleday, 1972. Of course, social scientists also are vulnerable to these pressures and temptations. For a discussion of their role in aiding counter-insurgency in Viet Nam see Noam Chomsky, *American Power and the New Mandarins*, New York: Vintage Books, 1969. For further accounts of corporate distortions of scientific and professional activity see Ralph Nader, Peter Petkas, and Kate Blackwell, *Whistle Blowing*, New York: Grossman, 1972, and Rosemary Chalk and Frank Von Hippel, "Due Process for Dissenting 'Whistle-Blowers,'" *Technology Review*, 81, 7, 1979, pp. 49–55.

62. *Cf.* Basil Georgopolous and Floyd Mann, "Supervisory and Administrative Behavior," in Robert A. Sutermeister, ed., *People and Productivity*, 2nd edition, New York: McGraw-Hill, 1969, pp. 359–363.

63. Cited in Meiksins, *op cit.*, p. 133. A 1979 Ontario survey found that about one-half of professional engineers were no longer employed as engineers; most of them were in management positions. This survey is discussed in Mark Thompson, "Collective Bargaining by Professionals," in John Anderson and Morley Gunderson, eds., *Union–Management Relations in Canada*, Don Mills: Addison-Wesley, 1982, pp. 379–397.

values and administrative skills. Leonard Silk, an astute observer of the corporate world and former editor of *Business Week*, writes: "Scientists or engineers customarily strive to achieve power within the business world by making themselves into businessmen rather than by remaining technicians. One route that leads in the direction of genuine corporate power is through graduate work in business or executive training courses paid for by their employers, and schools of business administration endow their graduates not with the values of a new technological elite, but with the attitudes of the existing profit-oriented business management."[64] Finally, professionals-turned-managers are responsible to higher authorities and to organizational objectives rather than to the pursuits and standards of their professional peers.

Alienation of professionals from the purposes of work has not been accompanied by alienation from the work process itself. The professional's relative autonomy in this realm tempers his or her resistance. Architects, engineers, accountants, attorneys, natural and social scientists, and so on have retained their level of professional knowledge and technical skills and are still able to exercise control over the immediate context of their jobs. Intrinsic gratifications, challenge, and opportunities for continuous learning are features of professional work. Professionals tend, naturally, to develop an attachment to work and on-the-job discipline that not only aligns their activities with organizational imperatives but that also keeps them preoccupied with questions of technique. Autonomy in the work process and the relatively lucrative rewards and privileges consequently mutes the potential conflict between bosses and professionals. Means rather than ends dominate their attitude toward work.[65] Professionals often disavow having a concern for the morality and ethics of their projects,

---

64. Cited in Tanzer, *op. cit.*, p. 16.
65. This relative autonomy also helps to account for the disinclination of professionals to unionize. However, some professional occupations are vulnerable to being "deprofessionalized." A case in point is computer programming, which has been progressively deskilled and standardized with the development of new computer languages, canned programs, structured programming,

disclaim interest in or responsibility for the social uses to which their labour is put, and preoccupy themselves with narrow issues of skill, technical competence, and the appropriateness of means and methods of work. In addition, the ideology of their discipline often insulates professionals even further from considering the social implications of their activities. The enjoinment of scientists to remain "objective" and "neutral" by not allowing moral or political considerations to "contaminate" their research is a case in point.

It is misleading to claim that the growth of the professional–technical stratum (see Table I) translates into a corresponding expansion of knowledge workers. Bona fide professionals constitute only a small portion of individuals placed in this category by Statistics Canada. The majority of persons listed as professional–technical workers possess neither the training, knowledge, or level of autonomy that mark the true professional. Surveyors, draftsmen, referees, and athletes hardly meet the distinguishing criteria of a profession. Moreover, one-half of the professional–technical stratum comprises elementary and secondary school teachers as well as nursing and nursing-related occupations. These groups, along with social workers, have been labelled as near professions or semi-professions, terms signifying, more than anything else, a lack of control over work. As Simpson and Simpson state, "In comparison with professional employees, semi-professionals lack autonomy; they are told what to do and how to do it."[66] Technicians, who constitute another sizable segment of the professional–technical category, occupy positions that, in terms of training, work

---

and program modules. As a result of these changes the all-around computer programmer has now given way to a three-tiered system: lower-level specialists, more skilled programmers and, at the top, systems analysts. Pay and perquisites are scaled accordingly. On the degradation of computer programming see Philip Kraft, *Programmers and Managers: The Routinization of Computer Programming in the United States*, New York: Springer–Verlag, 1977 and "The Industrialization of Computer Programming: From Programming to Software Production," in Zimbalist, *op. cit.*, pp. 1–17.
66. Richard L. and Ida Harper Simpson, "Women and Bureaucracy in the Semi-Professions," in Amatai Etzioni, ed., *The Semi-Professions and Their Organization*, New York: Free Press, 1969, p. 197.

content, and control, are among the least desirable of this stratum. Aronowitz equates the degree of discretion exercised by technicians with that of semiskilled production workers.[67] Braverman elaborates:

> ... the distinguishing characteristic of the technician is that he or she functions as "support" for the engineer or scientist; the routine which can be passed to a lower-paid and slightly trained person goes to the technicians. Most have no special training or education apart from what they learned on their jobs; but with the growth of attendance in higher educational institutions, employers are increasingly using graduates of two-year technical institutions and even holders of four-year degrees.[68]

If the vast majority of professionals and technicians are remote from positions of power in their own institutions, or if in assuming managerial positions they cease to employ their expertise, how can they be regarded as exercising control over broader political and economic affairs? If we examine the individuals to whom professionals and technicians are subordinate, we can get closer to the real seat of power. It is to this stratum that we now turn.

The Bosses

Managers of both public and private organizations are paid to ensure that the organization's objectives are achieved. This involves administration, co-ordination, and, above all, control. Under capitalist relations of production, the chain of command is larger and more elaborate than in enterprises where exploitation and stark differences of reward and power are absent.[69] Co-ordinating and administrating organizational activities are necessary functions in any conceivable organization, but man-

67. Stanley Aronowitz, "Does the United States Have a New Working Class?", in George Fischer, ed., *Revival of American Socialism*, New York: Oxford University Press, 1971, pp. 188–216.
68. Braverman, *op. cit.*, pp. 245–246.
69. This issue is discussed in Chapter 6.

agement in the capitalist firm is required to surveil, regulate, and control the activities of subordinate employees because the interests of the employers are often antithetical to those of the workers. The management structure of capitalist enterprises thus proliferates above and beyond what would be required in an organization not defined by a conflict of interests among its members. In the capitalist organization, a considerable differentiation of authority emerges, ranging from top executives of giant corporations, who may blend into the capitalist class, to middle managers and low-level supervisors, subject to subordination themselves.

Since the publication of Berle and Means' *The Modern Corporation and Private Property* (1933), many people have been convinced that ultimate corporate power is held by chief executives rather than owners.[70] They believe that with the development of the joint-stock company, ownership has become too diffuse to allow any identifiable group of stockholders to exercise control over corporate objectives and policies and that with this separation of ownership and control, the dominant propertied class was replaced by managers.[71] Although this managerial revolution is supposed to have occurred in all advanced capitalist nations, Porter has persuasively argued that, in Canada, management control is not as extensive as it purportedly is in the United States. "Boards of directors [i.e. not managers] are governing bodies of corporations. Although their decision-making does not concern the day-to-day operations of the firm, they hold ultimate power and establish the boundaries of over-all operations."[72] Porter's position was corroborated by

70. Adolph Berle, Jr. and Gardiner Means, *The Modern Corporation and Private Property*, New York: The Macmillan Company, 1933.
71. One important corollary of this thesis holds that because managers are less interested in corporate profits than owners, the former strive to create "soulful" corporations that are sensitive to community needs. Sophisticated data are not required to reject this hypothesis. One need only think of current problems like auto safety and pollution to dispel the notion of the soulful corporation.
72. John Porter, *The Vertical Mosaic*, Toronto: University of Toronto Press, 1965, p. 255. Porter also shows that the propertied class collectively dominates

a study of 136 large Canadian companies. Only 32 percent of these companies could be classified as being under management control, that is, where inside executives sat on the board of directors *and* owned substantial shares of the company's stock.[73] Most executives simply do not own enough stock to qualify as major shareholders. In 1975 the richest executives owned an average of $250 000 worth of shares, a drop in the bucket compared to a select core of groups and families with stocks and bonds valued at between $20 million and $500 million. Top shareholding executives represent, at best, a subordinate segment of the class with real wealth and power (the bourgeoisie).[74] Birnbaum, referring to all advanced capitalist nations, observes: "None of the evidence adduced for the existence, real or imaginary, of a technocratic elite has been able to explain away the continuing existence of large concentrations of power and property in industrial society."[75] The real issue, then, is not to determine *if* the propertied class dominates corporations and the economy, but to find out *how* this class exercises control.

the corporate world in particular and the economy in general. "They are the ultimate decision-makers and coordinators within the private sector of the economy. It is they who at the frontiers of the economic and political systems represent the interests of corporate power. They are the real planners of the economy, and they resent bitterly the thought that anyone else should do the planning."

73. Niosi, *op. cit.* Niosi believes his calculations overstate the extent of management control due to the unavailability of data allowing determinations of external control.

74. *Ibid.* According to investment ethics consultant J. Richard Finlay, fewer than 12 families account for over half the trading on the Toronto Stock Exchange. See Toronto *Globe and Mail*, March 8, 1986.

75. Norman Birnbaum, *Toward a Critical Sociology*, New York: Oxford University Press, 1971, p. 404. Maurice Zeitlin has challenged the "managerial revolution" thesis by showing that the evidence upon which it rests is unconvincing. See his "Corporate Ownership and Control: The Large Corporation and the Capitalist Class," *American Sociological Review*, 79, 1974, pp. 1073–1119. Even if ownership and control were in fact distinct, it does not follow that managers behave in ways which differ significantly from owners, for the fundamental aim of both is profit. Zeitlin writes that "profits constitute both the only unambiguous criterion of successful managerial performance and an irreducible necessity for corporate survival."

While major stockholders, it is true, do not generally interfere in the day by day operations of the enterprise, this simply means that the job of managing is distinct—but not divorced—from ownership. In most large corporations, final power remains in the hands of the major stockholders. Those who accept the Berle and Means thesis fail to differentiate between those who establish the general guidelines for organizational performance and those who, while exercising formidable powers inside the organization, must operate within these guidelines.

Generally speaking, managers, particularly at the executive level, are structurally less prone to alienation than most other workers because of the scope of their jobs and their capacity to make decisions. Nevertheless, like most other workers, executives are subject to the alienating effects of the capitalist market—the struggle for profit and the hyper-competitiveness that accompanies it.[76] When asked to describe the ideal colleague, one executive in the electrical industry replied, "Guys who are tigers, who approach their jobs like tigers on the prowl. Hungry guys, motivated guys." In describing their own personal sense of satisfaction a common response is, "What I like most is the big win."[77] An ex-president of several large corporations reiterated the typical analogy between the corporate world and the jungle, a jungle not simply characterized by the struggle for survival but by the drive to become the conqueror.

The danger starts as soon as you become a district manager. You have men working for you and you have a boss above. You're caught in a squeeze. The squeeze

---

76. In *The Holy Family* Marx states: "The propertied class [and presumably executives] and the class of the proletariat represent the same human self-alienation. But the former feels comfortable and confirmed in this self-alienation, knowing that this alienation is its own power and possessing in it the semblance of a human existence." Cited in Lloyd D. Easton and Kurt H. Guddat, eds., *Writings of the Young Marx on Philosophy and Society*, New York: Doubleday, 1967, p. 367. The bracketed words do not appear in Marx's statement.

77. Richard Todd, "Notes on Corporate Man," *The Atlantic*, 228, 1971, p. 93.

progresses from station to station. I'll tell you what a squeeze is. You have guys working for you that are shooting for your job. The guy you're working for is scared stiff you're gonna shove him out of his job.[78]

This situation is exacerbated as one moves further up the corporate ladder:

As he struggles in this jungle, every position he's in, he's terribly lonely. . . . To give vent to his feelings, his fears, and his insecurities, he'd expose himself. This goes all the way up the line until he gets to be president. The president really doesn't have anybody to talk to, because the vice-presidents are waiting for him to die or make a mistake and get knocked off so they can get his job.[79]

For corporate managers, competition and profits often take precedence over the substance of what it is they are competing for. As Ollman has recognized, managers (as well as stockholders) view the product of their business enterprise simply as a means to derive profit. "[They are] as indifferent to what it is actually used for and who will eventually use it as [they are] to the process by which it came into being."[80] Todd gives the example of the head of a company that manufactured a ballpoint pen made of exotic wood and trimmed in gold. The executive complains that the expensive pen is not selling. "But the pen itself has caught your interest. What about the pen; how does he feel about the thing? Should it have been made? He says you have misunderstood. The pen is just an example. *'The product is irrelevant.'*"[81]

Well paid and commanding a high degree of prestige in and outside of their company, the managerial stratum generally identifies with the company's goals and policies; their political

78. Studs Terkel, *Working,* New York: Pantheon Books, 1974, pp. 405–406.
79. *Ibid.,* p. 408.
80. Bertell Ollman, *Alienation: Marx's Conception of Man in Capitalist Society,* Cambridge: University Press, 1971, p. 155.
81. Todd, *op. cit.*

conservatism is well known.[82] As a result of their uncritical support of the status quo, managers who do experience alienation from work react to it differently than ordinary workers. They are inclined to identify their feeling of alienation with a more generalized malaise about the meaning of work and life. For example, middle managers tend to seek early retirement and mid-career job changes. Tanzer claims that managers often feel they are misdirected by the very company they supposedly run: They resent having traded away their skills and integrity for money. "The extent of this feeling in the corporate community is much greater than the outsider might suspect. Many individuals, for their own peace of mind, have developed elaborate mechanisms to repress these feelings. . . ."[83]

Middle and low-level managers are subject to direct scrutiny and control from executives above. Their main job is to transmit orders and see to it they are carried out, and they are acutely aware of their ambiguous position in the hierarchy of organizational authority.[84] A supervisor in an auditing department of a large bank illustrates the middle manager's plight. He has twenty people under him but he considers himself a pawn because there are fifty people above him. The supervisor complains:

When they come in we take a head count. You see who's late and who's not. You check around and make sure they start at eight-thirty and not go in the washroom and powder their nose for fifteen minutes. You make sure when they go for breaks they take fifteen minutes, not twenty. You check for lunch hours, making sure they take forty-five minutes and not an hour. And that they're not supposed to make personal telephone calls on the bank's phone. All you're doing is checking on people. This goes on all day.[85]

82. *Cf.* Michael Ornstein, "Canadian Capital and the Canadian State: Ideology in an Era of Crisis," in Robert Brym, ed., *The Structure of the Canadian Capitalist Class*, Toronto: Garamond Press, 1985, pp. 129–161.
83. Tanzer, *op. cit.*, pp. 136–137.
84. See Joe Kelly and Daniel Bilek, "White Collar Unions: Does Middle Management Want Them," *Canadian Business*, 46, 1973, pp. 56–58.
85. Terkel, *op. cit.*, p. 400.

The above discussion focussed exclusively on managers in privately-owned enterprises. The extent to which there is a convergence of circumstances, duties, and attitudes of managers in the public and private realms remains largely unanswered. Since public sector organizations are not subject to pressures arising from the necessity to generate profits and accumulate capital, it could be argued that public employees work in a more relaxed milieu and are protected from work rationalization measures, job insecurities, and strict subordination. Yet if this were so, one would expect management personnel to be occupied less with supervision and more with administrative and co-ordinative tasks. However, while higher civil servants are not propelled by the same profit criterion as business executives, it is not by accident—for reasons to be discussed in the next section—that state and private sector organizations operate similarly. Like large private firms, government activities are organized along bureaucratic lines. In fact, the centralization of authority in the Canadian public service is so pronounced that one expert on the subject described government department heads as having responsibility without authority.[86] For individuals lower in the chain of command the situation is even worse, as indicated in the following statement of a government employee:

> As a first-line supervisor, you're where the action is and therefore you aren't quite into the management group. You're expected to act and behave as management, for management, but you're not in on the decision-making. You get it filtered down through. And here there's an awful lot of chiefs; it becomes just a bit top-heavy.[87]

We may surmise that many of the dilemmas and frustrations experienced by middle and low-level managers in private business are shared by their counterparts in government offices. It

86. J.E. Hodgetts, *The Canadian Public Service: A Physiology of Government, 1867-1970*, Toronto: University of Toronto Press, 1973.
87. Pat Armstrong and Hugh Armstrong, *A Working Majority: What Women Must Do for Pay*, Ottawa: Canadian Advisory Council on the Status of Women, 1983, p. 13.

is also fair to say that managers in the public sector have become more preoccupied with control as governments at all levels undertake restraint measures, impose cut-backs, and intensify the rationalization of the work process.

THE SERVICE SOCIETY: MILITANCY IN THE PUBLIC SECTOR

Impressive white-collar employment gains were registered in the public sector after 1941, a development arising from the growth in the scope and complexity of government operations. In 1946 under 10 percent of the labour force was employed in the public sector. By 1970 over 20 percent of all workers were employed by the state.[88] The growth of the public sector is often viewed in negative terms. Because the state bureaucracy has no competitors and does not have to operate in terms of the measurable criterion of profit, it is associated in the public mind with red tape and inefficiency. Public employees are conventionally viewed as plodding and unimaginative, traits allegedly nurtured by the security of lifelong tenure. These stereotypes, however, are contradicted by evidence which demonstrates that the public and private sectors are organized along parallel lines. There are several bases of this organizational similarity.

The private and state spheres interpenetrate in important ways. There are substantial connections between capitalists and corporate executives on the one hand and the state elite (prime ministers, premiers, federal and provincial cabinet ministers) on the other. Business moguls are often elected or appointed to key state positions, and when prominent political figures leave the government they often end up in corporate offices and boardrooms. The state elite is also linked to big business leaders via both kinship and personal ties; as Clement shows, they run in the same social circles. Corporate executives and owners regularly sit on advisory boards to cabinet minis-

88. Hugh Armstrong, "The Labour Force and State Workers in Canada," in Leo Panitch, ed., *The Canadian State: Political Economy and Political Power*, Toronto: University of Toronto Press, 1977, pp. 289–310. The public sector includes federal, provincial, and municipal employees, health care and education employees, and employees of government enterprises such as Air Canada.

ters and royal commissions. Both the Liberal and Progressive Conservative parties depend heavily on financial contributions from the corporate world. Finally, government-owned corporations are controlled by the Canadian bourgeoisie.[89] Clement has demonstrated that owners and executives of big businesses are active in both the state and political systems and that the alliance between the two sectors is dominated by the interests of corporate capitalism.[90] Consequently, the top echelons of government bureaucracies—deputy ministers, assistant deputy ministers and their counterparts in state departments and agencies—are subordinate to elected and appointed officials who, for the most part, defend capitalist norms and practices. The state bureaucracy, as Miliband has shown, "is a crucially important and committed element in the maintenance and defense of the structure of power and privilege inherent in advanced capitalism."[91] Even the reform-minded civil servant finds him or herself constrained by political realities and obliged to formulate and adhere to policies (including internal operations) that are not offensive to the interests of higher business circles. Given these circumstances, it is not surprising to learn that the values and practices operative in the capitalist firm "invade" the public realm, inclining government organizations to adopt the rules and practices employed in profit-making enterprises. As Olsen remarked: "Whether or not practices derived from profit-making corporations *should* be applied to the not-for-profit public departments, the fact is they *are* applied."[92]

The "invasion" of government organizations by capitalist practices can be traced back to the period immediately following World War I, when an American firm of consultants was

89. *Cf.* Jorge Niosi, "Continental Nationalism: The Strategy of the Canadian Bourgeoisie," in Brym, *op. cit.*, pp. 53–65; Dennis Olsen, *The State Elite*, Toronto: McClelland and Stewart, 1980; Wallace Clement, "The Corporate Elite, the Capitalist Class, and the Canadian State," in Panitch, *op. cit.*, pp. 225–248.
90. Wallace Clement, *The Canadian Corporate Elite: An Analysis of Economic Power*, Toronto: McClelland and Stewart, 1975, p. 347.
91. Ralph Miliband, *The State In Capitalist Society*, London: Weidenfeld and Nicolson, 1969, pp. 128–129.
92. Olsen, *op. cit.*, p. 68.

hired to rationalize the Federal Public Service. While the firm's recommendations led to the abolition of patronage, it also initiated a detailed system of job classifications and hierarchies whose effects are still felt today.[93] Beginning in the early 1930s the popular writings of Gulick and Urwick, emphasizing that an administrative science propounding efficiency was applicable to any human association, irrespective of its goals, had a lasting influence on the organization of the public sector. A number of practices suggested by the principles of orthodox organization theory (which is akin to scientific management) were incorporated in the public services of Canada, Great Britain, and the United States. The composition and recommendations of the 1960 Royal Commission on Government Organization (Glassco Commission) illustrate to what degree these orthodox theories still prevail in the public sphere. Approximately one-half of the 170 persons staffing the Glassco Commission were drawn from management consulting firms, while the remainder were executives from private industry. Naturally, the Commission's report mirrored the predilections and philosophies prevalent in these business circles. It concluded: "The pervasive assumption that the differences between private and public organizations are not so substantial as to prevent the incorporation of the best practices and principles from the realms of private business management into the public service."[94] The "reforms" to the Canadian Public Service generated by the Glassco Commission Report exhibited, as Hodgetts pointed out, a narrow concern with technical efficiency.

While the work environment of government employees has long been shaped by the philosophies and operating criteria of the capitalist class, the current problems of state personnel are further compounded by governments' (at all levels) conservative response to the world economic crisis. As the recession

93. Extensions and modifications of the original classification system have eventuated in approximately 3700 job categories in the federal service, including such job titles as Assistant in Fruit By-Products and Assistant Investigator of Values. This complex system creates not only the usual constraints on individuals but also makes career advancement problematic. See "Management and Control of the Civil Service," in J.E. Hodgetts and D.C. Corbett, *op. cit.*, pp. 250–264.
94. Hodgetts, *op. cit.*, p. 26.

deepened in the 1970s, Keynesian economics were discarded in favour of government restraint measures. Social, educational, and medical services were cut back, resulting in staff reductions and hiring freezes in all government jurisdictions.[95] Public servants' right to bargain collectively as well as their right to strike were curtailed by federal and provincial wage controls, wage roll-backs of existing contracts, expanded definitions of "essential" workers (i.e. those prohibited from striking), and back-to-work legislation. For example, between 1950 and 1970, there were thirteen provincial and federal acts ordering strikers back to work; forty-one similar pieces of legislation were passed between 1975 and 1984.[96] At the same time social services were being cut, the state stepped up efforts to facilitate private investment and profitability, offering businesses a wide range of loans, grants, and tax concessions.[97]

As a result of these measures restiveness and militancy among public sector workers escalated. Prior to the 1960s, nearly all government workers settled differences with their employers either through consultative mechanisms or compulsory arbitration. Strikes were forbidden. During the 1960s and 1970s, however, public sector unions grew enormously (facilitated by the 1967 Public Service Staff Relations Act). In 1951 fourteen public sector unions in Canada claimed 54 000 members; by 1981, there were seventy-one public employee unions with over 1 347 000 members.[98] Grievances submitted to the Federal Public Service Staff Relations Board increased

95. John Calvert, *Government Limited: The Corporate Takeover of the Public Sector in Canada*, Ottawa: Canadian Centre for Policy Alternatives, 1984.
96. Royal Commission on the Economic Union and Development Prospects for Canada, Ottawa: Ministry of Supply and Services Canada, 1985, p. 680; Leo Panitch and Donald Swartz, "Towards Permanent Exceptionalism: Coercion and Consent in Canadian Industrial Relations," *Labour/Le Travail*, 13, Spring, 1984, pp. 133–157.
97. To make matters worse, the burden of financing these corporate welfare measures has fallen more and more onto working people. In 1950 government revenues were equally dependent on corporate and personal taxes. In 1982 corporate taxes as a percentage of total government revenue was 6.4, compared to 39.2 percent of revenue collected from individuals. See Calvert, *op. cit.*, pp. 88–91.
98. Rose, *op. cit.*

sevenfold between 1975 and 1982.[99] Strikes in the public sector increased from 155 in 1972–73 to 478 in 1980–81.[100] In 1980 one notable work stoppage involved 45 000 federal government clerical workers, some of whom were forbidden to strike because of having been designated as "essential." The strike was the largest in the history of the Federal Public Service.[101] While the 1980 walkout of clerical workers was unprecedented, several important groups of public employees, most notably postal workers, health care workers (including registered nurses), and teachers have been engaged in more protracted struggles. A closer look at their activities belies the idea that white-collar workers, even those who are professionally trained, are unwilling to use measures traditionally employed by manual wage earners.

Postal Workers

The 1965 postal strike, the first major walkout of federal employees in more than a generation, shattered the prevailing calm of public service labour relations and revealed a degree of rank and file militancy not ordinarily associated with non-manual workers.[102] Union executives were opposed to the strike and warned their membership that it would constitute an illegal walkout. Over the objections of the central leadership, rank and file postal workers initiated, co-ordinated, and directed the seventeen day strike to a successful conclusion. The workers learned that they had to struggle against two hostile parties, and that to succeed the rank and file would have to challenge the authority of union executives as well as that of management. In the end, the conservative central leadership of the union was replaced by officials who were more militant and

100. Douglas A. Smith, "Strikes in the Canadian Public Sector," in *Ibid.*, pp. 197–228.
99. Mark Thompson and Gene Swimmer, "Summary," in Thompson and Swimmer, *op. cit.*, pp. xiii–xiv.
101. Gene Swimmer, "Militancy in Public Sector Unions," in *Ibid.*, pp. 147–195.
102. Inside postal workers are classified by Statistics Canada as clerks. The account of the postal strike and its aftermath draws heavily on H.W. Arthurs, *Collective Bargaining by Public Employees in Canada: Five Models*, Ann Arbor: University of Michigan Institute of Labor and Industrial Relations, 1971.

more sensitive to the concerns and needs of the rank and file. "The intense and ubiquitous discontent within the post office and the cohesion of the employees in the major centres certainly made the strike possible. That it succeeded despite the opposition of the union leadership is some measure of the depth of their feelings."[103]

The strike and the ensuing events alerted the public to the similarity of many white-collar and blue-collar jobs. Following the strike, a commission of inquiry was formed to investigate working rules and conditions in the post office. In briefs to the Commission, the Canadian Union of Postal Workers (CUPW) and the Letter Carriers Union of Canada detailed their grievances, some of which were reminiscent of the early days of industrialization in Canada. Complaints were raised against dilapidated, poorly ventilated and heated, and often windowless quarters. The briefs criticized disciplinary codes and merit-rating procedures, and called for the elimination of fines. The unions were particularly incensed by the practice of managerial spying, which involved supervisors observing postal clerks through peepholes—a practice ostensibly used to guard against theft from the mails.[104] The Commission's findings, published under the title of the *Monpetit Report*, upheld many of the grievances documented by the unions. The report concluded that the post office was run along paramilitary lines, and it set forth a series of recommendations directed at humanizing the work situation of postal employees. Despite the fact that many of these recommendations have never been implemented, the report was significant in that it "helped dispel the myth of benevolence which had surrounded the traditional public employment system."[105]

Jamieson described the walkout of postal workers as one of the most important strikes in recent Canadian history because

103. *Ibid.*, p. 63.
104. An ex-president of CUPW recalls that "spy galleries were everywhere, including the washrooms, so that every sneeze, scratch and piss was potentially a public event. The investigator's job is to protect the mail, but it was widely believed that they reported the results of their spying to the supervisory staff to help them tighten up infractions of discipline." Joe Davidson and John Deverell, *Joe Davidson*, Toronto: James Lorimer, 1978, p. 51.
105. Arthurs, *op. cit.*, p. 67.

of its broad impact on the pattern of labour relations in the public sector. The strike was illegal, nation-wide in scope, and it was carried out by white-collar employees, a group previously regarded as unsusceptible to unionization and opposed to confrontation tactics.[106] One important outcome of the strike was that postal workers, in recognition of the collusion between employers and public service associations, joined the Canadian Labour Congress. These actions tended to pull other public employees and their associations in a more militant direction.

Like the conditions which prompted it, the aggressive stance adopted by postal workers in 1965 was not a temporary phenomenon: CUPW struck again in 1968. Although this time the main issue was wages, the workers returned to work with little in the way of economic gains. However, many of the changes recommended in the *Monpetit Report* had not been implemented, and substantial concessions in these areas were won by the strike. Since 1968, the major arena of conflict has been automation and its impact on the content of work, job classifications, and job security. The implementation of automation and the use of part-time labour precipitated rotating strikes in 1970, nation-wide wildcat strikes in 1974, a 42–day work stoppage in 1975, and a national strike in 1978 that was eventually halted by back-to-work legislation and threats to dismiss workers. Because he refused to order a return to work, CUPW president Jean Claude Parrot was imprisoned. All of these actions by the state were taken despite the fact that CUPW had been in a legal position to strike.

Underlying the contentiousness of the automation issue at every point was the intransigent position of management. In 1969 a post office adjudicator described Canada Post as "an establishment which still adheres to the nineteenth century master and servant precepts," and characterized its management as "arrogant and high-handed."[107] On October 31, 1974, the Toronto *Globe and Mail* reported: "Post office employees

106. Stuart Jamieson, *Times of Trouble: Labour Unrest and Industrial Conflict in Canada, 1900–1966*, Ottawa: Task Force on Labour Relations, 1968.
107. W.S. Martin, PSSRB (Public Service Staff Relations Board), Adjudication Report, 1969, p. 32.

can still find few reasons to be happy with their work; there is still an unduly authoritarian management, and workers' fears about mechanization have not been calmed." Peepholes were replaced by electronic surveillance equipment—a move workers believed was geared more to timing peoples' work speeds than any attempt to guard against theft. In 1975 a management attitude survey conducted by a private firm (The Hay Report) found major, pervasive problems in the *administration* of the post office. In the aftermath of the 1978 strike, a Toronto *Globe and Mail* business analyst wrote: "There is sufficient evidence to suggest that even if all CUPW officials were put in jail and the 23 000 inside workers fired and replaced, the mail would continue to be slow and unreliable ... the prime culprit is the post office's $1 billion automation program and the way management officials have gone about implementing it."[108] Conflict was supposed to abate when Canada Post became a crown corporation in 1981, but the battle between labour and management continues. In 1986 Conservative finance minister Michael Wilson set April, 1988 as the date by which he expected the post office to become financially self-sufficient. This goal can only be reached through the adoption of draconian measures: by contracting-out portions of postal operations to private, profit-making businesses, through extensive reductions in postal services, and by implementing major cut-backs in the hiring of unionized postal workers. "The Finance Minister, if he sticks to his guns, is setting the stage for a vigorous new round of conflict between Canada Post and the unions representing 60 000 employees."[109]

Health Care Workers and Teachers

The pressures exerted on government employees were also being felt by nurses as workloads grew and as the overall terms and conditions of their work deteriorated. Nurses have evinced a growing propensity to redefine their conventional position of subservience by challenging the unilateral right of hospital authorities to determine their conditions of employment. Over

108. Toronto *Globe and Mail*, January 3, 1979.
109. Toronto *Globe and Mail*, March 22, 1986.

the past several decades, nurses have gradually moved in the direction of collective bargaining, unionization, and the use of pressure tactics, including the strike, to achieve change. In 1965 union membership in the health care field was 28 000; by 1981 the membership rolls had reached 205 000. Much of this union growth was accounted for by registered nurses. Today, about 80 percent of registered nurses and non-office hospital staff are covered by collective agreements. During 1979, health professionals struck in Newfoundland, Quebec, and British Columbia.[110] In January of 1981 about 10 000 health care workers in fifty Ontario hospitals struck in defiance of provincial laws prohibiting strikes by hospital employees.[111] As the state continues to put the financial squeeze on medical services, further manifestations of conflict are likely.

School teachers offer another illustration of the heightened militancy of public employees. The 1960s were boom years for education in Canada, and enrollments and staff expanded rapidly. However, near the end of the decade, educational spending slowed down and spending ceilings were imposed, resulting in a deterioration of the terms and conditions of teachers employment. Staff cut-backs and hiring freezes brought about larger classes and heavier workloads at all levels of education. A manifesto issued in 1972 by the major teachers' union of Quebec offered a blunt assessment of the circumstances: "At one point in its evolution, capitalism reduced the craftsman to anonymity by setting up factories for mass production. Similarly, capitalism has reduced the teacher to anonymity by setting up factories for the mass production of ideology. They are now both common labourers."[112] In response to this situation, teachers opted for unions instead of professional associations, which in the past considered collective

110. Rose, *op. cit.*; Mark Thompson, "Collective Bargaining by Professionals," in Anderson and Gunderson, *op. cit.*, pp. 379–397.
111. John Deverell, "The Ontario Hospital Dispute, 1980–81," *Studies in Political Economy: A Socialist Review*, 9, Fall, 1982, pp. 179–190. For a discussion of alienation among physicians and health care workers see Martin Shapiro, *Getting Doctored: Reflections on Becoming a Physician*, Kitchener: Between the Lines, 1978.
112. Cited in Daniel Drache, ed., *Quebec—Only the Beginning*, Toronto: New Press, 1972, p. 118.

bargaining, strikes, and other militant actions inimical to the image and best interests of professionals. Union membership in education soared from 19 000 in 1965 to 335 000 in 1981. Between 1960 and 1969, there were twenty-six teachers' strikes in Canada, twenty-one of which took place in Quebec (eight of these being illegal).[113] In 1973 Ontario teachers "pink-lettered" school boards, struck, engaged in work-to-rule tactics, and submitted mass resignations. In December, 1973 thousands of teachers throughout the province held demonstrations to protest a controversial bill that would have forced them back to work.[114] Teachers' strikes in Canada have continued sporadically into the 1980s (with the exception of Quebec, where such strikes have occurred more frequently). While the demand for higher salaries remains important, the right of teachers to influence policy-making and exercise control over their work is also at stake. At the heart of many disputes are working rules and conditions such as job security, classroom size, grievance procedures, assignment and transfer of teachers, and length of working time. To the extent that the state continues to hold back expenditures on education, these kinds of demands will become ever more urgent.

Mass Struggles

Struggles of postal workers, teachers, and health care workers provide notable instances of restiveness and militancy among white-collar employees. But the most sweeping expressions of discontent have appeared at the provincial level, where a broad spectrum of public employees has acted in unison to challenge provincial authorities. Nowhere has this unrest erupted more dramatically than in Quebec. Events in this province revealed a

113. J. Douglas Muir, "Collective Bargaining by Canadian Teachers," *Education Canada*, 10, 1970, pp. 40-50.
114. The "pink-letter" notifies members of a teachers' association that a school board is being boycotted. Teachers are instructed not to apply for jobs in this area under threat of withdrawal of the association's support for the teacher in case of future difficulties. Work to rule refers to the practice of confining work activities to tasks which are legally required. For teachers this entails refusing assignments such as lunchroom and playground supervision, athletic coaching, and so on.

degree of radicalism among working people unrivalled in the rest of the country.

During the 1960s, the union movement in Quebec doubled its membership; the majority of the new unionists were public employees, many of whom wore white collars.[115] In early 1972 the bargaining units representing these diverse employee groups banded together, as the "Common Front," to bargain as a single unit with their employer, the Quebec government.[116] In negotiations with the government, the Common Front initially asked for equal pay for equal work (irrespective of sex), wage hikes, job security, a larger voice in decision-making, and a $100 a week minimum wage. Negotiations dragged on for months. On April 10, 1972, a public employee strike began. The Quebec government responded by imposing injunctions on hydro and hospital workers, some of whom were fined and received jail sentences for violating the terms of the injunctions. The strike continued. In desperation, the government passed a bill ordering an end to the walkout under threat of heavy fines and jail sentences. For having urged workers to ignore the bill, Yvon Charboneau of the teachers' union, Louis Laberge of the Quebec Federation of Labour, and Marcel Pepin of the Confederation of National Trade Unions (CNTU) were sentenced to one-year jail terms on May 8, 1972.

The response to this government action was immediate. Thousands of workers across the province walked off their jobs. The general strike was neither planned nor directed by union leaders. In fact, the scope and intensity of the outburst caught union leaders as much by surprise as it did the government. Clearly, the imprisonment of the three union leaders only served as a catalyst that brought to the surface the workers' profound discontent with the structure of work and politics in Quebec. The strike received support in large cities as well as in small towns; it erupted in affluent cities like Sept-Isles and in depressed areas with heavy unemployment like the Gaspé and

115. The account of events in Quebec which follows draws on an article by Nick Auf der Maur. See his "The May Revolt Shakes Quebec," *The Last Post*, 2, 1972, pp. 10–25.
116. The Common Front represented 210 000 of the 250 000 employees of the Quebec government.

St. Jerome. In addition, a wide spectrum of occupational groups participated: blue- and white-collar workers as well as public and private sector employees. The white-collar participants included civil servants, library workers, office workers, teachers, liquor board employees, hydro workers, and newspaper staffs. Common Front strike committees of rank and file workers were formed across the province, and in some cases entire cities were taken over by the strikers. Local radio stations were seized and strikers broadcast revolutionary music and union statements. The *Last Post* described the strike as "one of the greatest displays of solidarity this century has seen since the Winnipeg General Strike in 1919."

More recent confrontations between public sector employees and the Quebec government have not matched the magnitude or volatility of the actions of 1972. Divisions within the ranks of public employees (for example, the withdrawal of Hydro-Quebec workers from the Common Front and a major split within the CNTU) have made concerted actions difficult. Despite these barriers to unity, every round of negotiations subsequent to 1972 has been characterized by protracted strikes and special legislation forcing employees back to work. And each round of bargaining has been accompanied by rank and file workers' defiance of injunctions and back-to-work legislation.[117]

Labour militancy has also been mounting in British Columbia. Premier William Bennett's reigning Social Credit Party was met with a massive display of opposition when the government introduced a wave of anti-labour legislation in the summer and fall of 1983. The pending legislation (twenty-six bills all told) was aimed at eliminating collective bargaining and job security of provincial employees, abolishing agencies and laws that offered protection to disadvantaged people, and drastically reducing social services and economic support in the areas of education, welfare, and housing. The government justified this set of bills by claiming restraint on government spending was needed to deal with the economic crisis faced by the province.

117. Gérard Hébert, "Public Sector Bargaining in Quebec: A Case of Hypercentralization," in Thompson and Swimmer, *op. cit.*, pp. 229–281; Jean Boivin, "Labour Relations in Quebec," in Anderson and Gunderson, *op. cit.*, pp. 422–456.

Tens of thousands of citizens held a different view of the legislation. The Social Credit government demanded concessions, Palmer maintains, in order to ensure that both the rising costs of unionized labour and of the welfare state would not discourage future investments in the province, nor impede capital accumulation and the Socreds general plan for restructuring the political economy.[118]

Two prominent organizations were formed to oppose the proposed legislation: Operation Solidarity (a coalition of unions whose vital core consisted of public sector unions) and Solidarity Coalition (a coalition of diverse groups and activists whose funding came from the unions). Operation Solidarity organized what turned out to be the largest demonstration ever held in the city of Victoria: 25 000 protesters crowded onto the lawns of the provincial legislature. Two weeks later (August 10), more than 50 000 persons joined a protest rally at Vancouver's Empire Stadium, while demonstrations were held the same day in smaller communities across the province. Groups associated with Solidarity Coalition occupied the Vancouver offices of the provincial cabinet and staged street theatre dramatizing the plight of the disadvantaged in front of the home of a cabinet minister. On October 15, more than 60 000 protesters joined together at the Vancouver hotel where the Social Credit Party was holding its annual convention. So huge was this march that it took some six hours for the line to pass by the hotel.[119] While a general strike was often discussed—and the idea was endorsed by the Vancouver District Labour Council—leaders of Operation Solidarity instead decided on a plan of gradually escalating strike action, starting with the British Columbia Government Employees Union (BCGEU), a week later adding the teachers, then ferry workers, then municipal employees and bus drivers, and finally hospital and health care workers. To the disappointment of many workers involved in the movement, union leaders heading Operation Solidarity narrowed their

118. Bryan Palmer, "The Rise and Fall of British Columbia's Solidarity," in Bryan Palmer, ed., *The Character of Class Struggle*, Toronto: McClelland and Stewart, 1986, p. 183.
119. Thom Quine, *How Operation Solidarity Became Operation Soldout*, Toronto: International Socialists, 1985.

concern from the entire legislative package to the two labour-relevant bills. On November 1, BCGEU's 35 000 workers walked out. A week later, amidst much doubt about their willingness to strike, about 90 percent of the province's teachers and school support staffs joined the strike. Just as the momentum was building, the union officials of Operation Solidarity ordered the ferry workers to delay their walkout. Finally, on November 13, International Woodworkers' president, Jack Munro, met with Premier Bennett to "negotiate" a settlement: "A gentlemen's televised agreement on the premier's porch, in which nothing was signed, nothing was sealed, and no concrete settlement terms were stated. Thus ended one of the most dramatic labour and social confrontations in British Columbia's history."[120] The only accomplishment arising from months of protest activity was the withdrawal of several bills pertaining to government employees; the rest of the legislative package, which would negatively affect tens of thousands of British Columbians, remained intact.[121]

White-Collar Workers and Unions

Events in the public sector over the past several decades demonstrate that white-collar workers, even those with advanced training and professional trappings, can be committed and militant unionists. The significance of white-collar unionism cannot be discounted by the argument that there are important differences in blue-collar and white-collar unions. The central functions of any union are collective bargaining

120. Palmer, *op. cit.*, p. 196.
121. While not on the same scale as the Quebec or British Columbia struggles, in March of 1986 1700 transportation and public works employees of the Newfoundland Association of Public Employees (NAPE) struck illegally. As a result 72 arrests were made and two union leaders jailed. Seventeen days after the strike began the original strikers were joined by 3500 administrative and clerical workers—all members of NAPE. Included among these workers were secretaries, dental assistants, clerks, social workers, and computer operators. The strike was undertaken for wage increases and to repeal a provincial law requiring a portion of workers in any government bargaining unit to be designated as "essential." Because "essential" workers are prohibited from striking, the union argued that the law effectively negated the right to strike by keeping a minimum crew of workers on the job. See Toronto *Globe and Mail*, March 20, 1986.

and the defense of the interests of members, even if this entails the use of confrontation tactics. Moreover, unionization involves a rejection of the belief that a single individual can, through a mere display of competence, receive just rewards for work performance. To accept the idea of unionism is to realize that only through collective efforts can individuals guarantee some measure of justice and bring about improvements in wages and working conditions. Unionization is also based on the realization that the interests and objectives of management are not the same as those of employees. At issue, then, are control and power. Although this contest for power may not always be well articulated by workers or actively pursued by unions, it is always implicitly present because rejection of the principle of an identity of interest between employees and employers denies management's "right" to unilaterally establish and maintain working rules and conditions. The rationale behind blue-collar and white-collar unions, then, is the same.

White-collar unions, like their manual counterparts, have been formed as a response to alienation, but they are not an adequate solution to it. To evaluate unions favourably, then, is not tantamount to viewing them as a panacea for the problems generated by the content and organization of work. Unions do benefit workers: they are one of the few viable vehicles to defend workers' interests. But at the same time, they have only timidly challenged the issue of management dominance. Even the most militant unions have been unable to do more than temper or deflect management's capacity to organize and control the labour process. Despite this caveat, unionization still represents a progressive movement for white-collar workers, for it entails recognition of the existence of a structural conflict at the workplace and the need for collective rather than individual action in order to handle it. Considering the political and psychological history of white-collar employees, unionization must be regarded as a giant step forward.

A sudden surge of idealism and metamorphosis of political consciousness is not about to occur which would drive non-organized white-collar employees to eagerly embrace unionism. But alienating work and deteriorating working conditions of many white-collar employees, especially office and sales workers, will ultimately impel them to take more aggressive measures to defend their own interests. As more and more white-collar workers grasp the necessity of unionizing, we can anticipate mounting anti-union practices from employers and top managers. It would be a mistake to underestimate the lengths to which employers and the state may go to avoid, curb, or destroy collective bargaining and the right to strike. The conflict and struggle in white-collar worlds is bound to continue under these circumstances; only the outcome of the contest is uncertain.

SUMMARY AND CONCLUSIONS

By exploring the worlds of white-collar workers we have been able to evaluate critically the vision of the future set forth by theorists of post-industrial society. According to this view, advances in science, technology, and the tertiary sector of the economy are transforming the social relations of production as well as the class structure of advanced capitalist nations. Knowledge institutions and knowledge workers are central to the vision of post-industrial theorists. The expansion of complex and personally gratifying white-collar occupations purportedly requires a highly educated labour force. Moreover, the power of businessmen is being eclipsed as professionals and scientists begin to take over the command posts of modern society's central institutions. These trends are seen as converging to reduce and ultimately eliminate alienation and class conflict.

The evidence, however, hardly compels us to draw the same conclusions. While the number of white-collar jobs has grown appreciably, this development has come at the expense of agricultural pursuits rather than blue-collar jobs. The proportion of the Canadian labour force comprising blue-collar workers today remains roughly equivalent to what it was at the turn of this century. Of greater concern, though, is the question of the degree of complexity of white-collar jobs. Post-industrial theorists grossly exaggerate this point. The bulk of the white-collar segment of the labour force consists of clerical and sales jobs, whose two most prominent characteristics are specialization and subordination. The trend in this sphere of the world of work is toward mechanization and the imposition of Taylorist criteria of efficiency. Moreover, employees in the stratum that comes closest to embodying "knowledge"—professionals, scientists, and technicians—for the most part find themselves labouring under restrictions similar to those experienced by all dependent wage workers. A large portion of this stratum is made up of sub-professionals and technicians, whose defining trait (relative to the ideal of what constitutes a professional) is an inability to exercise control over their work lives. Even the activities of full-fledged professionals and scientists are shaped by the dictates of their bosses in both private and public organizations. Furthermore, there is no data to support the contention that professionals and scientists are on the threshold of seizing power from traditional ruling elites. When they do ascend to managerial positions or assume advisory roles in government, their activities continue to be carefully defined by the priorities and interests of administration and management.

That the eradication of alienated labour and class conflict is more myth than reality is indicated most pointedly by the actions of workers in the public sector of the Canadian economy. It is precisely those occupational groups, supposedly the true offspring of "post-industrial" developments, that have manifested the most dynamic forms of opposition in modern society. The explosion of opposition in Quebec in 1972 and the ill-fated British Columbia Solidarity movement in 1983 are only the most dramatic expressions of unrest among public employees and working people in general. These intense displays of unity and radicalism are relatively infrequent, but recent activities of postal workers, teachers, health care workers, and other public employees have demonstrated conclusively that growth of the tertiary sector of the economy has not ushered in the harmonious labour relations and consensus politics forecast by some observers. On the contrary, this sector is a dynamic arena of conflict in contemporary Canadian society. As events over the past several decades have shown, labour relations in the public sector are characterized more by dissension and conflict than consensus and co-operation.

From whatever vantage point they are viewed, the social and

political trends projected by adherents of the post-industrial thesis do not hold up. This assessment is borne out both by an analysis of developments in the structural properties of white-collar work and the activities of white-collar workers.

5 Blue-Collar Work

Sociological literature and the popular media frequently depict workers in stereotyped and even derogatory ways. Workers are portrayed as members of powerful trade unions that have improved wages and working conditions so much that workers now enjoy a state of affluence. Affluent workers, so the standard image would have it, are avid consumers whose life-styles are not unlike those of the middle class. Affluence is linked to an *instrumental* orientation to work: Manual workers are said to have such an overriding interest in the size of their paycheque and what it can buy that they do not much care about the conditions or the content of their jobs, nor about the amount of control they exercise over the work process or the degree of the skill and expertise they use on the job. It is also commonly believed that improvements in wages and working conditions have moderated the workers' political philosophies and practices, resulting in a politically contented, even reactionary, manual working class. Like all stereotypes, these typifications contain an element of truth. A careful assessment of the manual working class, however, reveals to what extent this portrait of the affluent and contented worker is misleading and inaccurate.

IS THE WORKER AFFLUENT?

Modern workers are undeniably better off than their historic counterparts. Statistics showing workers' economic gains *over time*, however, are very often used to argue that the *current* financial position of working people is one of affluence. In fact, historical statistics say little about the modern worker's financial status relative to the rest of society, and the term "affluent worker" makes little sense when viewed from an ahistorical perspective.

The incomes earned by blue-collar workers range from somewhere near the very bottom of the income scale to the relatively high wages received by skilled tradesmen. But the majority of wage earners falls somewhere between these two extremes, and most of them struggle just to "get by." In 1981 the Social Planning Council of Metropolitan Toronto calculated the amount of gross income that individuals and families of various sizes needed to live modestly. For a four-person blue-collar family the budget figures ranged from $19 942 (for renters without a car) to $25 562 (for homeowners with a car). These budgets were indeed modest. Despite the fact that three of five urban families incur debts from charge accounts and loans, no money was budgeted for credit of any kind. Moreover, the budgets did not provide for savings (not even for the children's education), and the insurance allotment covered only burial expenses and a six-month period of adjustment after death.[1] Viewed from another perspective, the low budget figure of $19 942 was only $3581 above the 1981 Statistics Canada poverty line for a family of four living in urban areas with populations of 500 000 or more.[2] In contrast to these budget standards, the average annual gross earnings of Toronto manufacturing wage earners employed full-time in 1981 was only $16 766.[3] In many families, women worked in paid jobs to compensate for the inadequate wages of their husbands. But even when the earnings of all family members were added to those of the household head, the total in many cases failed to meet budget standards. In 1981 about one-quarter of the four-person, blue-collar families in Toronto earned less than $20 000

1. See Social Planning Council of Metropolitan Toronto, *Guides for Family Budgeting,* 1981.
2. See National Council of Welfare, *1984 Poverty Lines: Estimates by the National Council of Welfare,* Ottawa, March 1984, Table 2.
3. This figure was calculated from average *weekly* wages. See Statistics Canada, *Employment Earnings and Hours,* Ottawa, May 1981, Table 4.

and nearly 40 percent grossed less than $25 000 (the upper figure for the budget).[4]

If many working people earn only enough to satisfy their most modest needs, still fewer meet the requirements of a strict definition of affluence or "middle classness." Porter offers the following insight into what constitutes a middle-class style of life:

> *Middle-class mothers exchange opinions with each other about their obstetricians, pediatricians, and orthodontists. They discuss the relative merits of various nursery schools, private schools, ballet lessons, music classes, summer camps. They talk about their cottage communities or their touring holidays . . . it is the ability to consume these things, which can neither be bought with a small down payment and three years to pay nor be used as the security for a chattel mortgage, which identifies the real middle class.[5]*

It is clear, according to Porter's definition, that the vast majority of Canadians fail to qualify as members of the middle class.

We should also bear in mind that a sizable minority of workers falls at or below officially defined poverty lines. The largest single category of poverty consists of the "working poor." Almost one-half of all poor individuals and family heads derive most of their income from employment. Considering only poor persons under the age of 65 (i.e., only those expected to be in the labour force), nearly nine of every ten household heads are employed at full-time jobs and four of every ten work fifty or more weeks a year.[6]

In examining the notion of working-class affluence, economic insecurity deriving from unemployment must also be considered—particularly in Canada's case. In 1970, when the

4. These calculations were based on data from Statistics Canada's "Public Use Sample Tapes" for the 1981 census.
5. John Porter, *The Vertical Mosaic*, Toronto: University of Toronto Press, 1965, p. 126.
6. National Council of Welfare, *The Working Poor: People and Programs*, Ottawa, 1981. Also see David P. Ross, *The Working Poor: Wage Earners and the Failure of Income Security Policies*, Toronto: James Lorimer, 1981.

unemployment rate stood at 5.7 percent, a labour economist observed that Canada had the "sorriest record of continuous unemployment of any advanced economy in the world."[7] Five years later the average annual unemployment rate, having reached 6.9 percent, began a steady ascent. In 1982, 11 percent of the labour force was jobless, the highest figure recorded since the depression years of 1938–39. By the mid-1980s, the economy showed signs of a modest recovery, but the jobless rate hovered around 10 percent with no relief predicted for the foreseeable future. Unemployment is not the exclusive property of manual wage earners, but they—particularly the young ones—experience it most directly.[8] In increasing numbers, however, workers across the spectrum of occupations and ages are suffering not only from the economy's incapacity to expand at a rate commensurate with the growth of the labour force, but also from lay-offs and permanent job losses.

The official unemployment rate underestimates the real amount of joblessness. Statistics Canada does not count as unemployed (a) those who have given up looking for jobs (discouraged workers) or (b) those who are forced to work part-time because of the unavailability of full-time jobs (underemployed workers). In March of 1982 a special Statistics Canada survey found that there were 407 000 "discouraged workers," that is, persons without work but not officially defined as unemployed. This figure was equivalent to one-third the number of persons *officially* regarded as unemployed during the

7. Stephen G. Peitchinis, *Canadian Labour Economics,* Toronto: McGraw-Hill of Canada, 1970, p. 229.

8. In 1982, the unemployment rate among blue-collar workers (14.8 percent) was twice as great as that among white-collar workers (7.1 percent); the unemployment rate of individuals between the ages of 15 and 24 was 70 percent higher than the national average. See Rick Deaton, "Unemployment: Canada's Malignant Social Pathology," *Perception,* Spring–Summer, 1983, pp. 14–19. Conservative thinkers like to attribute unemployment to some combination of personal traits of the jobless (e.g., lack of ambition, unreliability) and government welfare and unemployment insurance programs. The inadequacy of this "blame the victim" argument is exposed by data showing that on any given day in Canada there are some 50 000 to 75 000 jobs vacancies being sought by one and a half million persons—a ratio of one job opening for every 20 or 30 job-seekers. See Cy Gonick, "The Twisted Mind of Donald MacDonald and Co.," *Canadian Dimension,* January–February, 1986, pp. 19–23.

same period.[9] Stirling and Kouri revealed a major discrepancy between official and real unemployment rates. In their count of the unemployed, these researchers included discouraged workers, underemployed workers, and persons not in the labour force who would take paid jobs if they were available on reasonable terms. With these revised definitions, the percentage of the unemployed was roughly double the rate calculated by Statistics Canada.[10] To get some idea of the real extent of failure of the economy, however, it would be necessary to consider yet another category of the uncounted: those who work full-time but still cannot make ends meet.

The branches of the economy hit hardest by unemployment are construction and resource industries like logging and mining. The critically important manufacturing sector is vulnerable as well. Between 1965 and 1970, unemployment in manufacturing rose by 76 percent. Over a one-year period in the early 1970s in Ontario—the heartland of Canadian manufacturing—over 16 000 persons were laid off or lost their jobs permanently because of 138 plant shutdowns.[11] Because of the implementation of labour-replacing technology, recession, and the growing propensity of industrialists to relocate their operations in regions where labour is politically suppressed and cheap, the manufacturing sector continues to be a major source of employment insecurity. Between 1979 and 1983, 170 000 manufacturing jobs were eliminated in Canada.[12] For these workers, especially the older ones and the semiskilled, re-employment possibilities are often quite bleak. If they do find

9. Deaton, *op. cit.*
10. Robert Stirling and Denise Kouri, "Unemployment Indexes—The Canadian Context," in John Fry, ed., *Economy, Class and Social Reality: Issues in Contemporary Canadian Society*, Toronto: Butterworths, 1979, pp. 169–205. Further evidence that government figures grossly underestimate the true level of unemployment was provided by Statistics Canada in 1976. While 25 000 persons in Newfoundland were *officially* without work, an additional 28 000 said they wanted a job. See *The Report of the Peoples' Commission on Unemployment in Newfoundland and Labrador*, St. Johns: Newfoundland and Labrador Federations of Labour, 1978. Also see Cy Gonick, *Out of Work*, Toronto: James Lorimer, 1978, pp. 18–23.
11. Cf. "Unemployment: A New Analysis," *Our Generation*, 8, 1972, pp. 6–26.
12. Edward B. Harvey and John Blakely, "Education, Social Mobility and the Challenge of Technological Change," in *Transitions to Work*, University of Manitoba, Institute for Social and Economic Research, 1985, pp. 46–65.

another job, it entails a loss of seniority and, often, a reduction in pay.[13]

BLUE-COLLAR WORK

Proponents of the thesis of working-class affluence and political contentment ignore the fact that workers are producers as well as consumers. If we are to approach an understanding of the manual working class, it is imperative to examine the way work is structured and the way wage earners respond to their work. The remainder of this chapter focusses on these issues.

In 1981 blue-collar workers comprised 42.2 percent of the Canadian labour force. These workers constitute a heterogeneous stratum marked by differences in income, age, sex, ethnicity, and occupation. As Table II shows, manual wage earners are distributed among five major occupational categories, the two largest being the manufacturing and mechanical sector (essentially factory jobs) and the service sector. Within each of the occupational groups there is an enormous range of jobs and of workplaces, from small taverns to huge factories. Women occupy an increasing majority of service jobs, while in all other spheres of blue-collar work, males predominate. Despite these differences, there are common threads which run through the fabric of most blue-collar labour, and these common features are the focus of the discussion that follows.

13. The negative effects of the general economic slowdown being experienced in all capitalist countries are compounded in Canada by a long-standing emphasis on the resource-exporting sector and a corresponding neglect of manufacturing. In comparison with manufacturing industries, the resource sector provides fewer jobs because it is primarily capital-intensive. Moreover, resources shipped out are ordinarily finished in the recipient countries. See Glen Williams, *Not For Export: Towards a Political Economy of Canada's Arrested Industrialization*, Toronto: McClelland and Stewart, 1983. Canada's dependence on foreign (mainly U.S.) capital makes it difficult for any government so disposed to undertake an industrial development strategy aimed at a balanced and vital economy which would provide Canadians with greater employment stability.

TABLE II
Blue-Collar Occupational Groups,
Percentage Employed and Sex Composition, 1981

Sector	Percent	Male	Female	Total
Manufacturing and Mechanical	34.8	79.2	20.8	100.0
Construction	15.6	98.1	1.9	100.0
Transportation and Communications	17.2	86.4	13.6	100.0
Service	28.4	47.3	52.7	100.0
Fishing, forestry, and mining	4.0	95.6	4.4	100.0
TOTAL	100.0			

SOURCE: Adapted from 1981 Census of Canada, Vol. I, Cat. 92–917, Table 1, Ottawa: Statistics Canada, 1983.

The Content of Work

Throughout the twentieth century, the pursuit of profits has driven employers and managers to dilute workers' skills and worker control through the introduction of increasingly sophisticated technology and highly fragmented, standardized, and supervised work procedures. This trend towards the degradation of labour has enveloped more and more industries and occupations. Human skills have been increasingly replaced by machines, and the workplace philosophy of Taylorism has engineered a good deal of the complexity and control out of craft work. Consequently, the differences between skilled and non-skilled work have become less clear.[14] Many jobs currently defined as skilled bear little resemblance to the tasks performed by traditional craftsmen, a fact reflected by the limited importance of apprentice training requirements. Even workers whose labour retained aspects of craft-like autonomy (e.g., newspaper printers, miners, skilled machinists, and longshoremen), have been subjected over the past several decades to a rationalization of work procedures made possible by develop-

14. *Cf.* Stanley Aronowitz, *False Promises,* New York: McGraw–Hill, 1973.

ments in computer technology.[15] Despite the complexity of
many skilled jobs, most workers in traditional blue-collar
industries occupy semiskilled or unskilled positions. These
jobs usually entail the performance of repetitive tasks and
require little skill or training. Semiskilled and unskilled workers literally sell their capacity to work: They sell the ability to
learn a specific job, any job, in a particular work organization.
When they change jobs, their "skills" are not ordinarily trans-
ferable (unlike those of craftsmen or professionals), and they
are obliged to acquire new "skills" for new jobs. This state of
affairs gives substance to the observation that manual workers
are replaceable parts or cogs in the operations of the modern
business enterprise[16]

Because blue-collar jobs are so fragmented and simple to
learn, many workers find themselves permanently locked into
their situations. Once settled into semiskilled work, the individual has no place else to go. Promotions to supervisory or office
positions are almost non-existent. The low ratio of foremen to
production workers precludes most workers from this kind of
advancement. It is also extremely rare to move from semiskilled
work into skilled work, because the former offers no opportunity for continuous learning and skill accumulation. Most
skilled labour requires apprenticeship or special training either
on the job or at school. For those individuals who do not receive
this training early on in life there is often no escape from non-

15. Wallace Clement, *Hardrock Mining: Industrial Relations and Technological Changes at Inco,* Toronto: McClelland and Stewart, 1981. Also, see the
relevant articles in Craig Heron and Robert Storey, eds., *On the Job: Confronting the Labour Process in Canada,* Montreal: McGill–Queen's University Press,
1986, and in Andrew Zimbalist, ed., *Case Studies on the Labor Process,* New
York: Monthly Review Press, 1979.
16. A British study of jobs occupied by male manual workers who had not
served an apprenticeship (which includes the great majority of manual jobs,
including most of those defined as skilled) concluded: "Eighty-seven percent
of our workers exercise less skill at work than they would if they drove to
work. Indeed, most of them expend more mental effort and resourcefulness in
getting to work than in doing their jobs." The jobs examined in this study were
not concentrated in the classical site of repetitive work—mass production
factories—but were located in a wide range of industries, from manufacturing
and construction to dairy and railway. See R.M. Blackburn and Michael Mann,
The Working Class in the Labour Market, London: Macmillan Press, Ltd., 1979,
p. 280.

skilled jobs. The most the non-skilled worker can realistically expect within the organizational job ladder is to acquire, through seniority, a "gravy job" which is less repetitive or less physically demanding than jobs performed by younger workers.

Technology has progressively displaced workers from their traditional sites of manual employment, as in manufacturing. More and more workers have been drawn to service jobs, which have been comparatively unaffected by mechanization. Consequently, over the past several decades the number of people employed in service work has grown more rapidly than in any other major occupational group.[17] The inclusion of service workers in the manual segment of the labour force increases the proportion of non-skilled workers in the blue-collar category. Approximately twenty percent of the service category in Canada consists of protective service jobs like policemen, firemen, plant guards, and night watchmen. The remainder of the category consists largely of personal service occupations like waiters and waitresses, housekeepers and servants, barbers and hairdressers, and janitors, charworkers, and cleaners. Although relatively immune from mechanization, many service occupations have been no less subject to rationalization—in some cases to a degree that would evoke envy in the most efficiency-conscious factory manager. For example, time and motion studies are used in the fast food industry to standardize procedures and time spent for the assembly of, say, a hamburger, including the number and placement of pickles, onions, lettuce, and tomato slices; the amount (one-half ounce) and proper mode of dispensing ketchup ("evenly in a spiral motion over the pickles starting near the outside edge of the sandwich and ending near the centre"); the frying and packaging of french fries, and so on.[18] These highly standardized operations (which are codified in corporate manuals) are enforced by numerous diligent managers who preside over a part-time work force made up almost entirely of teenagers and married women.

17. In the U.S., MacDonalds restaurants now employ more persons than the basic steel industry.
18. Ester Reiter, "Out of the Frying Pan Into the Fryer—The Organization of Work in a Fast Food Outlet," Ph.D. Thesis, University of Toronto, 1985, p. 197.

As an executive for Burger King observed, "fast food restaurants operate like manufacturing plants today—not restaurants."[19] While fast food chains represent an extreme case of work rationalization, this approach is not unrepresentative of the service industry. Service jobs are generally characterized by low wages, employment insecurity, high quit rates, and growing numbers of female and part-time workers.[20] Not surprisingly, the training required for service jobs is often "conspicuous by its absence."[21]

To grasp the nature of typical blue-collar labour, consider the following job descriptions:

Food processing plant—

> Basically, I stand there all day and slash the necks of the chickens. You make one slash up on the skin of the neck and then you cut around the base of the neck so the next person beside you can crop it. . . . The chickens go in front of you on the line and you do every other chicken or whatever. And you stand there for eight hours on one spot and do it.[22]

Nickel mine—

> Every day you say to your wife, 'I'll see you tonight,' but you may not see her tonight because that's mining. It's dirty; it's wet. . . .
>
> He was reaching under to cut the other one (chunk of rock) and this piece fell. It slipped down off the bolt and fell on top of his back. He was not a hefty guy and one leg was out here and the other one was back this way. It never dropped from much height. It maybe dropped a couple of inches onto his back, but still it was solid rock. The thing must have weighed tons. It took nine guys to get it off him.

19. Cited in *Ibid.*, p. 138. Also see Ester Reiter, "Life in a Fast Food Factory," in Heron and Storey, *op. cit.*, pp. 309–326.
20. Pat and Hugh Armstrong, *A Working Majority: What Women Must Do For Pay*, Ottawa: Canadian Government Publishing Centre, 1983.
21. Lee Taylor, *Occupational Sociology*, New York: Oxford University Press, 1968, p. 563.
22. Armstrong, *op. cit.*, p. 128.

We had no big timbers to pry it off him, and then it was too late. There was not a bone broken or anything. He was all squished.[23]

Garment factory—

All the finishing you can learn is speed. Everything is the same . . . it's standard: You make the buttonhole. You make the facing. You put on shoulder pads. Anybody can do it. That's why finishers are looked down on.

I hate it because it's physically hard. Because not a great deal of intelligence is required. It's not challenging. Usually while I'm working I think about other things . . . all kinds of things. Oh God. My mind wanders because I'm so used to doing my job now, I can do it automatically.[24]

Luggage factory—

In forty seconds you have to take the wet felt out of the felter, put the blanket on—a rubber sheeting—to draw out the excess moisture, wait two, three seconds, take the blanket off, pick the wet felt up, balance it on your shoulder—there is no way of holding it without tearing it all to pieces, it is wet and will collapse—reach over, get the hose, spray the inside of this copper screen to keep it from plugging, turn around, walk to the hot dry die behind you, take the hot piece off with your opposite hand, set it on the floor—this wet thing is still balanced on my shoulder—put the wet piece on the dry die, push this button that lets the dry press down, inspect the piece we just took off, the hot piece, stack it, and count it—when you get a stack of ten, you push it over and start another stack of ten—then go back and put our blanket on the wet piece coming up from the tank . . . and start all over.[25]

23. Clement, *op. cit.*, pp. 219–220.
24. Charlene Gannagé, *Double Day, Double Bind: Women Garment Workers*, Toronto: Women's Press, 1986, pp. 106–107.
25. Studs Terkel, *Working*, New York: Pantheon Books, 1972, pp. 289–290.

Fast food restaurant—

> *At Burger King, hamburgers are cooked as they pass through the broiler on a conveyor belt at a rate of 835 patties per hour. Furnished with a pair of tongs, the worker picks up the burgers as they drop off the conveyor belt, puts each on a toasted bun, and places the hamburgers and buns in a steamer. The jobs may be hot and boring, but they can be learned in a matter of minutes. The more interesting part of the procedure lies in applying condiments and microwaving the hamburgers. The popularity of this task among Burger King employees rests on the fact that it is unmechanized and allows some discretion to the worker . . . management is aware of this area of worker freedom and makes strenuous efforts to eliminate it by outlining exactly how this job is to be performed.*[26]

Candy factory—

> *One of the jobs is the trays . . . they have these little plastic trays to put the chocolates in. One woman sits there the whole day and she just moves the tray from her hand to the table. . . . The days that are really bad are the thirteen hour days when the machine doesn't break and the kind of chocolate being done on the line doesn't change.*[27]

Auto factory—

> *The line lumbers steadily . . . bringing an endless procession of brown and grey metal skeletons. Each time a car skeleton comes past, the worker picks up the portable grinder that is his only tool and presses it onto bubbled welds, grinding them to flat smoothness in a shower of sparks and a screech of metal against metal. That is it. . . . He does this 'job' forty-eight times an hour.*[28]

26. Reiter, *op. cit.*, pp. 317–318.
27. *Women at Work in Nova Scotia*, Halifax: Halifax Women's Bureau, 1973, pp. 17–18.
28. Don Wells, "Autoworkers on the Firing Line," in Heron and Storey, *op. cit.*, p. 329.

Although more and more spheres of work have become rationalized, the trend toward labour degradation has proceeded unevenly. Tight labour markets and workers' determined opposition have sometimes retarded management's attempts to rationalize the labour process.[29] Volatile product markets can also inhibit the standardization and routinization of production. Similarly, in certain industries, often involving the supply of raw materials or the use of high technology, there are unpredictable though not uncommon events in the production process (e.g., impediments to extraction in coal mining, machine malfunctions in chemical processing) that render the managerial ideal of maximum job fragmentation and minimum worker discretion less profitable than more flexible modes of organizing work.[30] Developments in technology at times necessitate the acquisition of new worker skills, as in the cases of maintenance personnel, heavy equipment operators, and job setters. Then too, there are still a few genuine craft workers, like cabinet makers and toolmakers. Even in highly rationalized manufacturing there still exists a minority of jobs that are personally absorbing and that provide opportunities for continuous learning.

Management's goal of complete skill and knowledge dilution

29. Paul Thompson, *The Nature of Work: An Introduction to Debates on the Labour Process,* London: Macmillan, 1983; Craig Heron and Robert Storey, "On the Job in Canada," in Heron and Storey, *op. cit.,* pp. 3–46; John Bellamy Foster, "On the Waterfront: Longshoring in Canada," in Heron and Storey, *op. cit.,* pp. 281–308. Also see Stephen Wood, ed., *The Degradation of Work? Skill, Deskilling and the Labour Process,* London: Hutchinson, 1983, and David Noble, *Forces of Production: A Social History of Automation,* New York: Alfred A. Knopf, 1984.

30. For example, in chemical processing plants production problems must be quickly detected and remedial action taken immediately. Otherwise, substantial costs are likely to be incurred. Since the appropriate responses to unpredictable events cannot be predetermined, and since specialization inhibits workers' capacity to deal with such contingencies, a situation of highly unbalanced workloads arises, with some specialized workers being overwhelmed with work while others remain idle. John Kelly, *Scientific Management, Job Redesign and Work Performance,* New York: Academic Press, 1982; Charles F. Sabel, *Work and Politics: The Division of Labor in Industry,* New York: Cambridge University Press, 1982; also see James Rinehart, "Improving the Quality of Working Life Through Job Redesign: Work Humanization or Work Rationalization?", *The Canadian Review of Sociology and Anthropology,* Vol. 23, no. 4, 1986, pp. 507–530.

has been held in check because, when all is said and done, work can never be completely standardized; unexpected problems with materials, methods, and machines frequently arise, and consequently, even the most unskilled workers acquire through daily work experience a valuable and irreducible stock of on-the-job knowledge. The worker's repertoire of knowledge and responses, as Kusterer emphasizes, often goes beyond what can be taught in job-training or codified in standard operating manuals.[31] Nevertheless, intrinsically gratifying blue-collar jobs are the exception rather than the rule, and are found mainly among the skilled trades. Consider the following statements:

Toolmaker—

> *You make different kinds of tools. It isn't monotonous—everything's different. Sometimes you have to plan out your own work—it's a challenge. It's doing something different always.*[32]

Cobalt treatment operator—

> *I find it interesting because I make a game out of it; a lot of people complain because it's a pretty common job. But my job is more interesting than most because it's easier to make little innovations. It is a batch, and you are in full control of it. You are not responsible to a control room. There is no control room or mechanism monitoring what you are doing, and you are left alone. So, you have a lot more opportunity to play little games with yourself and with the batch. And you also have the opportunity that if you are not feeling well, you don't have to work so hard; on other days, if you feel a little energetic, you work more.*[33]

31. Ken C. Kusterer, *Know-How On The Job: The Important Working Knowledge of "Unskilled" Workers,* Boulder: Westview Press, 1978. Additional examples of working knowledge may be found in Jim Peterson, " 'More News From Nowhere': Utopian Notes of a Hamilton Machinist," *Labour/Le Travail,* 17, Spring, 1986, pp. 169–223.
32. Gavin Mackenzie, *The Aristocracy of Labor,* London: Cambridge University Press, 1973, p. 37.
33. Clement, *op cit.,* p. 196.

Sewing machine operator—

I don't work the same as others do. In my case it has to be just perfect. And if it isn't the way I understand it to be, then I rip it and sew it over. That's what I mean by a good operator. . . . When you do something, you plan before. You think about it. How it's going to be, how it's going to come out. You look at it like a painter paints a picture.[34]

Stonemason—

Usually it takes about three years of being a hod carrier to start. And it takes another ten or fifteen years to learn the skill. . . . It's a pretty good day layin' stone or brick. Not tiring. Anything you like to do isn't tiresome. . . . If I got some problem that's bothering me, I'll actually wake up in the night and think of it. I'll sit at the table and get a pencil and paper and go over it, makin' marks on paper or drawin' or however . . . this way or that way.[35]

Typesetter—

It takes a good five years. . . . I'm still learning . . . it's true. I never stop learning. . . . You discover certain things on the machine. . . . It's a work of art we do.[36]

Piano tuner—

Piano tuning is not really a business, it's a dedication. There's such a thing as piano tuning, piano rebuilding, and antique restoration. There's such a thing as scale designing and engineering, to produce the highest sound quality possible. I'm in all of this and I enjoy every second of it.[37]

Subordination and Discipline
The capitalist workplace is characterized by relations of domi-

34. Gannagé, *op. cit.,* p. 104.
35. Terkel, *op. cit.,* p. 22.
36. Armstrong, *op. cit.,* p. 159.
37. Terkel, *op. cit.,* p. 318.

nation and subordination, and manual workers occupy the subordinate positions. As Goldthorpe and his associates point out, a worker "can double his living standards and still remain a man who sells his labour to an employer in return for wages; he can work at a control panel rather than an assembly line without changing his subordinate position in the organization of production."[38] The precise character of subordination varies from workplace to workplace, from the arbitrary and paternalistic exercise of power in small shops, laundries, and restaurants, to the impersonal, bureaucratic authority of large factories. In small workplaces (usually not unionized) workers have little or no protection against the personal and absolute dictates of employers or supervisors. Large companies, on the other hand, depersonalize management's power by establishing regulations covering most aspects of personnel relations: discipline, promotion, grievances, seniority, and the evaluation of the work performance of both workers and supervisors.[39] While these measures to some extent mitigate the arbitrariness of management's decisions, the overall imbalance of power is not altered. Bureaucratic blandishments leave untouched the traditional domains of centralized decision-making and are superimposed on a labour process that is defined and directed by management personnel.[40]

Some rules in the workplace are designed to protect workers from hazards, but others define and punish insubordination as well as behaviour that interferes with the realization of production standards or worker output. Firms often post rules on bulletin boards throughout the workplace prohibiting activities such as horseplay, unauthorized demonstrations (including illegal strikes or work slowdowns), loitering, leaving one's work

38. John Goldthorpe, *et al., The Affluent Worker in the Class Structure,* Cambridge: The University Press, 1969, pp. 162–163.

39. Richard Edwards refers to these modes of domination as "simple control" and "bureaucratic control." See *Contested Terrain: The Transformation of the Workplace in the Twentieth Century,* New York: Basic Books, 1979.

40. This generalization is applicable to firms that have relaxed supervisory controls over the immediate work process, i.e., by forming semi-autonomous work groups which can determine such matters as job allocation and work pace. For a fuller exposition of the character and implications of such practices see Chapter 6.

station or plant without permission, leaving one's work station prior to quitting time, and failure to follow or refusal to follow instructions (insubordination).[41] As Trower states:

> *Anyone who has ever been a worker in any mine, mill, or factory in Canada, no matter how good his contract, no matter how powerful his union, will be quick to testify that there is no democracy in industry. By virtue of the fact that he is an employee, he must obey the orders of others in return for a wage. Whether he agrees with the orders or not, whether the orders make sense or not, so long as he is not asked to perform an unsafe or criminal act, he must obey or be guilty of insubordination.*[42]

Penalties for rule violations range from reprimands to dismissal. Not infrequently, penalties are applied immediately after management has "detected" the prohibited behaviour. This raises an interesting legal point. In the world of work, the Canadian system of jurisprudence is suspended. Generally, workers are required to submit to whatever decisions managers make. Even where grievance procedures are in effect, the individual must still accept management's ruling until the dispute has been settled. In effect, infractions of workplace "laws" bring an immediate, if temporary, verdict of guilty, and the onus is on the worker to prove his or her innocence. The punishments meted out by management remain in effect unless or until an arbitrator decides otherwise—a process that can drag on for months. During the interim, the fired or suspended worker must cope with a substantial loss of income. "Since workers often live from paycheque to paycheque, it is not unknown for a worker who is unable to keep up payments to lose appliances, the family car, perhaps the family home while waiting for the arbitrator's ruling."[43]

41. These rules are reinforced by the union contract, especially that section known as the "Management's Rights Clause." For an example of such a clause, see Chapter 6, pp. 195-196.
42. Chris Trower, "Collective Bargaining and Industrial Democracy," in Gerry Hunnius, G. David Garson, and John Case, eds., *Workers' Control*, New York: Vintage Books, 1973, pp. 139–140.
43. Wells, *op. cit.*, p. 339.

The Physical Environment

A great deal of manual labour is performed in environments where there are persistent problems of comfort, health, and safety. Poor ventilation, excessive heat or noise, dirt or pollution, and inadequate safety measures are dangers commonly faced by the manual labourer. Hundreds of thousands of workers in factories, mines, and construction sites are exposed to unsafe conditions and harmful pollutants, including toxic gases, acids, radioactive substances, and mineral dusts. These pollutants have been shown to be directly linked to diseases such as cancer, asbestosis, emphysema, black lung, byssinoisis, white lung, and silicosis. Hazardous conditions are an everyday threat to construction workers, miners, wire repairmen, and cleaners of moving machinery. An Economic Council of Canada report estimated that one worker is injured in Canada every 16 seconds, and that during each eight-hour work day 4000 wage earners are injured on the job.[44] Between 1968 and 1978 disabling injuries grew by 65 percent, and an average of 1005 fatalities occurred each year. Among a work force of eight and one-half million persons, over one million work injuries and illnesses were reported in 1978 alone.[45] As Ashford demonstrated, the majority (two-thirds) of job-related injuries are due *not* to the carelessness of workers but to illegal and/or unsafe working conditions.[46] This grim situation is allowed to persist because (a) government regulations are inadequate, (b) the regulations are inadequately enforced, and (c) the light penal-

44. Pran Manga, Robert Broyles, Gil Reschenthaler, *Occupational Health and Safety: Issues and Alternatives,* Ottawa: Economic Council of Canada, 1981.

45. Charles Reasons, Lois Ross, Craig Patterson, *Assault on the Worker: Occupational Health and Safety in Canada,* Toronto: Butterworths, 1981. The magnitude of the problem can be gauged by the following figures: between 1961 and the end of 1969, approximately 46 000 Americans were killed in Vietnam. Over the same nine-year period, 126 000 workers were killed in industrial accidents in the United States. *Cf.* Patricia Cayo Sexton and Brendan Sexton, *Blue Collars and Hard Hats,* New York: Vintage Books, 1971, p. 102. The majority of people affected by dangerous and unhealthy workplace conditions wear blue collars. See, for example, *Employment Injuries and Occupational Illnesses 1972-1981,* Ottawa: Labour Canada, 1984.

46. Nicholas Ashford, *Crisis in the Workplace,* Boston: MIT Press, 1976.

ties for non-compliance to the regulations do not deter corporate offenders.[47] Workers' powerlessness is also an important component of these dangerous circumstances since neither workers nor their unions have much say in establishing health and safety guidelines.[48]

THE WAR AT THE WORKPLACE

Opinion surveys that ask blue-collar workers to state their level of job satisfaction in terms of four or five fixed response alternatives ranging from "very satisfied" to "very dissatisfied" have repeatedly produced a surprisingly high degree of positive responses. Can we reconcile the objective content and conditions of blue-collar work and the structure of workplace authority with surveys that project an image of the "happy worker"? As mentioned earlier, these positive responses can be interpreted as indicating "satisfaction" only within a context of limited job alternatives, the permanent existence of a large reserve army of unemployed workers, and the persistent threat of lay-offs, permanent job loss, and plant shutdowns. This backdrop of constraints and insecurities helps to explain why a job, any job, can be viewed in a positive light by working-class individuals. Moreover, open-ended queries which allow people to express their feelings about work in their own words often reveal disturbingly high levels of dissatisfaction. Over and over again, such research indicates that many workers regard their work as unpleasant, feel that others look down on what they do for a living, would change occupations if they had their lives to live over again, and, finally, would do everything in their power to ensure that their children will not have to spend their lives in similar circumstances.[49]

Blue-collar workers and their orientations to work are signif-

47. Manga *et al., op. cit.*
48. *Ibid.*; Lloyd Tataryn, "A Tragically Repeating Pattern: Issues of Industrial Safety," in Katherina Lundy and Barbara Warme, eds., *Work in the Canadian Context,* Toronto: Butterworth, 1981, pp. 293–307.
49. See Peter Archibald, *Social Psychology as Political Economy,* Toronto: McGraw-Hill Ryerson, 1978, Chapter 8; James Rinehart, "Contradictions of Work-Related Attitudes and Behaviour: An Interpretation," *The Canadian Review of Sociology and Anthropology,* 15, 1, 1978, pp. 1–15.

icantly more complex than the simplistic portrayals derived from surveys that rely on limited multiple-choice question-naires. Manual wage earners ordinarily regard the time spent on the job not as their own but as the company's, and the job is defined simply as that—"just a job." Yet this absence of commitment is often accompanied by an active and constant struggle to humanize work and turn it into a meaningful and pleasurable experience. The tendency to avoid work, to do as little as possible, to strike, or to mutilate the instruments or products of work is accompanied by a counter-tendency to produce as effectively as possible, to race the clock in order to meet production quotas, and to take pride in building quality items or offering effective service. It is just such contradictory tendencies which elude simplistic attitude surveys and belie stereotypes of the instrumental worker. The activities and consciousness of working people can only be comprehended as a process that develops out of the concrete realities of their daily lives. The sections that follow examine the dimensions of these workplace activities.

Strikes

While strikes can be easily and fairly reliably quantified, they are only one of many manifestations of workers' reactions against the industrial system. Despite this caveat, one might expect an increasingly affluent and contented working class to have become less prone to engage in work stoppages. Statistics indicate, however, that there is no such trend. Canada has experienced four major strike waves in the twentieth century—in 1919–20, in 1946–47, in 1965–66, and in 1974–75.

Many strikes in the past ten or fifteen years have been precipitated by the erosion of workers' real wages. But we should be wary of purely economic interpretations of strike action. Strikes are complex phenomena arising out of complex and inter-related issues, and the relative importance of these issues often shifts as a strike progresses.[50] Even if we assume (with government statisticians) that the causes of a strike can be "ranked," a substantial number of work stoppages in any

50. Richard Hyman, *Strikes,* London: Fontana/Collins, 1972.

year are rooted not in pecuniary disputes but in grievances over working conditions and management decisions. This is not to say that wages are not a major concern to blue-collar workers. Rather, the wage question is often inextricably tied in with non-economic issues. For example, disputes instigated by non-economic concerns are sometimes focussed onto economic demands, primarily because collective bargaining does not facilitate resolution of non-economic issues. As Hyman observes, "pay claims are readily negotiable, since they provide ample scope for bargaining and compromise; whereas non-wage demands often involve questions of principle in which compromise is far more difficult. Trade union negotiators are usually far happier pursuing demands which offer reasonable prospects of peaceful settlement."[51]

Wildcat Strikes
While wildcat strikes are included in official strike statistics, they are so different from strikes called by the union that they warrant special attention. Wildcat strikes are illegal: They violate the contract negotiated between the company and the union, an agreement upheld by the legal authority of the state. Participants in such walkouts are subject to severe fines and penalties. The very fact that workers can be provoked to participate in what they know represents a serious breach of workplace laws underscores the seriousness of the problems that such walkouts seek to redress.

Wildcat strikes are a form of protest with clear-cut radical dimensions. These militant uprisings of rank and file workers are rarely openly supported by the union. In fact, union officials usually try to discourage workers from participating in walkouts or try to end them as quickly as possible. Wildcats strikes, then, involve a rejection of the formal and "legitimate" mechanisms established by the company and the union to resolve disputes and, as such, pose a direct challenge to

---

51. Richard Hyman, *Industrial Relations: A Marxist Introduction*, London: Macmillan, 1975, pp. 27–28.

workplace authorities—both of the company and of the union.[52]

While some wildcat strikes are planned in advance, many take place spontaneously, and in either case they are usually led by workers who do not hold official leadership positions in the union. The element of spontaneity may be seen in the fact that many workers not involved in the initial decision to leave work simply take it for granted that the strike must be supported. When a wildcat develops, workers often act first and ask questions later—outside the workplace. One participant writes:

> *One of the forms . . . short wildcats usually take, is that you're working on a machine or on a line and you see some people coming down the aisle heading toward the time clock and it isn't quitting time and there are too many people to be going to the tool crib. So you know they're leaving the plant. So what you do is literally shut down your machine. If you've got tools, you put them in your tool box, you walk out, you punch out. You have no idea what's happening—none whatsoever. All you know is that the plant's being struck. . . .*[53]

Wildcat strikes often involve only a segment of the plant work force, but at times they are supported by thousands of workers. Consider the case of a Ford plant located in Ontario:

> *The wildcat grew out of a worker sit-down in one area to protest the firing of two probationary workers. The sit-downers were jubilant when management agreed to rehire the two workers and conduct an investigation into the original firings. But when management refused to guarantee that there would be no punishment for those who had taken part in the sit-down, the sit-downers decided to call for a wildcat by the entire work force. The next day, they*

52. *Cf.* Maxwell Flood, "The Growth of the Non-Institutional Response in the Canadian Industrial Sector," *Relations Industrielles*, 27, 1972, pp. 603-615.
53. Martin Glaberman, *Theory and Practice*, Detroit: Facing Reality, 1969, p. 16.

rushed down the aisles, yelling "Hey, you scab, we need some support" and "This could happen to you." In hundreds and then thousands, workers gladly downed their tools, grabbed their street clothes, and joined the parade out of the plant. They marched through a sister plant and shut it down too, to the slack-jawed surprise of the supervisors.[54]

Workers ordinarily do not initiate wildcats over wage issues; these eruptions more commonly result from problems in the specific nature and organization of work and in the structure of workplace authority. Production speed-up, dangerous and unhealthy working conditions, arbitrary disciplinary action, violations of union work rules concerning job allocation and transfer—these are the kinds of problems which typically precipitate wildcats. In some instances, illegal strikes are the outcome of an accumulation of grievances. In his investigation of wildcats at Inco and Stelco, Flood found that hostility resulting from a build-up of grievances is often directed as much against the union as against management.[55] Finally, Flood's research demonstrated that the impetus for most wildcat strikes is a fundamental desire for "changes in social relations or objective environmental conditions."[56]

Restriction of Output

It is worth repeating that strikes, especially those that are legal, are only the most visible manifestation of industrial conflict. Even more revealing of the continuous struggle of workers to humanize their working time are the covert workplace actions that are usually known only to those who participate in them.

54. Wells, *op. cit.*, p. 328.
55. *Cf.* Flood, *op. cit.* Also see Maxwell Flood, *Wildcat Strike in Lake City*, Ottawa: Information Canada, 1970.
56. Flood, "The Growth of the Non-Institutional Response in the Canadian Industrial Sector," *op. cit.*, p. 603. Another kind of wildcat strike which takes place inside the plant and which does not show up in strike statistics is the sit-in. While this tactic was used effectively in the 1930s as a union organizing tool, today it is used by the rank and file to deal with grievances. For a description of a sit-in in a Canadian factory see Jim Monk, "Working on the Assembly Line," in Walter Johnson, ed., *Working in Canada*, revised second edition, Montreal: Black Rose Books, 1983, pp. 49–56.

The remainder of this chapter focusses on these daily workplace activities.

It has been said that Elton Mayo re-discovered the importance of the primary group in modern society through his studies of the Hawthorne Works of the Western Electric Company.[57] What he "discovered" was that workers organized themselves into cohesive groups which established a set of workplace rules that differed from, and often interfered with, the attainment of managerial production standards. There were three basic rules established by workers: Don't overproduce (rate-busting); don't underproduce (chiselling); don't report fellow workers to supervisors (squealing).[58] Since Mayo's time such counter-norms have become recognized as a common feature of the workplace. Years after Mayo's investigation, Whyte wrote: "We find almost universally that workers set a quota on what constitutes a fair day's work and refuse to go beyond this amount even when it is well within their ability to do so."[59]

One sociologist, who worked as a radial drill operator in a machine shop, took part in this "ceaseless war with management." He observed three types of output restriction: quota restriction, goldbricking, and slowdowns. Quota restriction involves limiting production to a norm established by management but below what could be easily produced. Meet the quota but do not exceed it is the rule. Goldbricking is a more common practice than quota restriction, partly because management is more likely to time worker output so that an all out effort is required. Goldbricking involves a decision by workers, either individually or collectively, not to produce up to management's expectations. Several techniques of goldbricking are described by a Canadian auto worker: "Going in the hole" (deliberately getting behind in your work); arguing with the foreman in order to stop working; running out of stock so that machines must be turned off.

57. For a discussion of Mayo's investigation see Chapter 6, pp. 173–179.
58. Cf. F.J. Roethlisberger and William J. Dickson, *Management and the Worker*, Cambridge: Harvard University Press, 1939.
59. William Foote Whyte, *Money and Motivation,* New York: Harper and Brothers, 1955, p. 4.

Running out of stock usually requires the co-operation of the stock chaser and jitney drivers who must arrange to be conveniently busy elsewhere when we begin to run low on something. Often a worker will strike up a conversation with his foreman as a distraction while others hide stock material or quickly use up what little is left.[60]

A final type of output restriction is the slowdown. What distinguishes a slowdown is that it involves even less expenditure of effort than the other two forms of withholding work. In addition, slowdowns are often used as explicit forms of protest or as a means of settling grievances.[61]

The restrictive practices described above are not only generalized responses to highly rationalized and regimented work; they are also based on the well-founded belief that the company tries to get as much work as possible out of as few workers as possible. Working to or beyond management's standards often results in a re-timing of jobs, an increased work-load, and most importantly, in a reduction in the plant work force. Consider the following explanations of workers:

Don't you know that if I turned in $1.50 an hour on these pump bodies tonight, the whole God-damned Methods Department would be down here tomorrow? And they'd re-time this job so quick it would make your head swim!

---

60. Monk, *op. cit.*, p. 50.
61. Work-to-rule is an overt, publicly announced form of slowdown that is used as a bargaining tactic. In describing the Canadian railway conflict of 1974, one group of workers stated: "Slowdowns and work-to-rule have been used by railworkers very effectively in an industry which hypocritically sets hundreds of safety rules that work loads demand be disregarded. If one works according to the rules, however, no work is carried out." See "Up Against the State: Experiences of a Railworkers Group," *Newsletter*, April, 1974, p. 50. Also see P.K. Edwards and Hugh Scullion, *The Social Organization of Industrial Conflict: Control and Resistance in the Workplace*, Oxford: Basil Blackwell, 1982.

And when they re-timed it, they'd cut the price in half!
And I'd be working for 85 cents an hour instead of $1.25! [62]

You just work so fast and you do just so much work.
Because the more you do, the more they'll want you to do.
If you start running, they'd expect you to do a little bit
more. [63]

Sabotage

There are few published accounts of industrial sabotage. In the
first attempt to analyze this phenomenon in sociological terms,
Taylor and Walton defined industrial sabotage as "conscious
action or inaction directed towards the mutilation or destruction of the work environment" (including the commodity being
produced). [64] Drawing on a variety of sources outside sociology,
Taylor and Walton grouped acts of sabotage in three categories
according to the *motives* or *purposes* of persons committing the
acts. The three types fall under the headings of attempts to (1)
reduce tension and frustration deriving from work, (2) facilitate
or ease the work process, (3) assert direct control over work.
The following discussion illustrates each of these types of
industrial sabotage.

One way of venting frustration at work is to mutilate or spoil
the product. The possible variations of this kind of sabotage are
virtually endless, and their particular form depends on the
nature of the commodity being produced. Heavy, durable items
such as cars and refrigerators are deliberately scratched or
dented, rattles are built in, parts are omitted, bolts are not
fastened securely. Textile workers rip garments, brewery workers put water in beer bottles, printers insert ridiculous or
obscene phrases in type matrices, food processing workers add

62. Donald Roy, "Quota Restriction and Goldbricking in a Machine Shop," in
William A. Faunce, ed., *Readings in Industrial Sociology,* New York: Appleton-
Century-Crofts, 1967, p. 316.
63. Terkel, op. cit., p. 170. The most common and least deliberate form of
output regulation is simple indifference to work—showing no initiative and
doing no more than what is absolutely necessary to keep one's job.
64. Laurie Taylor and Paul Walton, "Industrial Sabotage: Motives and Meanings," in Stanley Cohen, ed., *Images of Deviance,* Harmondsworth: Penguin
Books, 1971, p. 219.

absurd colouring agents to the product, and so on.[65] In what was undoubtedly one of the most extreme and costly cases of sabotage ever recorded, workers in 1974 razed the LG–2 construction site at James Bay. Electric generators were toppled by bulldozers, fuel storage tanks were slashed, and the buildings of the main campsite were set afire. The damage amounted to about $2 million and work on the project was delayed a full year.[66]

Workers constantly attempt to ease the tension of rationalized production schedules by instilling an element of play into work. In some cases this practice involves sabotage. One sociologist, who spent a year working in a large automobile factory, described a rod-blowing contest which continued for several weeks, resulting in the loss of 150 motors.

The inspectors organized a rod-blowing contest which required the posting of lookouts at the entrances to the shop area and the making of deals with assembly, for example, to neglect the torquing of bolts in rods for a random number of motors so that there would be loose rods. When an inspector stepped up to a motor and felt the telltale knock in the water-pump wheel he would scream out to clear the shop, the men abandoning their work and running behind boxes and benches. Then he would arc himself away from the stand and ram the throttle up to first 4000 and then 5000 rpm. The motor would knock, clank, and finally blur to a cracking halt with the rod blowing through the side of the oil pan and across the shop. The men would rise up from their cover, exploding

65. *Cf. Ibid.* A pet food company lost an entire day's production when a worker put green dye into a storage hopper. See *Banque Canadienne Nationale, Bulletin Mensuel,* Montreal, January, 1974.
66. Cf. Nick Auf Der Maur, "James Bay: The Hatred Behind the Explosion at the LG–2 Construction Site," *Last Post,* 4, 1974, pp. 21–4. The causes of the destruction are obscure. Apparently three factors contributed to the incident: inter-union rivalry, miserable working conditions, and the arrogance of American executives of the Bechtel Corporation, one of whom referred to workers as "frogs" and publicly stated, "You Canadians know fuck all."

> *with cheers, and another point would be chalked on the
> wall for that inspector.*[67]

Workers also sabotage production in order to facilitate the
work process, to shorten the length of the working day, and to
gain "free time." Taylor and Walton report that railworkers
block tracks with trucks to delay shunting operations, and farm
workers "choke" agricultural equipment with tree branches. In
factories, materials are hidden and machines and conveyor
belts jammed.[68] Within the space of several days one large
Canadian branch plant reported that the assembly line had
been jammed with bolts, coveralls, springs, tubing, boards,
chains, and iron pipes. One enterprising worker locked the
steering column and threw away the keys so that the car could
not be removed from the final assembly line.[69] Other ways of
gaining time are less dramatic but no less effective. One means
of accomplishing control over time is to make deliberate
mistakes so that production is eventually halted as defective
products pile up and as repairmen attempt to fix them.

The most sophisticated type of industrial sabotage is that
which involves a restructuring of social relations and the
establishment of workers' control over production. The following cases exemplify this kind of sabotage.

Roy reported a situation where workers from different sections of a plant acted in collusion to systematically evade
managerially determined methods of work designed to meet
production standards. Workers replaced managerial rules with
their own collectively determined work techniques. In effect,
the workers established an elaborate system of counter-plan-
ning production.[70]

---

67. Bill Watson, *Counterplanning on the Shop Floor,* Boston: New England
Free Press, 1972, p. 6. The workers undertook this action to protest management's deliberate policy of producing poor quality engines in order to meet
high output quotas.
68. Taylor and Walton, *op. cit.,* p. 219.
69. Seymour Faber, "Working Class Organisation," *Our Generation*, 11,
Summer, 1976, pp. 13–26.
70. Donald F. Roy, "Making Out: A Counter-System of Workers' Control of
Work Situation and Relationships," in Tom Burns, ed., *Industrial Man*,
Harmondsworth: Penguin Books, 1969, p. 359.

A roughly similar case, although one in which the element of sabotage was much more prominent, occurred in an auto factory. An engine had been carelessly designed by the company, and workers' suggestions for improving the motor were ignored by management. Consequently, the workers began to counter-plan production of the sub-standard engine. During breaks and lunch hours they met to plan a plant-wide sabotage campaign. Assemblers left out gaskets, inserted faulty spark plugs, failed to tighten bolts, or mixed up sparkplug wires. Engines that got through assembly without defects were sabotaged in the inspection department, even though rejected motors were piling up there. This practice continued until the plant was finally forced to shut down.[71]

The various acts of sabotage are difficult to place in the categories of Taylor and Walton. Each instance may be prompted by numerous and complicated reasons. Moreover, this disposition to categorize overlooks the one thing most acts of sabotage have in common: through them the workers gain *de facto* control over production. This is true not only of workers who act in unison to counter-plan production, but also of workers who jam assembly lines to gain a respite from work. The latter exercise control over production by stopping it.[72]

Making the Workplace Livable

Disrupting or curtailing production are reactions to work whose organization answers to managerial canons of profitability rather than to the needs of working people. But such practices are only one aspect of daily workplace activities. Workers constantly devise ways of making the workplace a more livable habitat and work a more satisfying endeavour. Work is never completely devoid of all meaning and gratification, if only because working people fall back on their own

71. Watson, *op. cit.*
72. This discussion of resistance is not exhaustive. For example, some—probably a substantial—proportion of absenteeism and turnover can be regarded as a reaction of disgruntled workers to the manner in which work is structured. This is the predominant form taken by resistance in situations where workers are constantly watched and unable to develop durable work groups, as in the fast food industry. See Reiter, *op. cit.* Also see Edwards and Scullion, *op. cit.*

imaginative and ingenious means of making it a more enjoyable experience.

One response to rationalized and regimented work is to instill an element of play into it. Long hours of monotonous, repetitive labour are often interrupted by talk, horseplay, and coffee and food breaks. Among punching machine operators, for example, the long work day was marked off into recognizable intervals and was made to pass more quickly by such regular breaks as banana time, coffee time, peach time, and coke time. While perhaps senseless at first glance, these practices are in fact attempts to deal with the "elemental problem of psychological survival."[73] On the assembly line, "workers like to let the work pile up so they can race to catch up with the line. This creates a few minutes of seemingly purposeful exertion. It makes hills and troughs, minor goals and fulfillments while you're waiting for the day to end or the line to break down."[74]

While the invention of production games in which workers exhaust themselves in races against the clock in order to *meet* production standards may appear as a predictable response to piecework incentives or as compliance with managerial norms, from the workers' point of view meeting the quota has quite different purposes and meanings. Workers transform quota attainment into a game which furnishes a number of personal satisfactions. The "game" serves as a vehicle for the self-expression denied by ordinary work. "The element of uncertainty of outcome provided by the ever-present possibilities of bad luck made quota attainment an exciting game played against the clock on the wall, a game in which the elements of control provided by the application of knowledge, ingenuity, and speed, heightened interest and led to exhilarating feelings of accomplishment."[75] The "game" not only challenges workers but it also lessens fatigue, reduces boredom, and makes the long working day pass more swiftly. In cases where workers are

73. Donald F. Roy, "Banana Time: Job Satisfaction and Informal Interaction," *Human Organization*, 18, 1960, pp. 158–168.
74. Barbara Garson, *All the Livelong Day: The Meaning and Demeaning of Routine Work*, New York: Penguin, 1977, p. x.
75. Donald F. Roy, "Work Satisfaction and Social Reward in Quota Achievement: An Analysis of Piecework Incentive," *American Sociological Review*, 18, 1953, p. 511.

responsible for a set quota of labour and no more, "making out" (achieving the quota) early in the day furnishes "free time" (the expression is revealing), that is, time which is controlled by workers rather than the company. Finally, meeting quota before the end of the working day is a way of expressing resentment against management and going "one-up" over the "despised time-study men." "The greater the ease in making out, the less time it took to achieve the quota, the greater the beating administered to the men who set the piece rates."[76] The worker-initiated speed-up in a Windsor truck plant shows, as the description below suggests, that even a modicum of temporary control by the direct producers, undertaken in the spirit of play, can be threatening to supervisory personnel:

They couldn't believe their eyes. There was nothing for them to do but stand around uselessly and watch. The workers started kidding the foremen saying they "weren't needed, get out of the way, go home, go have a coffee and come back Monday." Something extraordinarily unusual began happening—the foremen began pushing the trucks back trying to slow the work down. It was so funny, so out of context, that we all started yelling and laughing at them.[77]

A more dramatic example of fusing work and play was

---

76. *Ibid.,* p. 512. Michael Burawoy views "making out" as a game which involves the collusion of management. The game masks exploitation and generates consent on the shop floor, because it creates limited choices for workers (giving them an illusory sense of power) and establishes a common interest (in the game, its rules, and its outcomes) between managers and workers. Consent to the rules of the game, then, allegedly becomes consent to capitalist production. See *Manufacturing Consent: Changes in the Labor Process Under Monopoly Capitalism*, Chicago: University of Chicago Press, 1979. "Making out" may have the functions ascribed to it by Burawoy, but is is only one of many games initiated by workers—most of which cannot be viewed as being in the management's interest. In addition, workers who cannot or do not engage in "making out" (probably the great majority) do not appear to be any more or less conscious of exploitation than their game-playing counterparts. A balanced discussion of Burawoy's thesis is contained in Chapter 6 of Paul Thompson, *op. cit.* Also see Peterson, *op. cit.*
77. Faber, *op. cit.,* p. 19.

recorded by Watson, who described a water fight in one section of a large auto plant.

> *The fight usually involved about 10 or 15 unused hoses, each with the water pressure of a fire hose. With streams of crossfire, shouting, laughing, and running about, there was hardly a man in the mood for doing his job. The shop area was regularly drenched from ceiling to floor, with every man completely soaked.*[78]

Workers also invent techniques and devices to make work easier. They "change gears when the foreman is not about. Some make special tools and fixtures to make it easier for themselves. They keep their improvements secret so the company doesn't benefit."[79] One common form of easing work on the assembly line is "doubling up," where one worker takes over the job of another as well as his or her own for a period of time. Thus, both workers enjoy more "free time" than that prescribed by managerially determined work methods. Moreover, workers insist that the stimulation of doubling up enhances their work performance, resulting in a higher quality product.[80]

Production organized by management is a continuous, uninterrupted process. Production games, horseplay, sociability— devices to ease production—are all important ways of interrupting, shortening, and humanizing work. These patterned behaviours reveal a keen desire among workers to schedule their time as they see fit and to do so according to their own inclinations.

78. Watson, *op. cit.*, p. 6.
79. Paul Romano and Ria Stone, *The American Worker*, Detroit: Bewick Editions, 1972, pp. 36–37.
80. David Moberg, "No More Junk: Lordstown Workers and the Demand for Quality," *Insurgent Sociologist*, 7, 1978, pp. 63–69.

CONCLUSION

In this chapter we have shown that the image of manual workers as affluent, instrumentally oriented to work, and politically conservative is grossly misleading. Most working people simply "get by" economically; many are poor. Even the incomes of the best-paid workers fall short of providing the trappings of a middle-class style of life. But the myth of the "happy worker" is objectionable not only because it represents workers as being affluent—which they are not, but also because it ignores the fact that working people are producers as well as consumers. Many wage earners hold jobs that are defined and controlled by others, that require little training and are repetitive, and that are easy to get locked into for life. In modern society "happy workers" are not behaving as if they are happy. Beneath the open forms of conflict like strikes and defiance of institutional authority, we can detect covert struggles at the workplace—struggles to evade, subvert, and sabotage production. At the same time, individuals take pride in making quality items or providing effective service, seek recognition as "good workers," test their skills and endurance through self-imposed speed-ups, and strive to fuse work and play by devising production games or simply through horseplay and sociability. If manual workers were purely instrumental, if all they really cared about was the size of the paycheque, such responses to the organization and content of work would not occur. What underlies these seemingly disconnected and contradictory activities is the character of capitalist production. Under capitalism work is a unity of production for profitable exchange, and of the production of useful goods and services. Conflicting pressures are generated by these aspects of capitalist production. In their pursuit of profits, employers and managers subjugate workers, speed up and routinize work, implement labour-replacing machinery, and keep wages as low as possible—actions inviting resentment and resistance from workers. By contrast, involvement in the production of useful goods and services creates among workers a concern for the *quality* of their output and their work performance. Struggles against work and efforts to make work socially meaningful and pleasurable can, however, be understood within the same conceptual framework: Both are attempts to transcend alienation. Workers react to work when it is not their own, when it is defined and directed by others; they react by trying to humanize it and, at the same time, extend their control over it.

6 Solutions to Alienated Labour

A society that will abolish alienation,
will abolish not labour, but its alienating
conditions.
SHLOMO AVINERI

In the preceding chapters we demonstrated that discontent with work is not confined to isolated or anachronistic segments of Canadian working people. Alienated labour extends throughout the world of work, affecting the traditional manual labour of heavy industry as well as reaching up through the ranks of white-collar jobs—including the professional, scientific, and technical positions prototypical of post-industrial society. Even managers at the upper levels of the hierarchical authority structures of public and private organizations are not immune from the effects of alienation. But the burning issue is this: Can alienated labour be transcended? In this chapter we will critically evaluate five possible solutions to alienation: leisure, automation, human relations and quality of work life (QWL) programs, unions, and workers' control.

LEISURE

Industrial capitalism not only dramatically altered the way people worked, it also brought about significant changes in the way people lived outside of work. The industrial revolution created a sharp separation between the work and non-work spheres of life. In striking contrast to this institutional differentiation, the economic activities of non-literate societies are embedded in the social relations of family and community. Their approach to work is no exception. Anthropologist George

Dalton writes: "Production is often undertaken by intimate communities of persons sharing a multitude of social ties and functions, one of which happens to be the production of material goods."[1] The allocation of work tasks and the composition of work groups are rooted in familial and community ties. Rewards for work are not based on measures of time, production quotas, or marketable skills; rather, intimate communities of people engage in production as an extension of social life with the goal of satisfying the needs of the community and its individual members. The boundaries between the public and private spheres, between work and leisure, are blurred institutionally and psychologically. So fused are these two activities that in some non-literate societies a single word refers to both work and play.[2] As we noted in Chapter 3, there was considerable overlap between work and leisure and between workmates, family members and friends in pre-industrial Canada as well.

The social and economic processes that severed the production process from community values and control—a division resulting in the compartmentalization of work and non-work—are regarded by some observers as necessary and even desirable. Alienated labour is seen as a reasonable price to pay for the benefits of an advanced technology that provides the material basis for the consummation of the "good life." For example, Kerr and his associates believe that in advanced industrial societies alienated labour is consistent with the "great new freedom" that leisure time has to offer:

The great new freedom may come in the leisure-time life of individuals. Higher standards of living, more free time, and more education make this not only possible but almost inevitable. Leisure will be the happy hunting ground for the independent spirit. Along with bureau-

---

1. "Traditional Production in Primitive Societies," in George Dalton, ed., *Tribal and Peasant Economies*, Garden City: The Natural History Press, 1967, p. 63.
2. Cf. Marshall Sahlins, *Stone Age Economics*, New York: Aldine–Atherton, 1972. Also see Wilfred Pelletier, "Childhood in an Indian Village," in Bryan Finnigan and Cy Gonick, eds., *Making It: The Canadian Dream*, Toronto: McClelland and Stewart, 1972, p. 14.

*cratic conservatism of economic and political life may
well go a New Bohemianism in the other aspects of life—
partly as a reaction to the confining nature of the productive side of society. There may well come a search for
individuality and a new meaning to liberty. The economic
system may be highly ordered and the political system
barren ideologically; but the social and recreational and
cultural aspects of life should be quite diverse and quite
changing.*[3]

A common response to alienating work is to regard it as a
means to other more important ends. One of the consequences
of industrialism, Peter Berger contends, is that the individual's
search for meaning and identity is confined to the so-called
private sphere of his or her life.[4] C. Wright Mills summed up the
situation rather dryly when he stated: "Each day men sell little
pieces of themselves in order to try to buy them back each
night and weekend with the coin of fun."[5] These observations
are not lacking evidence. Faunce cites an impressive array of
evidence showing that blue-collar and low-level white-collar
workers are alienated from work in that their low status in
work organizations progressively wears away their self-esteem
and, consequently, their commitment to work and work organizations. Having defined alienation in terms of status and self-
esteem, which Faunce assumes are of paramount importance to
human beings, he goes on to argue that individuals can insulate
themselves from the potentially devastating impact of alienating jobs by seeking out other areas of life in which to maintain
and confirm a favourable self-image. "One response to the
inability to confirm a favourable self-image at work is to

3. Clark Kerr, John T. Dunlop, Frederick H. Harbison, and Charles A. Myers,
Industrialism and Industrial Man, New York: Oxford University Press, 1969,
pp. 237–238.
4. "Some General Observations on the Problem of Work," in Peter Berger, ed.,
The Human Shape of Work, New York: The MacMillan Company, 1964,
pp. 211–241.
5. C. Wright Mills, *White Collar*, New York: Oxford University Press, 1956,
p. 237.

evaluate one's self exclusively with non-work related values."[6] This suggests that alienation is not an all-encompassing phenomenon but, rather, is specific to institutions, people, and activities; in other words, one can be alienated in one sphere of life and not in others. Individuals are seen as being flexible enough to shed the imprint of dreary work roles and to emerge at the end of the day or week contented consumers of leisure, ready to make up for the pleasure, self-realization, and autonomy their stultifying work has denied them.

The compensatory leisure thesis implies that if work is an activity in which individuals invest little of themselves and from which little is expected, then why worry about its rigidities? This question was partially addressed in the previous chapter's discussion of instrumentalism. That working people are not neutral towards nor immune from workplace experiences is obvious given workers' resistance to the organization of work as well as their attempts to humanize it. Work dominates our lives, consuming over one-third of our waking time. The sheer amount of time spent at work means that leisure pursuits can only be truncated experiences geared to and constrained by the rhythms of work. Work is a precisely scheduled activity; it goes on uninterrupted. By contrast, leisure must be enjoyed in small batches; it must be put aside until the end of another round of "productive" activity. Because work is such a time-consuming and time-dominating endeavour, the leisure–work trade-off is a poor bargain. But time is not the only constraint on the enjoyment of leisure. The institutional compartmentalization of work and leisure does not mean the two spheres are psychologically separate. The alienating experience of work in capitalist society invades consciousness and spills over into other areas of life.

In a study of workers in a Vancouver Island manufacturing company, Meissner found that the nature of an employee's job (how much the job prohibited discretion, the use of skill and talent, and social interaction) affected the character of his or her activities off the job. Workers with jobs that required little

6. William A. Faunce, *Problems of an Industrial Society*, Second Edition, New York: McGraw-Hill, 1981, p. 157.

or no discretion were not likely to involve themselves in activities outside of work which entailed planning or purposeful action. Similarly, socially isolating work was associated with solitary leisure pursuits.[7] The importance of variations in work was also underscored in a study of social values and child-rearing attitudes among large samples of middle- and working-class Americans and Italians. The degree to which these individuals exercised control over their work was shown to be a strong determinant of the manner in which they reared their children.[8] There is, in addition, a large body of research showing a relationship between undesirable jobs and mental and physical health problems. Coburne, for example, found that workers with repetitive, low-discretion jobs were particularly prone to poor health. Lowe and Northcott's comparative study of letter-carriers and inside workers for Canada Post revealed that the mail-sorters' (whose jobs were the most rigidly supervised) incidence of poor health was greater than that of the outside workers. Among the inside workers, those who worked with automated machinery suffered more job stress and health difficulties than individuals who worked with non-automated equipment.[9]

There is no question that individuals in modern society search for meaning, fulfillment, and autonomy outside of work. However, this desire is a response to the way work is structured; it is a desperate attempt by individuals to minimize or transcend alienation. But such efforts do not compensate for the "long stretches of gray weekdays."[10] Since work dominates time and penetrates all aspects of life, it necessarily limits the extent to which leisure can be utilized satisfactorily. No qualitative judgment about how people use their leisure time is being

7. Martin Meissner, "The Long Arm of the Job: Social Participation and the Constraints of Industrial Work," in W.E. Mann, ed., *Canada: A Sociological Profile*, 2nd edition, Toronto: The Copp Clark Publishing Company, 1971, pp. 362–377.

8. Melvin L. Kohn, *Class and Conformity*, Homewood: Dorsey Press, 1969.

9. David Coburn, "Work Alienation and Well-Being," in David Coburn *et al.*, eds., *Health and Canadian Society*, Toronto: Fitzhenry and Whiteside, 1981, pp. 420–437; Graham S. Lowe and Herbert C. Northcott, *Under Pressure: A Study of Job Stress*, Toronto: Garamond Press, 1986.

10. C. Wright Mills, *op.cit.*, p. 258.

implied. The point is that the way work is structured in contemporary society places constraints on the successful pursuit of *any* leisure activity. It is precisely the combination of alienated labour and unfulfilling leisure experiences that gives rise to the contradiction between the relief resonating in the phrase, "Thank God it's Friday," and the fact that people say they would work even if financially secure.

AUTOMATION

Computers, microtechnology, and other forms of automation could help to liberate us from alienating work, because the tremendous productive potential of automation could drastically reduce the amount of time people spend at paid labour. Robert Heilbronner believes we can look forward to "a time when as small a proportion of the labour force as now suffices to over-provide us with food will serve to turn out manufactured staples, the houses, the transportation, the retail services, even the government supervision that will be required."[11] Assuming for the moment that circumstances like those described by Heilbronner are even remotely possible, an expanded sphere of leisure could conceivably offer genuine opportunities for meaningful activities and self-fulfillment. It is likely, however, that such a society would be more of a nightmare than an Eden. Under capitalism, technological developments are utilized not to improve the lot of people in general but to enhance corporate profitability and augment the power and privileges of a tiny minority of the population. Consequently, the resolution of some problems in the realm of production would only compound problems in the sphere of distribution. Instead of universally high living standards and extensive leisure time, the scenario envisioned by Heilbronner would likely feature the widening of present inequalities: a large lumpen proletariat of unemployed and underemployed

11. *The Limits of American Capitalism*, New York: Harper and Row, 1965, p. 124.

citizens existing alongside an incredibly privileged and powerful minority benefitting from the new technology.[12]

Automation, it is suggested, eliminates the more menial and physically exhausting tasks and allows for the creation of more challenging jobs than those available under earlier forms of technology. This is the position of the post-industrial theorists. Their forecasts emphasizing benign shifts in investment and employment between sectors of industry are complemented by visions of a high technology that will provide challenging jobs in manufacturing industries.[13] Recent trends, however, indicate that projections of growing job complexity both in manufacturing proper and the overall economy are exaggerated.

Advanced technology has indeed created jobs requiring special training and professional-type knowledge, but its major effect has been to drive employment out of those industries where new technology has been introduced into industries relatively immune from technological innovations. In recent decades, the movement of employment from goods-producing to service-producing industries has brought with it in the United States a net increase of lower skilled, poorly paid jobs.[14] Declines in manufacturing employment and a rapid increase in Canada of part-time jobs suggest this tendency is not unique to the United States. Part-time jobs are, for the most part, held by women, are poorly paid, offer few or no benefits, and provide little job security. From 1979 to 1983, Canada lost 170 000 jobs

12. Unequal distribution of privileges and power within advanced capitalist societies is only part of the problem. An issue of even greater magnitude is inequalities between nations.

13. An early statement of this thesis is Robert Blauner's *Alienation and Freedom*, Chicago: University of Chicago Press, 1967. Blauner maintains that alienation is minimal in craft industries but increases greatly with the rise of mechanized and mass production industries. This trend allegedly is reversed with the emergence of automated production. Compared with mechanized production systems, Blauner contends that automated plants require proportionately fewer unskilled labourers, more skilled maintenance and repair workers, and operators who take on important production responsibilities and a substantial measure of discretion. An excellent critique of Blauner is found in Theo Nichols and Hew Beynon, *Living With Capitalism: Class Relations and the Modern Factory*, London: Routledge and Kegan Paul, 1977.

14. Markley Roberts, "A Labor Perspective on Technological Change," in Eileen Collins and Lucretia Dewey Tanner, eds., *American Jobs and the Changing Industrial Base*, Cambridge: Ballinger, 1984, pp. 183–205.

in manufacturing, many of which were in unionized companies and were relatively well paid. Between 1975 and 1981, part-time jobs were created at a more rapid rate than full-time jobs, and part-time workers as a percentage of all workers in Canada increased from 10.6 to 13.5 percent. If part-time work continues to grow at this rate, one-half of all jobs will be part-time in the year 2000. This surge of part-time employment has occurred alongside the rapid growth of the tertiary sector, large sections of which have been unaffected by recent advances in technology. Two-thirds of all part-time workers are in service, clerical, and sales occupations.[15]

It is often argued that the growth of high technology industries will not only relieve unemployment but will provide complex, challenging jobs as well. However, the progressive use of sophisticated technology in high tech industry and the small size of this sector limit its capacity to generate employment opportunities. For example, between 1971 and 1981, employment in Canada expanded annually by 3.1 percent, for a total of three million new jobs. In high tech industries, employment growth averaged 3.9 percent per year, but this translated into only 900 000 new jobs over the ten-year period.[16] Future developments can only be dimly perceived, but as micro-technology finds more and more realms of application in the 1980s and 1990s, the most rapidly growing jobs probably will require minimum skill and offer little remuneration. Forecasts by the Canadian government indicate there is no end in sight to the rapid growth of routine jobs. Table III shows projections to the year 1992 of the thirty fastest-growing Canadian occupations (in order of growth potential). Of the thirty occupations on the list, only one can be considered a high tech occupation—systems analysts—and this is number 28 on the list. It is evident that the majority of jobs on the list are routine, require only modest educational training, and are not well paid. After examining

15. Julie White, *Women and Part-Time Work*, Ottawa: The Canadian Advisory Council on the Status of Women, 1983; Edward B. Harvey and John Blakely, "Education, Social Mobility and the Challenge of Technological Change," in *Transitions to Work*, Winnipeg: University of Manitoba, Institute for Social and Economic Research, 1985, pp. 46–65.
16. Keith Newton, "Employment Effects of Technological Change," Ottawa: Economic Council of Canada, 1985.

TABLE III

Projections of Fastest-Growing Occupations, Canada, 1983–1992

RANK	OCCUPATION	PROJECTED 1983	EMPLOYMENT 1992	TOTAL REQUIREMENTS 1983–1992
1	Secretaries and stenographers	351 300	438 800	87 500
2	Bookkeepers	368 200	448 500	80 300
3	Truck Drivers	238 000	310 000	72 000
4	Financial Officers	140 000	180 000	39 100
5	Janitors	223 600	261 400	37 800
6	Cashiers and tellers	229 600	263 800	34 200
7	Carpenters	107 300	138 100	30 800
8	General office clerks	136 400	165 300	28 900
9	Waiters and waitresses	252 400	281 000	28 700
10	Guards and security personnel	76 900	101 500	24 600
11	Typists and clerk typists	95 700	118 400	22 700
12	Receptionists	90 400	112 000	21 600
13	Sales management occupations	169 900	191 100	21 200
14	Non-construction labourers	54 200	74 900	20 700
15	Graduate nurses, non-supervisory	185 500	206 100	20 600
16	Welders	79 800	99 800	20 000
17	Industrial farm mechanics	88 200	108 000	19 800
18	Auto mechanics	140 700	160 000	19 300
19	Sewing machine occupations	88 100	106 600	18 500
20	Bus drivers	49 000	67 400	18 400
21	Chefs and cooks	162 500	180 800	18 300
22	Non-construction supervisors	66 500	84 300	17 900
23	General managers	79 200	96 800	17 600
24	Nursery workers	58 800	75 900	17 100
25	E.D.P. equipment operators	71 300	88 100	16 800
26	Police officers	53 800	69 300	15 500
27	Stock clerks	91 500	106 600	15 100
28	Systems analysts	56 800	71 900	15 100
29	Shipping clerks	84 200	98 500	14 300
30	Commercial travellers	95 900	109 600	13 700

SOURCE: Adapted from Government of Canada Consultation Paper on Training, Ottawa: Supply and Services, 1984.

these thirty occupations, an Economic Council of Canada analyst concluded: "The great majority of jobs in the foreseeable future will not require major shifts in educational preparation. For a relatively small number of very specialized jobs in high tech occupations, qualifications in mathematics, computer science, and related disciplines will be in great demand. But for many jobs, even the recent emphasis on 'computer literacy for all' is increasingly questioned."[17]

It is also instructive to examine the kinds of jobs being created in high technology manufacturing industries, that is, in businesses that (a) manufacture equipment in communications, semiconductors, information processing, robots, and biotechnology, or (b) use advanced technology (such as drugs, plastics, chemicals, and electronic components) in production. Most of the jobs being created in this sector are hardly challenging. After examining the relevant research in the United States, one economist concluded: "It's not news that most jobs in high tech manufacturing industries are not high tech jobs, but it is surprising to learn that many are not even very good jobs."[18] In the semiconductor industry, for instance, 60 percent of the employees (mostly women) are semiskilled or unskilled production workers who occupy highly repetitive, poorly paid, and often unhealthy jobs. Even these unattractive jobs are insecure; high tech companies like Atari, Apple, and Wang have moved assembly operations to low-wage countries like Mexico, Taiwan, and the Phillipines.

Continuous-process industries, like chemical and petroleum industries, allegedly provide responsible, high-discretion production jobs aside from the necessary complement of highly skilled maintenance and repair personnel. The job of operators in such plants requires responsibility (for monitoring the expensive equipment) but not high skill. Moreover, the separation of the conception of the work from its performance prevails here every bit as much as it does under mechanized production. Continuous-process operators are relegated to the role of passive spectators of the production process; their main

17. *Ibid.*, p. 21.
18. Eileen Appelbaum, "High Tech and the Structural Employment Problems of the 1980s," in Collins and Tanner, *op. cit.*, p. 41.

responsibility is to ensure that dials and gauges are correctly set so that the quantity and quality of the throughput as programmed in the front office is maintained. Nor is much discretion involved in reading dials. Operator discretion comes into play when the equipment malfunctions or when there is some other operational problem. At these critical times, workers are required to detect quickly the sources of the problem and to take the appropriate corrective actions. Unpredictable malfunctions and other special production conditions in automated plants cannot be effectively and cheaply handled with a highly specialized division of labour and tight supervisory controls. Because a degree of worker flexibility and autonomy is the most profitable mode of operating continuous-process technology, workers ordinarily learn to perform multiple tasks and are accorded some control over such matters as job assignments and labour allocation.[19] But this measure of discretion may be transitory. In the most advanced continuous-process plants, worker discretion is being severely restricted. Decisions once made by operators are being made by computers capable of activating whatever work needs to be done. Instead of a number of operators periodically walking through the plant to check dials, a single employee sits before a television console monitoring the meters.[20]

The most comprehensive study of the effect of automation on the overall skill level of the manufacturing work force was conducted by James Bright.[21] From his survey of thirteen automated plants, Bright was unable to draw any firm conclusions as to the general impact of automation on skill levels. In some cases, a reduction in the skill of production workers was offset by a concomitant or proportionately greater increase in the skill levels of job setters and maintenance and repair personnel. In other cases, the net effect of the introduction of automated equipment was to reduce the overall skill level of

19. The relationship between continuous-process technology and flexible modes of labour organization is discussed below.
20. *Cf.* Gerald I. Sussman, "Process Design, Automation, and Worker Alienation," *Industrial Relations*, 11, 1972, p. 43; Stephen Hill, *Competition and Control at Work*, London: Heinemann, 1981.
21. James Bright, *Automation and Management*, Boston: Harvard University School of Business Administration, 1958.

plant workers. Had Bright undertaken his study more recently, he may have discovered a more pronounced tendency toward overall reduction of skill levels. In new continuous-process facilities, for example, management customarily minimizes its dependence on skilled workers by assigning maintenance and repair duties to semiskilled operators.

Automation has displaced skilled labour in other areas besides the continuous-process facilities and high tech industries named above. Machine shops, which until recently were repositories of production skill, have been invaded by numerically controlled (NC) machines. Mass production plants are turning more and more to robotics. According to Shaiken, "computer systems not only control the operations of machine tools, but track raw materials coming into the shop, inventory completed parts, monitor robots on the assembly line, and schedule production."[22] While the productive capacity of this technology is of no little interest to management, profits and power are the major considerations. Numerically controlled machines enable management to transfer the control and operation of the machine from skilled workers to a preprogrammed set of instructions recorded on a tape. From management's point of view, all that should be left for the worker to do is to load and unload the machine. But the stakes involved here are workers' skills and control. There is no technical or other reason why skilled workers could not assume programming tasks, but management customarily prefers to hire university-trained (non-union) personnel for this job. This preference attests to management's intent to destroy the shop floor and union power of skilled machinists.[23] The magazine *Iron Age* quite candidly stresses this managerial advantage: "Numerical control is more than a means of controlling a machine. It embodies much of what the father of scientific management,

22. Harley Shaiken, *Work Transformed: Automation and Labor in the Computer Age*, New York: Holt, Rinehart and Winston, 1984, p. 8.
23. *Cf. Ibid.*; David Noble, *Forces of Production: A Social History of Industrial Automation*, New York: Alfred A. Knopf, 1984. For a fascinating account of a machinist who taught himself programming and computer skills but whose efforts to apply this know-how on the shop floor were repeatedly frustrated by management, see Chapter 2 of Robert Howard, *Brave New Workplace*, New York: Viking, 1985.

Frederick Winslow Taylor, sought... [namely] taking the control of the machine shop out of the hands of many workmen and placing it completely in the hands of management."[24] Not only are the skills and power of skilled machinists threatened, even the high-tech jobs of programmers and other software personnel are insecure due to the introduction of what is known as computer aided design (CAD). Engineers can now use electronic pencils, press buttons, or give keyboard instructions to design objects on an electronic drawing board; these designs can then be relayed directly to the numerically controlled machines. "With conventional methods, an engineer would design the part, a draftsman would draw it, and a machinist would build it. Now CAD is capable of translating a design directly into a part program that guides the cutting tool on an NC machine, eliminating all intervening steps between design and production."[25]

Robot usage is also growing at an exponential rate, as this equipment is being refined and costs are dropping. Robots were initially employed to perform some of the most undesirable factory jobs like spot welding and spray painting, but as robots become more flexible they are beginning to take over more attractive jobs such as inspection. Finally, microtechnology has become the basis of new systems capable of monitoring workers' activities. These systems report, among other things, the rate at which parts are being produced on a machine and the length of time the operator is away from the machine.[26]

Fortunately, we can qualify the bleakness of the scenario

24. Cited in Shaiken, *op. cit.*, p. 49. David Noble, *op. cit.*, painstakingly describes the history of NC machines and explains why they were selected over an alternative technology, record-playback machines, which appeared earlier. In contrast to NC machines, record playback was not designed to eliminate but to reproduce the skills of machinists. As a machinist produced a part, the motions of the machine were recorded on magnetic tape. Once the tape was completed, parts identical to the first could be made by simply playing the tape; the skilled workers remained essential to the work process, even though their productivity increased enormously. Noble brilliantly demonstrates that NC machines were adopted and record-playback machines left to die not because the former were more productive but because they offered to management the opportunity to tighten its grip on production at the expense of skilled workers.

25. *Ibid.*, pp. 219–220.

26. Shaiken, *op. cit.*

portrayed above if only because management's expectations for technology are not always realized. New machinery is often much less automatic and reliable and more "temperamental" than management anticipates or than advertising brochures lead them to expect. As a result, the skill and judgement of workers may still be required to get out production.[27] In addition, workers and unions have resisted encroachments on shop floor skill and power, and, in some cases, they have succeeded in tempering the technology's degrading effects.[28] But these are holding actions. In North America, the introduction, deployment, and uses of technology are determined by owners and managers of the means of production. Unions have adopted, for the most part, a reactive approach to technological advances. Ideally, unions would challenge or veto management decisions about the character and purposes of new technology, but, as it is, they have largely restricted their concern to minimizing its adverse impact on employees. These tendencies are likely to persist as long as present configurations of political and economic power prevail.

It is not unreasonable to close this section on a pessimistic note. In the short run, there appears to be little likelihood that new, sophisticated forms of technology will have a liberating impact on the labour process and workers. This is not due to any intrinsically alienating properties of technology; it is a result of the manner in which technology is designed and selected, and the purposes for which it is employed.

HUMAN RELATIONS

Scientific management simplified and standardized jobs and tightened management's grip on the production process, but it was not fully successful in achieving its ultimate objective: maximum profitability and control. Taylorism was met by the

27. For instance, in a study of companies using computer-aided design (CAD), it was found that the system's capacities were not as great as suggested by manufacturers of this equipment. Most design applications are very complex and exceed the capacities of the CAD systems. See Harold Salzman and Philip Mirvis, "The Work Force Transition to New Computer Technologies: Changes in Skills and Quality of Work Life," in *Transitions to Work, op. cit.*, pp. 66–87.
28. *Cf.* Noble, *op. cit.*

resistance of workers who chafed under its rigidities. Workers subverted managerial objectives through such practices as absenteeism, turnover, work stoppages, sabotage and the restriction of output (which Taylor was so intent on eliminating). The failure of scientific management to provide a fully satisfactory solution to the "labour problem" led to the emergence of the human relations school: If workers could not be subdued by the stopwatch, perhaps a more "humane" approach was in order. It was this hope that inspired the famous series of experiments at the Hawthorne Works of the Western Electric Company from 1924 to the early 1930s.[29]

The Hawthorne Studies

The Hawthorne Works was considered by its management to be one of the more enlightened firms of the day.[30] The company had pension plans, sickness benefits, and recreational facilities. Yet, it was beset by costly "labour problems." Puzzled by the persistence of worker unrest, a team of company researchers was instructed to find out how to reduce labour tensions and increase the productivity of workers. Armed with the same behaviouristic conception of human action that informed Taylorism (what Miller and Form have called the image of the worker as a biological machine), company researchers initially designed a carefully controlled experiment to determine the effect of illumination on worker output.[31] Expecting to find a positive correlation between the intensity of lighting and output, the research team was amazed to learn that workers increased production throughout the course of the experiment, independent of variations in illumination.

At this point management called in Elton Mayo, a professor at Harvard University's Graduate School of Business. Mayo ac-

29. For an excellent critical analysis of human relations see John Calvert, "Authority and Democracy in Industry," Ph.D. dissertation, London School of Economics, 1976.

30. Despite its "enlightened" policies, Western Electric was fiercely opposed to unionization. In response to this threat, the company paid out about $26 000 in the early 1930s for industrial espionage. See J.A.C. Brown, *The Social Psychology of Industry*, Harmondsworth: Penguin, 1954.

31. Delbert C. Miller and William H. Form, *Industrial Sociology*, 2nd edition, New York: Harper and Row, 1964.

cepted the invitation and embarked on a long and felicitous association with the company. His first step was to select for intensive observation and experimentation six women who assembled the forty component parts of telephone relays. Mayo's objective was to determine what conditions, if any, facilitated or retarded worker output. Accordingly, he recorded the average productivity rates of the six operatives before the introduction of test factors as well as during the period in which experimental changes were introduced.[32]

The "benchmark conditions," that is, the conditions that prevailed prior to the modification of working conditions, were a 48-hour week with no rest period and no piece work rates. Having recorded these circumstances and the corresponding output rates, Mayo began to systematically alter working conditions in the relay assembly room. The women were put on a piece work system and their output increased. When they were given two five-minute breaks, output increased. Next, the rest pauses were extended from five to ten minutes; output rose again. In the subsequent phase, when six five-minute breaks were prescribed, output fell slightly. A return to two rest pauses (this time with a free meal thrown in) brought another increase in output. The assemblers' quitting time was changed from five o'clock to 4:30; productivity rose. They were let off at 4:00 instead of 4:30 and productivity remained the same as in the previous stage. In the final phase of the experiment, which lasted 12 weeks, all the earlier improvements were taken away; the women returned to a 48-hour week with no rest breaks, no piece work, and no free meal. The result: Output exceeded that registered in all previous phases of the experiment.

Mayo and his associates initiated another experiment in the mica room, where five women separated thick sheets of mica into thin strips of standard size. As in the relay assembly room, modifications in working conditions and material incentives were unrelated to output. At a third research site, the bank wiring room, the research team was content to simply observe and record workers' behaviour. Here, male workers assembled

32. The Hawthorne experiments are discussed in Elton Mayo, *The Human Problems of an Industrial Civilization*, Cambridge: Macmillan, 1933.

and inspected a piece of telephone equipment known as a "bank." The major finding was that the workers acted cohesively to establish a shop floor culture whose norms countered management expectations by systematically restricting output—even though greater production would have brought bonus payments.

It was clear to the researchers that variations in the material conditions of work had no discernable effect on productivity. What was not so obvious was how to interpret these results, which seemed to defy logical explanation. Initially, Mayo appeared to accept the explanation workers in the relay assembly and bank wiring rooms gave for their increased output. The workers said they produced more because they had the opportunity to participate in deciding important aspects of their work and because they were free from the constraints of heavy-handed supervision. The workers' perceptions were accurate, but Mayo was reluctant to concede a direct relationship between participation and output. One of his cohorts, T.N. Whitehead, was not, and, through him, participation became a lasting principle of human relations.[33] However, the most important conclusion Mayo and his researchers drew from the investigations was a more general one: Material conditions of work—job content, the working environment, financial incentives, and so on—had no direct or predictable effect on output; rather, they were mediated by workers' attitudes and feelings. These psychological states, the researchers surmised, were shaped by the social groups to which the workers belonged.[34] The salience of the social was evident in the relay assembly room where, as the experiment progressed, the women became more and more dependent on one another for support and security, as well as in the bank wiring room, where employees set their own output norms.

This insight prompted the research team to embark on a

33. T.N. Whitehead, *Leadership in a Free Society*, Cambridge: Harvard University Press, 1936.
34. Another explanation which emerged subsequently is known as the "Hawthorne effect." Because they were singled out for special attention from management and the research team, workers supposedly were flattered. Their needs for recognition and status having been satisfied, the workers were motivated to raise their output.

massive interviewing program at the Works. Over a period of several years, approximately 20 000 interviews were conducted.[35] The interviews revealed a preponderance of negative remarks, which the research team grouped into two categories. The first set of negative remarks had to do with physical conditions of work like excessive heat or malfunctioning machines. The second group comprised complaints about social relations: the methods of supervision and company policies on such matters as wage rates and promotion. Mayo deemed the first category of complaints as verifiable and valid, but he disregarded statements about social relations. After all, he reasoned, Western Electric was a progressive company "committed to justice and humanity in its dealings with workers."[36] These complaints, Mayo insisted, were "repugnant to common sense" and could not, therefore, be taken at face value.[37] Instead, Mayo interpreted workers' grievances as symptomatic of broader societal conditions and workers' experiences *outside* the plant.

In search of an explanation for worker discontent, Mayo turned to psychology, in particular, to the ideas of Freud and Janet. He concluded that modern societies produce more than their share of obsessional character types and neurotic predispositions and that these lead to exaggerated and distorted reactions to certain situations—like work. But Mayo was not content with a purely psychological explanation of worker unrest. He situated the abnormal personal responses of workers in the broader sociological framework of Emile Durkheim.

35. The interviewing program was put to uses other than serving the ends of "science," for it became tied to a counselling program whose purpose it was to cool out worker unrest through the medium of "sympathetic listeners." A manual published by the Western Electric Company delineated the functions of counsellors. Among his or her duties the counsellor "was to watch constantly for signs of unrest and try to assuage the tension by discussion before the unrest became active. He was to try to dilute or redirect dissatisfaction by helping the employees to think along 'constructive' lines." Loren Baritz, *The Servants of Power*, New York: John Wiley, 1965, p. 101. Jeanne Wilensky, who was a counsellor at Hawthorne, argued that the counselling service was begun to forestall unionization. See Jeanne Wilensky and Harold Wilensky, "Personal Counselling: The Hawthorne Case," *American Journal of Sociology*, 57, 1951/1952, pp. 265–280.

36. Mayo, *op. cit.*, p. 96.

37. *Ibid.*, p. 93.

Mayo alleged that industrialism and urbanism had led to the disorganization of contemporary society, and what is more important, that these massive changes had weakened the community's control over the individual. Workers' neurotic tendencies were nourished by the absence of effective normative control, predisposing them to obsessional and irrational responses to life and work. Industrial organizations were not only subject to these intrusions of the broader society, but, as microcosms of that society, these organizations reproduced the same kinds of normlessness within their own boundaries. Workers, Mayo lamented, have lost their capacity for co-operation, and "at no time since the industrial revolution has there been, except sporadically here and there, anything of the nature of effective and whole-hearted collaboration between the administrative and working groups in industry."[38] The most pressing problem facing industrial society, then, was to find a way of developing and maintaining co-operation in business organizations.

This line of reasoning eventually led the Harvard group to conceive of the business enterprise as a social system comprising two main sub-systems. The first sub-system, the technical system, epitomizes rationality: It is geared toward profitable production and, guided by scientific knowledge, seeks the most efficient means to achieve the goal of profitable production. Managers and engineers are located within the technical system. The second sub-system is the social system, consisting of subordinate employees who are non-rational in the sense that their relationship to production is determined by their social needs. The non-logical workers represent an obstacle to the scientific technology and work methods devised by industrial engineers as well as to the rational or "scientific" policies wrought by management. Within the human relations perspective, then, workers' resistance to management policies and actions is not viewed as a rational response to real conflicts of interest (for instance conflicts over work speed, revamped work procedures, and labour replacing machinery), but arises from their commitment to the maintenance of the work group and

38. *Ibid.*, p. 158.

their fear of social dislocation. The Mayoites also viewed the poor communications between the two sub-systems as problematic. Communication was a one-way street, moving from the top of the company to the bottom, never the reverse. As a consequence, the company was never prepared for workers' opposition to management directives.[39]

The solution to the problems of the business organization, according to Mayo, was to develop a science of human relations in industry capable of apprehending the conditions conducive to teamwork and co-operation and to train an administrative elite in the theory and practice of this new science. Fully versed in the principles of human relations, the administrative elite would be able to effectively elicit the collaborative efforts of workers. The Mayoites recommended supplanting top–down communications with a two-way flow of communication, so that management could anticipate workers' reactions to company policies. But the central task of this administrative elite was to construct cohesive groups of workers whose customs and sentiments conformed to the rational policies of management. Once in place, this pliant shop floor culture would be conducive to squeezing from workers their full productive potential as well as encouraging them to wittingly acquiesce to the inevitable and desirable march of new technology and work procedures.[40]

Human relations experts wanted to elicit workers' co-operation with corporate goals, but they foundered on what appropriate measures should be taken to create an organizational milieu conducive to achieving this objective. In the 1930s and 1940s, the lessons of the Mayo school were applied in two major forms: employee counselling and foreman training.

---

39. *Cf.* F.J. Roethlisberger and William J. Dickson, *Management and the Worker*, Cambridge: Harvard University Press, 1939.
40. Obviously, the thrust of human relations is not to contest scientific management but to establish the conditions on the shop floor that enable its principles to be smoothly implemented. The Mayoites never questioned specialized jobs, routinized and standardized work procedures, or technological innovations that might deskill workers or cost them their jobs. These practices were viewed as imperatives of successful business operations. Only in regard to work incentives and close supervision did the Harvard group part company with Taylorism, and these differences were far outweighed by large areas of concurrence.

Counselling was never adopted on more than a limited basis by North American corporations, but during the 1950s, human relations training gained momentum—though it was still in industry "primarily a training activity confined to the lower ranks of supervision."[41] In the late 1950s and early 1960s, two new strands of human relations emerged: participative management and job redesign. Participative management drew on, refined, and elaborated the participatory and teamwork themes of the original human relations literature. The second notion represented a departure from traditional human relations in that it directly challenged Taylorist and Fordist principles of work design.

Participative Management
Participative management is rooted in human relations research and in investigations undertaken from the late 1930s on by Kurt Lewin and his associates at the University of Michigan's Institute for Social Research (ISR). From experimental, observational, and questionnaire research methods in both factories and offices, the ISR staff linked worker co-operation and superior work performance to consultative and participative relationships between bosses and subordinates. The ISR data formed the basis for Rensis Likert's book, *New Patterns of Management* (1961). Likert concluded that organizational effectiveness is related to open communications and to the degree individuals at all levels of the enterprise are able to influence decisions. This perspective was reinforced in the 1960s by the influential writings of individuals like Chris Argyris, Warren Bennis, and Douglas McGregor, whose advocacy of organizational participation was grounded in social psychological theories.[42] McGregor, for example, criticized the set of assumptions about human behaviour (known as "Theory X") upon which orthodox management practice is based. Theory X involves the

41. F.J. Roethlisberger, *The Elusive Phenomenon*, Boston: Harvard University Graduate School of Business Administration, 1977, p. 217.
42. *Cf.* Douglas McGregor, *The Human Side of Enterprise*, New York: McGraw-Hill, 1960; Chris Argyris, *Integrating the Individual and the Organization*, New York: John Wiley, 1964; Warren Bennis, *Changing Organizations*, New York: McGraw-Hill, 1966.

following ideas: (1) Individuals dislike work and avoid it when-ever possible; (2) because people dislike work, they must be coerced or manipulated to work hard; (3) most individuals do not want to be self-directed and are content to let others tell them what to do. Against these ideas, McGregor set forth his own "Theory Y": Work is a natural activity and is not inherently distasteful; individuals under the right circumstances seek self-direction and responsibility, and such traits are lodged in the majority of people, not just a select few; when individuals are committed to work and its objectives the human potential for self-actualization becomes manifest. Central to McGregor's analysis is the concept of self-fulfilling prophecies. If workers are viewed and treated as if they detested work, then their behaviour will come to conform with this image, and the need for coercive forms of management will thus *appear* warranted. The answer to this pervasive problem, according to McGregor, is to establish a participatory milieu to bring out those human qualities which have been stifled and buried in business organizations operating on the basis of Theory X. McGregor was a staunch advocate of the Scanlon Plan, which offers a group bonus for savings on labour costs and productivity increases. Committees consisting of management and worker representatives encourage, evaluate, and implement workers' suggestions for improving efficiency. Ideally, the Plan unifies labour and management by giving both parties the same goal: increased output and profits.

Participatory theory was applied not only to the shop floor but also to the control apparatuses of large companies. This broadened focus of the participatory school arose from the growth, diversification, and elaboration of the managerial structure of large organizations. The modern corporation, was characterized by a large and unwieldy chain of command that created serious problems of communication, empire building, and interpersonal and interdepartmental rivalries. In the 1950s and 1960s, organizations manifested an interest in participa-tory techniques like T-groups (sensitivity training) to teach managers how to effectively get along with each other. Organi-zation Development (OD) was also, and still is, popular. OD is a set of techniques geared to improving co-operation and effectiveness among managers. OD consultants often use T-groups formed within rather than outside the corporation. A widely used OD approach is the managerial grid, which trains executives in the fundamentals of sound management and aims to improve interpersonal relations among managers and between managers and their subordinates. Management-by-objectives (MBO) is another common participatory technique directed at supervisory personnel. Consultations between all levels of management are encouraged so that personal and departmental goals can be "jointly" established. The purpose of MBO is to align managerial activities and departmental goals with the objectives of upper management.

In recent years, especially with the worsening of the economy, corporate executives have shown a renewed interest in applying participatory principles to the shop floor. Forms of workers' resistance and union opposition once tolerated by management are now viewed as serious impediments to the profitability of companies being squeezed by foreign competition. Scanlon Plans sprang up here and there, but the favourite participatory format was joint management–worker or management–union committees that collaborate to resolve issues of "mutual concern." The most popular type of joint committee is, currently, the quality control (QC) circle, which involves small groups of workers and a foreman who are trained and meet periodically to detect and solve problems of production.[43] The QC circle program drew its inspiration from the precepts of the earlier human relations school—the potential of this approach finally being recognized after its efficacy was demonstrated in Japanese firms.

QC circle programs are viewed by management consultants and corporations as a boon to workers, offering them better jobs, involvement in decision making, cordial relations with

43. This section on QC circles was informed by the following materials: Mike Parker, *Inside the Circle: A Union Guide to QWL*, Boston: South End Press, 1985; Don Wells, *Soft Sell: "Quality of Working Life" Programs and the Productivity Race*, Ottawa: The Canadian Centre for Policy Alternatives, 1986; James Rinehart, "Appropriating Workers' Knowledge: Quality Control Circles at a General Motors Plant," *Studies in Political Economy*, 14, 1984, pp. 75–97; Donald Swartz, "New Forms of Workers' Participation: A Critique of Quality of Working Life," *Studies in Political Economy*, 5, 1981, pp. 55–78.

bosses, improved working conditions, leadership skills, and employment stability. Apart from these benefits, the participation *process* itself is designed to be a source of gratification. In return, the company expects a more co-operative and diligent work force, a more "reasonable" union (if one is present), and workers' method-improving and cost-cutting ideas. What QC circle programs promise workers and what they deliver are, in most important respects, very different. The advantages of participation are restricted largely to the realm of psychological satisfactions. Some workers, for example, are gratified by feeling their ideas are listened to, by identifying with a small group, and by being on a first name basis with their bosses—whatever recognition this implies. In tangible areas like employment stability and workplace democratization, however, QC circle programs fall far short of their promises. In North America, QC circle programs not only may eliminate jobs (due to productivity gains arising from participation); they also provide no guarantee of employment security to a smaller, more productive work force. The general stability of a firm's work force is linked to such conditions as amount of customer demand, rate of technological innovation, and level of profitability but not to the success or failure of QC circle programs. In regard to the most fundamental promise of participatory schemes—the democratization of the workplace—Quality of Work Life (QWL) rhetoric is exposed. Participatory schemes invariably establish carefully defined limits on the *scope* and *degree* of workers' involvement in decision making. QC circles and other participatory mechanisms have as their focal point workers' immediate jobs and work areas. Workers or their representatives are thus kept from making decisions on matters such as what is to be produced, investments, distributions of profits, technology, size of the work force, or plant closures.[44] Just as the scope of workers' decision making is circumscribed, so too is their degree of influence. Participatory mechanisms grant employees

44. Exceptions to this restricted scope of involvement are found mainly outside North America. European participatory mechanisms include worker representatives on corporate boards, works councils, and joint union–management committees which deal with issues transcending workers' immediate jobs.

the right to be consulted, to influence, or to make suggestions, but management always retains the right to veto workers' ideas or practices. In QC circle programs, for instance, the disposition of workers' suggestions rests entirely with management.

Any benefits realized by workers must be weighed alongside the insidious and largely hidden purposes behind corporations' adoption of participation. Participatory schemes do not, nor were they intended to, establish a base of power among employees. In fact, a major, usually unstated, objective of participation is to dilute the power of independent workers' groups or unions by drawing them into a web of collaborative relationships and alliances that eventuate in actions consistent with the goals of upper management. QC circles may also weaken workers' attachment to their union by encouraging close relationships with bosses, by receiving benefits from the company which the union has been unable to obtain, and by pitting circle against circle in competition for management's recognition and favours. Training materials and circle meetings encourage workers to adopt a management perspective in relating to other workers and in determining and solving workplace problems.[45] Management justifies this training by arguing that in order to save jobs, the company must either match or surpass its domestic and foreign competitors. The objective is to eradicate the "we" (workers) versus "they" (managers) consciousness and replace it with the notion that both groups in a particular plant have the same interests. If workers can be induced to identify and co-operate with plant management, they might renounce

45. For example, the General Motors training manual contains a hypothetical case of an assembly group whose output is low. The circle trainees are instructed to ascertain the source of this problem. With the aid of statistical techniques, the trainees trace the source of the problem to an assembler with poor eyesight. The preferred solution—locating the assembler in a well-lighted area—is less important than the manual's attempt to persuade the trainees that sub-standard work performance is not just management's problem; workers are encouraged to put pressure on others who fail to meet company production goals. The manual also instructs trainees to use cost-benefit analysis in solving problems, and what constitutes a cost or a benefit is defined from management's perspective. Hence, in the manual's hypothetical case, reduced labour time is defined as a benefit and retraining workers as a cost. The criteria for these definitions are company profits, not workers' interests in acquiring new skills or job security. See Rinehart, *op. cit.*

militancy and temper their bargaining demands, paving the way for concessions to the company that reduce the quality of workers' lives on and off the job. As Wells concluded from his evaluation of participatory programs in two large Canadian plants, "The biggest problem both the union and the membership face in this quest for job security through increased co-operation with management is that QWL helps pit workers in one plant against workers in another in a fight for scarce jobs. Such competitions naturally lead to local productivity bargaining and are a direct threat to industry-wide collective agreements. Workers in different plants are played off against each other to achieve greater profits. The result is a massive disunity within the union, especially above the local level. The ultimate logic of these pressures is to destroy the union."[46]

Job Redesign

Since its emergence in the 1950s, job redesign has followed several trajectories, all of which have sought to overturn the design tenets of scientific management. The earliest approaches entailed simple despecialization, either through job enlargement or job rotation. In the late 1950s a conceptual approach to work redesign, called "job enrichment," was developed and popularized by the psychologist Frederick Herzberg. After combing the job satisfaction literature, Herzberg concluded that factors promoting dissatisfaction with work were qualitatively different from those engendering job satisfaction. Subsequent research by Herzberg found that five major factors contributed to job satisfaction: achievement, recognition, responsibility, advancement, and the job itself. The main factors responsible for job dissatisfaction were: company policy and administration, supervision, salary, interpersonal relations, and physical working conditions. The "satisfiers" dealt with what workers actually did at work, whereas the "dissatisfiers" dealt with the context or environment in which work was performed. The theoretical rationale for this conclusion was found in the assumption that humans have a dual nature. One facet of human nature is animal-like and strives to avoid unpleasant

46. Wells, *op. cit.*, p. 42.

experiences; the other side is specific to the human species and constitutes a need for development and self-actualization. Optimum working conditions ("hygiene factors") such as high wages and pleasant surroundings, since they do not facilitate human growth, can only produce a sense of not being dissatisfied. Factors associated with the content and reward structure of jobs, on the other hand, provide a matrix for self-development and promote involvement in and satisfaction with work. According to Herzberg, the goals of an enterprise (productivity and profitability) are often in conflict with the needs of individuals trapped in trivial and meaningless jobs. To develop motivated and diligent workers, jobs must be enriched. Herzberg insists that simple job enlargement (greater task variety or what he calls "horizontal loading") is not a sufficient motivator. What is required is "vertical loading," that is, adding tasks which call for skill and responsibility, offering recognition, and providing opportunities for advancement and self-development.[47]

A second, now dominant, approach to job redesign is associated with the research of London's Tavistock Institute of Human Relations. Labelled socio-technical systems, the objective of this approach is to find the best fit ("joint optimization") between an enterprise's technological system and its social system. An enterprise is believed to operate best when the tasks required by technology and the social-psychological needs of employees are both satisfied. Like job enrichment, the socio-technical systems school stresses expanding workers' tasks and discretion. Unlike Herzberg's emphasis on individual jobs, however, this school ordinarily implements changes through the medium of work teams (autonomous groups) which are collectively responsible for performing a set of tasks. Job enlargement takes the form of developing flexible workers; ideally, every team member should have the requisite skills and knowledge to perform all the separate tasks involved in the

47. See Frederick Herzberg, Bernard Mausner, and Barbara Snyderman, *The Motivation to Work*, New York: John Wiley, 1959, and Herzberg's *Work and the Nature of Man*, New York: Mentor Books, 1966; "One More Time: How Do You Motivate Employees?", *Harvard Business Review*, September–October, 1968, pp. 53–62.

work of the unit. The socio-technical systems approach fosters workers' discretion by letting the team decide (within limits) how fast to work, job assignments and rotation patterns, and work methods.[48]

Adherents of work redesign maintain that its potential for boosting productivity and profits arises from the motivating force of good jobs. This proposition has been challenged by recent research. Job redesign may improve employees' attitudes toward work, but the basis of its adoption and the corporate payoffs of restructured work have little to do with improving workers' motivation. Job redesign facilitates the achievement of corporate objectives not so much by reducing resistance and promoting co-operation among workers as by *rationalizing* the work process. While rationalization is usually associated with a highly specialized and routinized division of labour, there are conditions under which maximum job fragmentation and minimum worker discretion are not the most productive or profitable modes of organizing the labour process. In these cases, some degree of despecialization and restoration of workers' autonomy can cut labour costs and reduce necessary production time. In addition, job enrichment consultants not infrequently incorporate elements of scientific management into their programs. A few examples will suffice to illustrate these criticisms.

Large offices have provided the most fertile soil for job enrichment. In the 1950s and 1960s, office productivity stagnated, labour costs increased, and profits fell. Job enrichment provided one solution to the situation. At AT&T, for example, thousands of jobs were redesigned in the late 1960s. The redesign criteria applied to the jobs of keypunch operators typify the thrust of this massive program. Before "enrichment," an assignment clerk randomly distributed each day's work among keypunchers. The keypunchers sent obvious data errors to an error-corrector prior to punching. Punching errors were corrected by verifiers, who also checked all of each keypuncher's work. Under the enrichment program, the random

48. *Cf.* Eric Trist, G. Higgin, H. Murray, and A. Pollock, *Organizational Choice*, London: Tavistock, 1963; Eric Trist, *The Evolution of Socio-Technical Systems*, Toronto: Ontario Quality of Working Life Centre, 1981.

assignment of work was replaced by a "modular" system. Work to be done was classified by the department from which it originated, for example payroll, and a worker punched data coming from a specific department. The workload and due dates were now specified in advance, and operators scheduled their own time to meet these quotas. Only a portion of the keypunch operators' work was now verified, the two correction functions were handled exclusively by keypunchers, and they now kept output records. The quality and quantity of output improved, a result the redesign consultant attributed to improved worker motivation. Roughly similar changes were applied to hundreds of other AT&T job categories in Canada and the United States.[49]

The "success" of AT&T's redesign efforts resulted not from improved employee motivation—evidence for such improvement was equivocal at best—but from the work intensifying and job-reduction effects of the program. Under the old system, the responsibilities of non-supervisory employees had been so narrowly defined that a large and expensive supporting cast of verifiers, checkers, and supervisors had become necessary. By consolidating tasks, assigning some supervisory functions to subordinates, and reducing verification, fewer employees were now needed to handle the work. As the AT&T design consultant recognized, "The basic approach is to load people with responsibility—to build in direct personal feedback. Then . . . you find you don't need so many checkers, verifiers, work assigners, and 'pushers' of various kinds."[50] Indeed, after "enrichment," substantial numbers of employees were let go or transferred, saving the company large sums in labour costs. Moreover, redesign made it possible for AT&T to hold certain employees account-

---

49. This section on job enrichment at AT&T is based on data originally provided in Robert Ford, *Motivation Through the Work Itself*, New York: American Management Association, 1969. The analysis of job enrichment and the other major forms of work redesign is adopted from James Rinehart, "Improving the Quality of Working Life Through Job Redesign: Work Humanization or Work Rationalization," *Canadian Review of Sociology and Anthropology*, 23, 4, 1986, pp. 507-530. Also pertinent is John Kelly, *Scientific Management, Job Redesign and Work Performance*, New York: Academic Press, 1982.
50. Ford, *op. cit.*, p. 66.

able for specific and readily identifiable "modules" of work (recall that a keypunch operator was assigned work originating from a particular section of the firm). According to AT&T's redesign expert, the assignment of a module of work to an employee triggers the Herzbergian "motivators" of responsibility, achievement, and recognition. This technique is completely compatible with Taylorist principles. Whereas the original design had afforded the worker a degree of anonymity, "modularization" of jobs allows management to readily identify workers' output and hold them accountable, and to apply sanctions to those who fail to meet performance standards. As one AT&T executive remarked: "Before, we did not really know who was competent because verifiers or supervisors checked everything, making sure no one failed and seeing to it that errors were low. Now I know whom to drop. If they cannot do the job . . . then we cannot carry them."[51] In effect, modularization allowed management to impose a speed-up on a work force that had been decimated by job consolidations.

The situation is much the same in factories. Assembly line production (Fordism) is most profitable when there exists a large consumer demand for standard products. This cost-advantage is lost when mass production facilities must produce for volatile product markets that necessitate product diversification, frequent model changes, and short production runs. Under these conditions, the assembly line requires frequent line balancing measures by engineers to ensure that workers along the line are continuously busy. Job content must be frequently revised, causing adjustment problems and sagging output on the part of specialized workers. Line problems like time spent on inspection, the supply of assembly materials, and mechanical failures are also magnified. These difficulties have led some manufacturers to replace conveyors with assembly islands where a small group of workers is responsible for an enlarged sphere of operations. Workers get their own assembly materials, learn each others' jobs, and take on inspection and simple repair tasks. This revamped process enables changes in product and work procedures to be quickly implemented, and

51. *Ibid.*, p. 35.

flexible workers can readily adapt to new work methods. When product demand fluctuates, a firm can simply add or eliminate assembly islands rather than change the character and length of the assembly line through intricate and costly rebalancing measures. Restructured assembly operations, then, are adopted not because they improve jobs and workers' attitudes—though this may occur—but because they are a cost-effective mode of maintaining production in a market of diversified and fluctuating demand.[52]

In plants employing highly automated, continuous-process technology, flexible job definitions and self-regulating work groups are the rule. This enlightened mode of organizing work arises not from the humane concerns of employers but from the exigencies of profitably operating continuous-process technology. Since the work often is relaxed when the process is running to schedule, management keeps operators busy by having them perform tasks such as housekeeping, equipment maintenance, and repair. This not only minimizes idle time, it also lessens the wage costs of craft workers responsible for maintaining and repairing equipment. At Shell's continuous-process plant in Sarnia, Ontario, for instance, highly skilled craft workers only work on the day shift. Maintenance and repair problems emerging on the other two shifts are handled by less well paid operators.[53] Furthermore, process operators are not tied to a single machine or work station; they move throughout the plant, monitoring the machinery complex. Malfunctions must be rapidly spotted and corrected to avoid substantial costs. Since the appropriate responses to these unpredictable but regularly occurring events cannot be determined in advance, a highly specialized division of labour impedes workers' capacity to deal with such contingencies. When malfunctions occur, specialization creates highly unbal-

52. For an excellent description and explanation of restructured assembly operations at Olivetti see Federico Butera, "Environmental Factors in Job and Organization Designs: The Case of Olivetti," in Louis Davis and A. Cherns, eds., *The Quality of Working Life*, Vol. I, New York: Free Press, 1975, pp. 166–200.
53. *Cf.* Norman Halpern, "Sociotechnical Systems Design: The Shell Sarnia Experience," in J.B. Cunningham and T.H. White, eds., *Quality of Working Life: Contemporary Cases*, Ottawa: Labour Canada, 1984, pp. 31–69.

anced workloads; some specialized workers are very busy while others do nothing. Consequently, workers are trained to perform various jobs, and they can move as a unit to collectively deal with production problems.[54] Finally, work groups are granted a measure of self-regulation, because this reduces delays in reacting to operational emergencies. This form of work group regulation not only speeds up reaction time, it is less expensive than paying a cadre of supervisors to detect problems and co-ordinate workers' responses to them.

This rather extensive analysis of modern varieties of human relations is warranted by their popularity in corporate circles, and by the widespread belief that such programs represent reforms that benefit both employees and employers. In the early 1980s it was estimated that QC circles involving more than one million participants were in operation at 8000 locations in the United States, and by 1985, 41 percent of American firms with over 500 employees had worker–management participation programs.[55] An untold number of offices have job enrichment programs, although developments in micro-technology will undoubtedly render this approach superfluous in the future. And, as more and more plants implement advanced forms of technology, we can expect the already numerous instances of flexible work roles and autonomous groups to grow. While no comprehensive survey has been conducted in Canada, hundreds of companies have some form of QWL program in

54. Union work rules concerning job classifications and skill demarcations are increasingly under attack by corporations, especially those with advanced technology. By inhibiting management's capacity to allocate labour as it sees fit, these classifications, for example welder, inspector, forklift operator, and so on, protect workers against speed-ups, job consolidations, and management attempts to ignore seniority as a basis of job assignments. The contract between the United Auto Workers and General Motors for the proposed small-car Saturn plant in Tennessee incorporates such flexible work roles. This contentious contract is viewed by some as a model for future agreements. For an excellent discussion of the implications of job classifications see Parker, *op. cit.* For a good discussion of how a form of job enlargement undertaken at Inco subverted workers' interests, see Wallace Clement, *Hardrock Mining: Industrial Relations and Technological Changes at Inco*, Toronto: McClelland and Stewart, 1981, Chapter 8.

55. *Ibid.*; Charlotte Gold, *Labor*-Management Committees: Confrontation, Cooptation or Cooperation? Ithaca, N.Y.: New York State School of Industrial and Labor Relations, Cornell University, 1986.

operation. The list of known user companies includes Canadian General Electric, Domtar, General Foods, Ford, General Motors, Westinghouse, Inco, Macmillan-Bloedel, Petrosar, Shell Canada, Prudential Insurance, Esso, Union Carbide, Air Canada, Alcan, Cominco, Canadian Tire, Budd Canada, Eaton Yale, Steinberg's, National Cash Register, and Supreme Aluminum.[56]

Corporations generally introduce these programs under the banner of improving the quality of work life, indicating their commitment to progressive personnel policies. This is a profoundly cynical claim in those cases where QWL techniques are used to insulate companies from the prospect of unionization. As Parker warns, "Today there is an explosion in the number of corporate consultants, labour relations specialists, lawyers, workshops, and publications all available (at a hefty price) to advise in using 'communication' and 'participation' to crush any attempt to organize a union."[57] Management consultant M. Scott Myers says that the QWL program "in the non-union organization is harnessing talent in a manner that gives a competitive advantage to that organization, and also offers the only realistic strategy for preventing the unionization of the workplace." He discusses a large Canadian chemical firm where workers, after having been exposed to a QWL program, voted to toss out their union.[58] American companies that have employed QWL programs to keep out unions include Texas Instruments, IBM, the TRW conglomerate, and Coors Brewing.

Avowedly anti-union consultants are not representative of the QWL school, but the practices of even the best-intentioned consultants should be carefully scrutinized.[59] All adherents of QWL insist it is a game with no losers. On the one hand, work is

---

56. This partial list was culled from Terrence White, *Human Resource Management—Changing Times in Alberta*, Edmonton: Alberta Labour, 1979; Jacquie Mansell, *An Inventory of Innovative Work Arrangements in Ontario*, Toronto: Ontario Ministry of Labour, 1978; various issues of Labour Canada's *Quality of Working Life: The Canadian Scene* and the Ontario Quality of Working Life Centre's *QWL Focus*.

57. Parker, *op. cit.*, p. 113.

58. M. Scott Myers, "Overcoming Union Opposition to Job Enrichment," *Harvard Business Review*, 17, 1971, p. 38.

59. If all QWL consultants were pro-union, their programs still would have to be approached cautiously. This is because employers and managers are the final arbiters of the character of QWL programs.

made a more gratifying and democratic experience. On the other hand, the happy workers are more co-operative and diligent. This promise of "mutual benefits" is what constitutes the broad appeal of QWL programs. If QWL achieved what it claims to achieve, such efforts would be deserving of support from both labour and capital. It is true that maximum job fragmentation and minimum workers' discretion are directly challenged by QWL programs, but, as we have tried to demonstrate, this retreat from the precepts of Fordism and Taylorism is undertaken *by* management *for* management's purposes. In whatever form it is packaged, QWL is used by the corporation insofar as it is compatible with cost-reducing and profit-maximizing objectives. Job redesign is implemented not to humanize work but to intensify labour, lessen labour costs, or to meet production exigencies that a highly specialized division of labour cannot handle economically. Participatory mechanisms are introduced to appropriate workers' knowledge and to turn resistant workers and adversarial unions into willing collaborators with management and its policies. And what management has given it can also take away. Many companies that introduced reforms have, for various reasons (for example, because of employees' resistance or more often because management's objectives were not being met), returned to conventional modes of operating.

Skeptics of this line of reasoning may agree that QWL programs are advantageous to the company but add that this does not preclude improvements in the lot of workers. This is true, but because QWL programs are selected and constructed in terms of the criteria of profitability and the maintenance of workplace power relationships, no room is allowed for genuine reform. The most ambitious participatory programs lead only to a greater measure of discretion by workers over their *immediate* jobs and work areas. Loosening detailed supervisory controls may pose a threat to the first-line managers, but it leaves untouched, and possibly strengthens, the real locus of power at the upper reaches of management. Since participatory mechanisms are instituted by and for management, it would be naive to expect any fundamental redistribution of power. As the Nobel prize winner Herbert Simon forthrightly observed years ago, "The employer can tolerate genuine participation in decision making only when he believes that reasonable men, knowing the relevant facts and thinking through the problem will reach a decision that is generally consistent with *his* goals and interests in the situation."[60] Moreover, in many cases workers' interests are threatened by such programs. Participation is used to dilute the militancy of shop floor workers, to induce workers to assume managerial perspectives without management authority, and to weaken the power of labour unions. Such outcomes of participation are harmful because the militant initiatives of workers and unions are the only reliable means of improving the quality of work life in capitalist society. Job redesign does increase to some degree variety and discretion—changes workers might appreciate. However, redesign programs often add repetitive tasks to a highly fragmented job, resulting in jobs of "routine variety." But the most damning indictment of redesign is that it speeds up the work process— often without commensurate increases in pay—and eliminates jobs.[61]

It is clear that the human relations approach, from its auspicious beginnings at the Hawthorne Works to its sophisticated contemporary forms, has accepted the goals of the capitalist enterprise and has operated as an arm of management rather than workers. Because the entire school has assisted management in solving *management's* problems, there is in this approach an irreducible element of anti-labour bias and no remedy for alienated labour. When we ask the question that should be posed about all scientific information—"Knowledge for whom?"—the answer in this case is unequivocal. Here indeed is a science for managers.[62]

60. Herbert Simon, "Authority," in Conrad Arensberg *et al.*, eds., *Research in Industrial Human Relations—A Critical Appraisal*, New York: Praeger, 1957, p. 111.
61. A survey of North American and European redesign programs found that job loss resulted in 68 percent of the cases where redesign had been implemented, and that approximately one of every four redesigned jobs was made redundant. See Kelly, *op. cit.*
62. Mayo was often accused of having a pro-management bias. J.A.C. Brown regards this criticism as unfair, since "no industrial psychologist has ever shown anything else, and it is therefore hard to understand why Mayo should have been selected for this criticism." See Brown, *op. cit.*, pp. 92–93.

UNIONS

Working people have engaged in bitter and protracted struggles to form labour organizations of their own choosing. These efforts stem from a recognition by workers that acting alone as individuals they are powerless. Only through collective action can working people expect to receive some measure of economic and social justice at the workplace. Indeed, unions have improved the terms and conditions of employment. They have improved wages and benefits, increased job security, and protected workers from arbitrary and discriminatory managerial decisions. These obviously important gains have blunted the harsh edge of capitalist power, but the essential core of that power remains intact. Despite their achievements, unions have come to accept the practice if not the principle of managerial domination and worker subordination. What must be understood is that unions are paradoxical institutions: While they are the only effective vehicle workers have at present to advance their interests, they have also become a force for accomodating workers to corporate capitalism.

This accommodation to capitalist power was formalized in what is known as the post-World War II compromise forged in the midst of the intense class struggles of the 1940s. This settlement between labour, big capital, and the state featured the establishment of a new industrial relations system and stipulated a set of trade-offs. Unions were legally recognized (through PC 1003 and the 1948 Industrial Relations and Disputes Investigation Act) and accorded organizational security (through the automatic dues checkoff provided by the Rand Formula). Collective bargaining rights were institutionalized, and the state instituted programs, such as unemployment insurance, that protected working people from absolute deprivation. The *quid pro quos* were measures aimed at containing workers' unrest and reinforcing the right of employers to determine investments, profits, and the character of the production process. Specifically, contractual clauses enshrined management's right to govern the workplace, and striking while a contract was in force was legally prohibited.[63] Fundamental

---

63. As indicated in Chapter 3, the post-World War II compromise began to come undone in the 1970s; the state and employers attacked collective bargaining and workers won significant gains.

conflicts of interest between employees and employers, then, were institutionalized rather than resolved by the collective bargaining process, which enmeshed conflicts in a web of rules enshrined in contracts and labour laws enforced by the state. These are the institutional parameters within which unions are obliged to operate.[64]

Unions' acknowledgement of the power of property is contained in a section of the contract known as the management's rights clause. A contract between a union and an Ontario manufacturer illustrates the sweeping prerogatives of management:

The union acknowledges that it is the exclusive function of the company to: (a) maintain order, discipline, and efficiency; (b) hire, classify, direct, transfer, promote, demote, lay off, and discharge, suspend or otherwise discipline employees for just cause, provided that an allegation that the cause is unjust shall not preclude the company from imposing such penalty as it deems necessary prior to the issue being determined by grievance or arbitration procedure; (c) generally to manage the industrial enterprise in which the company is engaged, including all matters concerning the operation of business not specifically dealt with elsewhere in the agreement, and without restricting the generality of the foregoing, to determine the products to be manufactured, methods of manufacture, schedules of production, kinds and locations of machines and tools to be used, process of manufacturing, the engineering and designing of its products, the control of materials and parts to be incorporated in the products produced, and extension, limitation, curtailment, or cessation of operations.[65]

64. If trade unions ignore these constraints by engaging in radical *activities* (as distinct from espousing radical ideas), their very existence can be endangered.
65. Managerial power is further augmented by what is known as the "residual rights theory." This interpretation of the contract allows employers to take any action not explicitly forbidden in the contract, but it restricts workers to acting solely in accordance with what is contractually permitted.

Managerial authority is also shored up by the union's obligation to guarantee labour peace when a contract is in effect. When a grievance arises on the shop floor, the natural inclination of workers is to settle it immediately, if necessary, through actions like slowdowns and work stoppages. But since these actions are forbidden by the contract, the union is placed in the anomolous position of sometimes having to discipline its own members. Union officials, then, become "managers of discontent" who are legally bound in cases where workers disrupt production to take responsibility for the enforcement of workplace discipline.[66] In place of aggressive shop floor actions by workers to settle disputes, the contract substitutes an individualized, bureaucratically structured (and painfully slow) grievance procedure.[67] The resolution of everyday workplace problems, then, is transferred from the shop floor to the labour relations department of the firm.[68]

Unions emerged in response to alienation and exploitation, but collective bargaining, the defining characteristic and essential function of unions, takes as given the prevailing power relations at the workplace. The capitalist mode of production is the framework within which union demands are articulated and pursued. At best, unions nibble away at the margins of power, modifying but not altering in any fundamental sense relations of domination and subordination. And since capitalist power is at the heart of alienated and exploited labour, unions are not in a position to offer real solutions to these conditions.

---

66. C. Wright Mills was the first to label union officials "managers of discontent." See his *The New Men of Power*, New York: Harcourt, Brace, 1948.
67. Of course, workers' demands can be pursued through collective bargaining and strikes upon expiry of the contract. However, since World War II, these everyday grievances or "local issues" have been, for the most part, treated by union leaders as far less significant than economic issues. When issues of power do arise in collective bargaining, the union usually assumes a defensive stance—opposing management's attempts to alter or abrogate workers' traditional rights.
68. The revamped industrial relations order also ushered in an era of complex negotiations and contract language, leading unions to a greater reliance on university-trained legal, financial, and economic experts. The result of these developments was to shift the locus of decision making and the onus for initiating and directing struggles from the rank and file members to union leaders.

This does not alter the fact that, in capitalist society, unions constitute critically important organs of struggle and are still the only viable means workers have to realize better lives on and off the job.

WORKERS' CONTROL

Must we close this discussion on a thoroughly pessimistic note by arguing that all efforts to overcome alienation are futile? There is one answer to alienated labour that deserves serious consideration: workers' control. In contrast to participatory, stock purchase, or profit sharing programs implemented by management to lessen antagonisms between labour and capital, workers' control is initiated by workers for workers' purposes. It encompasses workers' struggles to restrain, challenge, assume, or seize traditional managerial authority. In its most advanced stage, workers' control takes the form of a democratically planned economy and workers' self-management at the point of production. While the concept and practice of workers' control has deep historical roots, it is a subject riven with strong differences of opinion as to its definition, strategies, and goals. It is beyond the scope of this book to evaluate the substance of these controversies. Furthermore, it would be premature to attempt to provide, let alone urge, workers to follow some kind of strategic blueprint of a self-managed economy. Such plans do exist, but they are only meaningful to the degree they resonate with the experiences, predilections, and activities of workers. Our concern is with the question of whether workers actually want to control the means and ends of production and whether they are capable of doing so. If it could be demonstrated that the attitudes and actions of people reveal either an unwillingness or an inability to manage production, discussions of workers' control would be meaningless. There are a number of past and contemporary cases that speak pointedly to the issue of individuals' concern and capacity to take charge of production. These examples are not exhaustive, but they do indicate that struggles by people to regulate their work lives take many forms and transcend national boundaries.

Workplace Struggles Over Control

At its most elementary and common level, workers' control has a defensive character; workers resist managerial encroachments on their customary domains of discretion. This level of struggle is a permanent feature of capitalist work organizations. Conflict over the frontier of control is a natural outcome of the antithetical interests of a non-producing, dominant minority (and their agents) and a producing, subordinate majority. Defensive struggles are not ordinarily impelled or informed by well-formulated theories of workers' power. It is the *practice* of workers' control rather than its ideology that distinguishes these struggles, and which we have referred to throughout this book as "resistance." As Carter Goodrich recognized years ago, "The roots and beginnings of the control demand are in the felt irksomeness of the present system of control, not in a conscious desire for a new field of activity."[69] Workplace resistance sometimes assumes a pro-active nature when workers begin to co-ordinate their activities and to take on, if only temporarily, functions ordinarily performed by management. There is, then, within workers' resistance a latent but nonetheless real possibility of more deliberate control demands that under certain historical circumstances may transcend the usual boundaries of struggle and provide a glimpse of a new order.

Revolutionary Situations and Workers' Control

There are examples from all over the world of insurgent movements by masses of working people to restructure power and establish organs of direct democracy: the Paris Commune of 1871; the Russian revolutions of 1905 and 1917; Italian and German factory occupations of 1918–1920; Spain in 1936; Hungary in 1956; France in 1968; Portugal in 1974; and Poland in 1981. At each of these historical moments, working people replaced, or attempted to replace, centralized, authoritarian structures of feudal, party, or class power with democratically organized bodies to regulate workplaces and communities. As Huxley remarks, these "spontaneous expressions of working

---

69. Carter L. Goodrich, *The Frontier of Control: A Study in British Workshop Politics*, London: Pluto Press, 1975, first published 1920, pp. 34–35.

class power... have arisen in every significant revolutionary upheaval in the twentieth century."[70] Events in Spain (1936) and Hungary (1956) illustrate the character of these expressions of working-class power and deserve amplification for two reasons. Both were massive popular movements at whose centre were workers rather than elitist elements acting in the presumed interests of workers. Second, the true dimensions of these events are relatively unknown.

The Spanish Civil War and the events surrounding it are usually related in terms of a script in which the leading roles are played by the Republican forces of democracy and the Fascists. Buried beneath this conventional scenario is the vital role played by the real *dramatis personae* of the period—the masses of urban and rural labourers who had radically transformed social and economic conditions in large sections of the country. Approximately 1700 villages, involving about three million people, were engaged in collective forms of agriculture. Workers' committees also controlled entire towns. The industrial city of Alcoy was run by a single, umbrella commune. While industrial collectivization was largely restricted to Barcelona and the province of Catalonia, the extent of democratic regulation was broad.[71] It embraced heavy industry and textiles, petroleum companies, harbour operations, the fishing industry, health services, railways and municipal transportation, and the utilities of water, gas, telephone, and electricity. Small trade was directed by collectives of barbers, hairdressers, and shopkeepers. In Barcelona, industry, commerce, and public services were effectively operated on a collective basis.[72] Signs were affixed to buildings and vehicles to indicate the liberated areas. They simply read, *incautado*—meaning "placed under workers' control."[73] Although the ideological foundation of this massive collectivization had been formulated during years of education

---

70. Christopher Huxley, "Council Communism," *Labour/Le Travailleur*, 12, Autumn, 1983, p. 216.
71. Industry was heavily concentrated in Catalonia. About one-half of all industrial production in Spain was carried out in this province.
72. Sam Dolgoff, ed., *The Anarchist Collectives*, Montreal: Black Rose Books, 1974.
73. Noam Chomsky, *American Power and the New Mandarins*, New York: Vintage Books, 1969.

and agitation by anarchists and socialists, it was, as Chomsky observes, a largely spontaneous movement without a revolutionary vanguard.[74]

One of the most remarkable displays of workers' solidarity and determination occurred in Hungary in 1956. After years of authoritarian rule by Soviet-dominated Hungarian communists, the people were ripe for any kind of movement for change. Their pent-up frustrations were brought out into the open when a group of student demonstrators were fired upon by the hated security police. News of the incident spread quickly and citizens were rapidly armed and on the streets. Soon after the fighting broke out a workers' council was established in Budapest; within three days a network of councils covered the entire country—in cities, villages, and rural areas. The councils were devised by manual and office workers as well as youth groups and professional associations. They took charge of factories, mines, hospitals, government bureaus, and state farms. Workers' councils organized freedom fighters, declared strikes, and "assumed managerial responsibilities that extended over the whole range of economic and social welfare problems pertaining to the respective plants or shops."[75] They dismissed managers, seized control of company funds, ran production, and paid out salaries. In many cases, they took over the administration of entire towns.[76]

The Hungarian Revolution was not directed by an official central revolutionary body. The important revolutionary institutions were organized only after fighting in the streets had begun. The workers' councils emerged on a more or less spontaneous basis, and they were, as Vali notes, "representative instruments for the expression of the will and opinions of the working class."[77] In summarizing the function and structure of the workers' councils, Zinner observed that they conformed to the ideal of pure democracy more closely than any institutional

74. *Ibid.*
75. Paul E. Zinner, *Revolution in Hungary*, New York: Columbia University Press, 1962, pp. 271–272.
76. Ferenc Vali, *Rift and Revolt in Hungary*, Cambridge: Harvard University Press, 1961.
77. *Ibid.*, p. 332.

form yet devised. The spontaneous development of the councils, their democratic composition, and their effective activities—all combined to furnish "a lesson not easily to be forgotten by the totalitarian and not lightly dismissed by the student of politics."[78]

Contrary to the elitist bias of much scholarly opinion, the failure of these popular movements for self-management in Spain and Hungary did not reside in the complexity of modern society or in the inexorable workings of the iron law of oligarchy.[79] Rather, both posed a tangible and immediate threat to traditional forms of authority. As such, these organs of democratic control were ruthlessly destroyed. In Hungary, of course, the revolution was smashed by the superior military power of the Soviet Union. And in Spain, enterprises run by workers were forced to a standstill because credit and necessary supplies were withheld by the Republican authorities. Ultimately, Spanish anarchists and socialists and their organizations were violently suppressed.[80]

Plant Seizures
The revolutionary activity in Spain and Hungary is only a dramatic illustration of peoples' desire and ability to manage their work and their communities. There are a number of more recent cases of narrower scope where workers have seized an individual enterprise, carrying out functions normally handled

78. Zinner, *op. cit.*, p. 313. Zinner's praise of the workers' councils is qualified. He alleges that their effectiveness is predicated on revolutionary enthusiasm, which ebbs away as time passes.
79. According to the iron law of oligarchy, democratic decision making is time-consuming, chaotic, and ineffective. In order to be viable, any large-scale organization—even one devoted to democratic procedures and goals—must be governed from the top by a small group of knowledgeable and committed experts and officials. See Robert Michels, *Political Parties*, New York: The Free Press, 1962. First published in 1915. While there are *tendencies* toward oligarchy in organizations, the cases of workers' control discussed in this chapter demonstrate that Michels' proposition cannot be considered a law.
80. *Cf.* Chomsky, *op. cit.* It is important to stress that these democratic organizations of Northern Spain were not suppressed by Franco's Fascist troops. Rather, they were destroyed by Republican forces, sometimes acting hand in hand with the Communist Party. For a personal account of the suppression of the Spanish anarchists and their allies see George Orwell, *Homage to Catalonia*, New York: Harcourt, Brace and World, 1952.

by owners and managers. In the late 1960s Italian workers in Regio Emilia occupied their farm equipment factory, which was scheduled to be shut down, and began to run it themselves. Eventually the state stepped in to lend financial support to the employee-operated enterprise.[81] A notable plant takeover occurred in France in the early 1970s at the Lip watch company. The impetus for the workers' actions was an announcement of bankruptcy by owners of the Lip company. Upon hearing the news, workers formed committees to deal with the situation, occupied the factory, and decided to resume production. The committees dealt with various aspects of the business, including finance, wages, production, and sales. The insurgents seized $2 million worth of watches, generated their own sales force, and paid wages from the proceeds. The government, however, ordered the plant closed, and riot police were dispatched to evict the workers. After a lengthy period of demonstrations and negotiations, the plant re-opened under the direction of an industrial consortium and backed by bank credit and government funds.[82] Inspired by the example of Lip workers, more than 200 French factories were occupied in 1974 and 1975.[83]

Such activities are not purely a European phenomena. In Chapter 4 we described how in 1981 workers occupied and ran the British Columbia Telephone Company. Having barred management from the premises, workers demonstrated to themselves and the public that they were quite capable of organizing and managing company operations. In the summer of 1973 Canadian television viewers were treated to the fascinating

81. Andre Gorz, "Workers' Control is More than Just That," in Gerry Hunnius, ed., *Participatory Democracy for Canada*, Montreal: Black Rose Books, 1971.
82. Mel Kliman, "L'Affaire Lip," *Canadian Forum*, 1974, pp. 4–8; Keven Mundy, "Lip Workers Win," *Canadian Dimension*, 10, 1974, pp. 13–14. The Lip story did not end at this point. A declining market for the watches and the French recession of 1975 and 1976 pushed the company toward bankruptcy, and workers once again occupied the plant. Eventually, the workers offered to purchase the plant themselves, a move they had resisted because it entailed giving up their status as workers to become owners. This, they believed, would cut them adrift from the rest of the French working class, with whom they strongly identified. See Chapter 4 in Martin Carnoy and Derek Shearer, *Economic Democracy: The Challenge of the 1980s*, White Plains, New York: M.E. Sharpe, 1980.
83. *Ibid.*

spectacle of townspeople and workers of Temiscaming, Quebec, riding rafts and armed with shotguns to prevent owners of a pulp mill from sending logs down the river. The episode was part of a broader struggle by workers to take over the mill, which had been closed down by Canadian Industrial Paper (CIP). After a series of worker and community protests, negotiations for a buy-out began. In July, 1975 an agreement was reached, and the plant reopening was financed mainly by the Quebec and federal governments, with smaller sums advanced by a three-person management group, workers, and the local population.[84]

Like the plant takeovers in France and Italy, this Canadian struggle was prompted by the need to save workers' jobs. That workers' control is often born of desperation simply illustrates that it is rooted in the concrete experiences and needs of the working class. Material conditions of life and work are the underlying catalysts to actions that can penetrate and transcend the ideological restraints of capitalist society. Whether worker-owned and controlled enterprises prefigure forms of a democratically planned economy and self-managed work organizations is a question to which we now turn.

Worker-Owned and Controlled Enterprises

Most of the cases of workers' control we described were unable to sustain themselves in the face of hostile economic and political environments. But workers' self-management is not limited to these transitory cases. Durable worker-owned and controlled enterprises not only exist in most countries of the capitalist world, but over the past ten or fifteen years this form

84. The democratic aspirations of workers were undermined by government officials, who were determined that the plant would be controlled and operated in a hierarchical fashion. Only two of the nine board directorships were assigned to workers, and the internal operations of the plant were arranged along conventional lines. Government was not "prepared to see in Tembec a genuinely worker-owned and controlled enterprise.... Tembec had to be given away to someone—but not to the workers." See Keith Bradley and Alan Gelb, *Worker Capitalism: The New Industrial Relations*, London: Heinemann, 1983, p. 112. For a more positive view of Tembec see Donald V. Nightingale, *Workplace Democracy: An Inquiry into Employee Participation in Canadian Work Organizations*, Toronto: University of Toronto Press, 1982, pp. 203–209.

of work organization has enjoyed growing popularity. In the mid-1970s, France had over 600 worker-controlled firms.[85] Spain and Sweden have well known co-operative movements. In the United Kingdom, the number of worker-owned and controlled enterprises grew tenfold between 1975 and 1980; by 1982, over 480 co-operatives were operating there.[86] Between 1970 and 1980, Italian worker co-operatives increased twelve-fold, totalling some 5000 firms in 1981.[87] Worker-owned businesses are growing rapidly in the United States, and they are becoming more common in Canada as well.[88]

Worker-owned firms arise out of diverse motivations and circumstances. Some are formed by individuals committed to democratic socialist principles; in other cases the only consideration is to preserve the jobs of workers faced with impending plant closures. Co-operative enterprises have also been established to create employment. A few firms have been given to employees by their original owners. While the decision-making structure of these enterprises varies, they are owned and operated by the employees themselves.

A well publicized case is the Mondragon group of some eighty-seven financial, industrial, and service co-operatives in the Basque region of Spain. Founded by a priest in the 1940s, the first producer co-operatives started up in 1956. There are

85. Eric Batstone, "Organization and Orientation: A Life Cycle Model of French Co-operativism," *Economic and Industrial Democracy*, 4, 2, 1983, pp. 139–161.
86. Chris Cornforth, "Some Factors Affecting the Success or Failure of Worker Co-operatives: A Review of Empirical Research in the United Kingdom," *Economic and Industrial Democracy*, 4, 2, 1983, pp. 163–169.
87. Jenny Thornley, "Workers' Co-operatives and Trade Unions: The Italian Experience," *Economic and Industrial Democracy*, 4, 3, 1983, pp. 321–344.
88. Howard Aldrich and Robert N. Stern, "Resource Mobilization and the Creation of US Producer's Cooperatives, 1835–1935," *Economic and Industrial Democracy*, 4, 3, pp. 371–406. There are only fragmentary data on Canadian co-operatives. Early in 1986, two bankrupt British Columbia saw-mills opened up under ownership of their employees, who are repaying loans through payroll deductions. See Toronto *Globe and Mail*, January 9, 1986. The Toronto *Globe and Mail* reported on June 16, 1986, that provincial support for co-operative ventures is now available in Manitoba and Quebec, and that there are some 300 worker-owned enterprises in the latter province. Current information on the subject can be obtained in *Worker Co-ops*, a journal published by the Centre for the Study of Co-operatives, University of Saskatchewan. Also, see Nightingale, *op. cit.*

now sixty industrial enterprises employing about 14 000 persons, five schools, a polytechnical college, a social security cooperative, and a bank with over fifty branch offices and 170 000 members. The industrial enterprises produce goods ranging from car parts and home appliances to excavators and small ships; their annual sales exceed $1.7 billion. The appliance cooperative is Spain's leading producer of stoves and refrigerators. All the Mondragon enterprises are owned exclusively by their workers, with the exception of the bank; it is half owned by its employees and half owned by all the other co-operatives. Each enterprise's board of directors is elected by the workers—one person, one vote. The board selects a chief executive, while a general assembly of worker-owners establishes overall policy and appoints a manager for a four-year term. In contrast to conventional firms, where the income differential of employees may range from a ratio of ten or twenty to one, the earnings ratio in the Mondragon enterprises does not exceed 4.5:1.[89]

There are eleven plywood firms in the northwestern United States (Oregon and Washington) that are fully owned and controlled by their "employees." Some of the firms have been in business for as long as 35 years. They range in size from 80 to 450 worker-owners and handle about one-fifth of all softwood plywood production in the United States. The worker-owners meet annually as a general assembly to elect (again, one person, one vote) from among themselves a board of directors, which establishes overall policy for the firm. Also elected annually are the president, vice-president, and secretary-treasurer. The company officers continue working at their jobs in the plant. The board of directors appoints a manager to handle co-ordination and daily operational decisions, and the general assembly of workers sets the manager's salary. All the worker-owners receive periodic financial reports on the business, and the general assembly has the power to veto decisions by the board of directors. In fact, the general assembly has the final say over

89. *Cf.* Carnoy and Shearer, *op.cit.*, Henk Logan and Chris Thomas, *Mondragon: An Economic Analysis*, London: George Allen and Unwin, 1982; Robert Oakeshott, *The Case for Workers' Co-ops*, London: Routledge and Kegan Paul, 1978; Daniel Zwerdling, *Workplace Democracy*, New York: Harper and Row, 1980.

and responsibility for all matters. Every worker-owner from the floor sweeper to the chairman of the board receives the same rate of pay; earnings are based on the amount of time worked.[90]

Obviously, many producer co-operatives fail, but the evidence suggests that the causes of failure reside primarily in factors having nothing to do with the democratic character of the co-operatives. For example, when workers buy out firms scheduled to close in order to preserve their jobs (which is common in North America), they begin on shaky grounds. These are risky ventures from the outset—ventures that private capital abandoned because they could not be operated profitably. More generally, worker-owned firms often find it difficult to raise capital because they are operating in sectors with declining markets and/or because they receive hostile treatment from conventional financial institutions. Mondragon has overcome this problem with its own banking system, but most worker-owned firms, especially in North America, have no access to alternative sources of credit.

Despite the failures, worker co-operatives often have excellent results in terms of normal criteria of business success. Earnings in the plywood co-operatives have generally been higher than what workers earn in regular plywood firms, and jobs are much more secure. If sales drop workers take pay cuts and collectively reduce their working hours. One economic advantage enjoyed by co-operatives is that workers' commitment and diligence is high. This produces a second advantage: Less supervision is needed than in conventional firms. Mondragon is an obvious success. None of its enterprises has folded, and its record of employment stability is outstanding. Comparative studies of French producer co-operatives and the worker-owned plywood firms revealed that they out-performed capitalist enterprises.[91] As Gunn concludes, "On balance, theoretical

90. *Cf.* Paul Bernstein, *Workplace Democratization: Its Internal Dynamics*, New Brunswick, New Jersey, Transaction Books, 1980; Carnoy and Shearer, *op.cit.*; Christopher Eaton Gunn, *Workers' Self-Management in the United States*, Ithaca, New York: Cornell University Press, 1984; Zwerdling, *op.cit.*
91. Batstone, *op.cit.*; Bernstein, *op.cit.*; Seymour Melman, "Industrial Efficiency Under Managerial Versus Cooperative Decision Making: A Comparative Study of Manufacturing Enterprises in Israel," *The Review of Radical Political Economics*, 2, 1970, pp. 7–34.

debates have done little to shake the basic case for the efficiency of the labour-managed firms, and empirical findings have tended to support that case."[92]

The economic success of co-operative enterprises demonstrates that workers are both willing and able to operate businesses, and that they can do it efficiently with democratic rather than hierarchical and coercive relations. Nevertheless, there are several reasons why worker-owned organizations do not portend a gradual erosion of capitalism and why they cannot be held up as a model for the transformation of work and society. The economies of advanced capitalist nations are dominated by giant corporations with huge sums of capital and monopolistic or oligopolistic market power. Ordinary people simply do not have access to the capital required to start up, let alone compete with, these huge organizations. Most co-operatives are relatively small and develop in labour-intensive economic sectors that do not rely heavily on innovations in product or technology. Opportunities to start up self-managed enterprises are quite limited; for most wage labourers, worker ownership is simply an unrealistic alternative. This aside, the fact that worker-managed organizations in stable capitalist societies are necessarily subject to the play of market forces and its rules also restricts the growth of co-operative enterprise. Richard Hyman warns that control structures established on a local level have little choice but to accommodate the coercive and intractable demands of market-forces or government requirements.[93] Worker-owned firms are set up to provide secure and permanent incomes for their owners, thus, they must gain access to a stable market and produce commodities or provide services for a profit. Profitability has to be an essential criterion of operating the business, and this exerts a powerful influence on the policies and operations of worker-owned firms. Consequently, the technology, division of labour, and work procedures of worker-owned enterprises come to

92. Gunn, *op.cit.*, p. 43.
93. Richard Hyman, "Workers Control and Revolutionary Theory," *Socialist Register*, 1974, p. 252.

resemble the structures that prevail in capitalist firms.[94] As Marx recognized over a century ago, "The co-operative factories of labourers themselves represent within the old form the first sprouts of the new, although they naturally reproduce, and must reproduce everywhere in their actual organization all the shortcomings of the prevailing system."[95]

CONCLUSION

In this chapter a number of possible solutions to alienated labour were considered. Leisure is no answer because work dominates our waking hours and affects the way in which we spend our time away from the job. Advanced technology provides no solution because its character and uses are decided by individuals and organizations interested in profitability and the perpetuation of class relationships. The net result of developments in automated technology is to shift employment toward the least desirable end of the occupational spectrum. Moreover, the monitoring capabilities of new electronic equipment enable managers to tighten their control over the labour process. Workplace reforms introduced by practitioners of classical human relations and its contemporary QWL versions have the appearance of striking at the core of alienation. Ostensibly, these programs democratize the workplace and provide more challenging jobs. Once the progressive rhetoric is penetrated, however, these measures are exposed as schemes implemented to achieve management's purposes. Similarly, job redesign is undertaken not to create challenging jobs but to enhance profits by rationalizing the labour process. Both the human relations approach and its more sophisticated contemporary variant—participative management—are used to promote collaborative relationships between bosses and workers and to erode and ultimately destroy the collective power of

94. For excellent critical discussions of worker-owned and controlled firms see *Ibid.*; Edward S. Greenberg, "Context and Cooperation: Systematic Variation in the Political Effects of Workplace Democracy," *Economic and Industrial Democracy*, 4, 2, 1983, pp. 191–223; Harvie Ramsay and Nigel Haworth, "Worker Capitalists? Profit-Sharing, Capital-Sharing and Juridical Forms of Socialism," *Economic and Industrial Democracy*, 5, 3, 1984, pp. 295–324.
95. Karl Marx, *Capital*, Vol. III, London: Lawrence and Wishart, 1974, p. 440.

workers and unions. Unions have improved workplace conditions and the terms on which employees are obliged to dispose of their labour power. At the same time, unions represent an institutionalization rather than a resolution of conflict; collective bargaining and the contract stabilize labour-management relations. Since unions operate within rather than challenging the essential boundaries of capitalist power, they are able to deal with some of the effects but not the causes of alienated labour.

We are left with one answer—workers' control. Recall that alienation in the first instance is a structural condition in which workers are detached from control of their labour and its products. The antithesis of alienated labour is workers' control—not just over their immediate jobs but over the entire work process and its objectives. Workers' control strikes at the fundamental sources of alienation; it would entail a transfer of power from elites to working people. Decisions about the purposes of work could thus be aligned with the interests, values, and needs of workers and their communities. Technology would be designed and deployed not to enhance profits and class power but to fulfill the needs of workers and the broader community. The specialization of labour could be attacked and jobs rotated and enlarged in accordance with the needs and dispositions of individuals. The gulf separating manual and intellectual labour could be bridged, in part by the act of conceptualizing and planning, which workers in control must do, and in part by mass education, which would arm ordinary working people with a knowledge of the processes of production and distribution. These goals cannot be reached through the medium of worker-owned enterprises operating in capitalist economies dominated by giant corporations. While worker-owned enterprises obviously relieve alienation, opportunities for beginning and successfully running such undertakings are limited. Moreover, the transforming potential of such enterprises is constrained by market forces and the necessity to generate profits. The only genuine solution to alienation involves a total restructuring of the workplace, the economy, and the state; that is, the establishing of a truly collective mode of production—a democratically planned economy and worker-managed enterprises. No less than such a radical change can overcome alienation. The most intransigent source of alienation is the market, which transcends national boundaries and exerts its centripetal pull over even the most reluctant nations. But the market is nothing more than a term which summarizes a very complicated set of human relationships. As such it is not a mysterious force and is amenable to change to the degree that the social relationships underlying it are transformed.

We harbour no illusions about the ease with which people could take control of their work and their communities. Those who presently dominate the political economies of advanced capitalist nations fiercely and, if need be, violently resist encroachments on their power and privileges. Only when working people take up the struggle on a massive basis will the full development of our personal and social lives become possible.

References

Abella, I., "Oshawa 1937," in *On Strike*, edited by I. Abella, Toronto: James Lewis and Samuel, 1974, pp. 93-128.

Acheson, T.W., "The National Policy and the Industrialization of the Maritimes," in *Canada's Age of Industry: 1849-1896*, edited by M. Cross and G. Kealey, Toronto: McClelland and Stewart, 1982.

Aitken, H.G.T., *Taylorism at Watertown Arsenal*, Cambridge: Harvard University Press, 1960.

Aldrich, H. and R.N. Stern, "Resource Mobilization and the Creation of U.S. Producers' Co-operatives, 1835-1935," *Economic and Industrial Democracy*, 4, 3, 1983, pp. 371-406.

Anderson, N., *Dimensions of Work*, New York: David McKay, 1964.

Appelbaum, E., "High Tech and the Structural Employment Problems of the 1980s," in *American Jobs and the Changing Industrial Base*, edited by E. Collins and L. Dewey Tanner, Cambridge: Ballinger, 1984.

Archibald, W.P., *Social Psychology as Political Economy*, Toronto: McGraw-Hill Ryerson, 1978.

Argyris, C., *Integrating the Individual and the Organization*, New York: John Wiley and Sons, 1964.

Armstrong, H., "The Labour Force and State Workers in Canada," in *The Canadian State: Political Economy and Political Power*, edited by L. Panitch, Toronto: University of Toronto Press, 1977, pp. 289-310.

Armstrong, P. and H. Armstrong, *A Working Majority: What Women Must Do for Pay*, Ottawa: Canadian Advisory Council on the Status of Women, 1983.

Armstrong, P. and H. Armstrong, *The Double Ghetto: Canadian Women and Their Segregated Work*, Toronto: McClelland and Stewart, 1984.

Aronowitz, S., "Does the United States Have a New Working Class?" in *Revival of American Socialism*, edited by G. Fischer, New York: Oxford University Press, 1971, pp. 188-216.

Aronowitz, S., *False Promises: The Shaping of American Working Class Consciousness*, New York: McGraw-Hill, 1973.

Arthurs, H.W., *Collective Bargaining by Public Employees in Canada: Five Models*, Ann Arbor: University of Michigan Institute of Labor and Industrial Relations, 1971.

Ashford, N., *Crisis in the Workplace*, Boston: MIT Press, 1976.

Auf Der Maur, N., "James Bay: The Hatred Behind the Explosion at the LG-2 Site," *The Last Post*, 4, 1974, pp. 21-24.

Auf der Maur, N., "The May Revolt Shakes Quebec," *The Last Post*, 2, 1972, pp. 10-25.

"Automating the Office," *Canadian Dimension*, 15, December, 1981.

Avery, D., "Canadian Immigration Policy and the 'Foreign' Navvy, 1896-1914," Canadian Historical Association, *Historical Papers*, 1972, pp. 135-156.

Avery, D., *"Dangerous Foreigners": European Immigrant Workers and Labour Radicalism in Canada: 1896-1932*, Toronto: McClelland and Stewart, 1979.

Bakke, E.W., *The Unemployed Worker*, New Haven: Yale University Press, 1940.

Baritz, L., *The Servants of Power*, New York: John Wiley and Sons, 1965.

Batstone, E., "Organization and Orientation: A Life Cycle Model of French Co-operatism," *Economic and Industrial Democracy*, 4, 2, 1983, pp. 139-161.

Beckett, E., *Unions and Bank Workers: Will the Twain Ever Meet?*, Ottawa: Labour Canada Women's Bureau, 1984.

Bell, D., *The Coming of Post-Industrial Society*, New York: Basic Books, 1973.

Bell, D., *Work and its Discontents*, New York: League for Industrial Democracy, 1970.

Bennis, W., *Changing Organizations*, New York: McGraw-Hill, 1966.

Bercuson, D., "The Winnipeg General Strike," in *On Strike*, edited by I. Abella, Toronto: James Lewis and Samuel, 1974, pp. 1-32.

Berger, P., "Some General Observations on the Problem of Work," in *The Human Shape of Work*, edited by P. Berger, New York: The MacMillan Company, 1964, pp. 211-241.

Berle, A. Jr. and G. Means, *The Modern Corporation and Private Property*, New York: The Macmillan Company, 1933.

Bernard, E., *The Long Distance Feeling: A History of the Telecommunications Workers Union*, Vancouver: New Star Books, 1982.

Bernstein, I., *The Lean Years*, Boston: Houghton-Mifflin, 1960.

Bernstein, P., *Workplace Democratization: Its Internal Dynamics*, New Brunswick, New Jersey: Transaction Books, 1980.

Bertram, G.W., "Economic Growth in Canadian Industry, 1870-1915: The Staple Model," in *Approaches to Canadian Economic History*, edited by W.T. Easterbrook and M.H. Watkins, Toronto: McClelland and Stewart, 1967, pp. 74-98.

Birnbaum, N., *Toward a Critical Sociology*, New York: Oxford University Press, 1971.

Blackburn, R.M. and M. Mann, *The Working Class in the Labour Market*, London: Macmillan Press Ltd., 1979.

Blau, P., *The Dynamics of Bureaucracy*, Chicago: University of Chicago Press, 1955.

Blauner, R., *Alienation and Freedom*, Chicago: University of Chicago Press, 1967.

Bliss, M., *A Living Profit*, Toronto: McClelland and Stewart, 1974.

Boivin, J., "Labour Relations in Quebec," in *Union-Management Relations in Canada*, edited by J. Anderson and M. Gunderson, Don Mills: Addison-Wesley, 1982, pp. 422-456.

Bradley, K. and A. Gelb, *Worker Capitalism: The New Industrial Relations*, London: Heinemann, 1983.

Bradwin, E.W., *The Bunkhouse Man*, Toronto: University of Toronto Press, 1973.

Brandes, S., *American Welfare Capitalism 1880-1940*, Chicago: University of Chicago Press, 1976.

Braverman, H., *Labor and Monopoly Capital: The Degradation of Work in the Twentieth Century*, New York: Monthly Review Press, 1974.

Bright, J., *Automation and Management*, Boston: Harvard University School of Business Administration, 1958.

Brown, J.A.C., *The Social Psychology of Industry*, Harmondsworth: Penguin Books, 1954.

Burawoy, M., *Manufacturing Consent: Changes in the Labor Process Under Monopoly Capitalism*, Chicago: University of Chicago Press, 1979.

Butera, F., "Environmental Factors in Job and Organization Designs: The Case of Olivetti," in *The Quality of Working Life*, Vol. I, edited by L. Davis and A. Cherns, New York: Free Press, 1975, pp. 166-200.

Calvert, J., *Government Limited: The Corporate Takeover of the Public Sector in Canada*, Ottawa: Canadian Centre for Policy Alternatives, 1984.

Calvert, J., "Authority and Democracy in Industry," Ph.D. Thesis, London School of Economics, 1976.

Canadian Conference of Catholic Bishops, *Ethical Reflections on the Economic Crisis*, Episcopal Commission for Social Affairs, January, 1983.

Canadian Industrial Relations: The Report of the Task Force on Labour Relations, Ottawa: The Queen's Printer, 1969.

Carnoy, M. and D. Shearer, *Economic Democracy: The Challenge of the 1980s*, White Plains, New York: M.E. Sharpe, 1980.

Carroll, W., "Dependency, Imperialism and the Capitalist Class in Canada," in *The Structure of the Canadian Capitalist Class*, edited by R. Brym, Toronto: Garamond Press, 1985, pp. 21-52.

Chalk, R. and F. Von Hippel, "Due Process for Dissenting 'Whistle-Blowers'," *Technology Review*, 81, 7, 1979, pp. 49–55.

Chomsky, N., *American Power and the New Mandarins*, New York: Vintage Books, 1969.

Clement, W., *Hardrock Mining: Industrial Relations and Technological Changes at Inco*, Toronto: McClelland and Stewart, 1981.

Clement, W., *The Canadian Corporate Elite: An Analysis of Economic Power*, Toronto: McClelland and Stewart, 1975.

Clement, W., "The Corporate Elite, the Capitalist Class, and the Canadian State," in *The Canadian State: Political Economy and Political Power*, edited by L. Panitch, Toronto: University of Toronto Press, 1977, pp. 225–248.

Coburn, D., "Work, Alienation and Well-Being," in *Health and Canadian Society*, edited by D. Coburn et al., Toronto: Fitzhenry and Whiteside, 1981, pp. 420–437.

Collette, R., "Operators Dial Direct Action," *Open Road*, 12, Spring/Summer, 1981.

Collins, R., "Functional and Conflict Theories of Educational Stratification," *American Sociological Review*, 36, 1971, pp. 1002–1019.

Copp, T., *The Anatomy of Poverty: The Condition of the Working Class in Montreal 1897–1929*, Toronto: McClelland and Stewart, 1974.

Cornforth, C., "Some Factors Affecting the Success or Failure of Worker Co-operatives: A Review of Empirical Research in the United Kingdom," *Economic and Industrial Democracy*, 4, 2, 1983, pp. 163–169.

Craig, A.W., *The System of Industrial Relations in Canada*, Second Edition, Scarborough: Prentice-Hall of Canada, 1986.

Craven, P., *An Impartial Umpire: Industrial Relations and the Canadian State 1900–1911*, Toronto: University of Toronto Press, 1980.

Crispo, J.H.G. and H.W. Arthurs, "Industrial Unrest in Canada: A Diagnosis of Recent Experience," *Industrial Relations*, 23, 1968, pp. 237–265.

Cross, D.S., "The Neglected Majority: The Changing Role of Women in 19th Century Montreal," in *The Neglected Majority: Essays in Canadian Women's History*, edited by S.M. Trofimenkoff and A. Prentice, Toronto: McClelland and Stewart, 1977, pp. 66–86.

Cross, M. and G. Kealey, eds., *Canada's Age of Industry: 1849–1896*, Toronto: McClelland and Stewart, 1982.

Cuneo, C.J., "Has the Traditional Petite Bourgeoisie Persisted?", *The Canadian Journal of Sociology*, 9, Summer, 1984, pp. 269–301.

Dahl, R.A., "The Science of Public Administration: Three Problems," in *Canadian Public Administration*, edited by J.E. Hodgetts and D.C. Corbett, Toronto: Macmillan Company of Canada, 1960, pp. 24–31.

Dalton, G., "Traditional Production in Primitive African Societies," in *Tribal and Peasant Economies*, edited by G. Dalton, Garden City: The Natural History Press, 1967, pp. 61–80.

Dalton, G., ed., *Tribal and Peasant Economies*, Garden City: The Natural History Press, 1967.

Davidson, J. and J. Deverell, *Joe Davidson*, Toronto: James Lorimer, 1978.

Deaton, R., "Unemployment: Canada's Malignant Social Pathology," *Perception*, Spring–Summer, 1983, pp. 14–19.

Deffontaines, P., "The 'Rang' Pattern of Rural Settlement in French Canada," in *French Canadian Society*, Vol. I, edited by M. Rioux and Y. Martin, Toronto: McClelland and Stewart, 1970, pp. 3–19.

Derber, C., "Toward a New Theory of Professionals as Workers," in *Professionals as Workers: Mental Labor in Advanced Capitalism*, edited by C. Derber, Boston: G.K. Hall, 1982.

Deverell, J., "The Ontario Hospital Dispute, 1980–81," *Studies in Political Economy: A Socialist Review*, 9, Fall, 1982, pp. 179–190.

Djilas, M., *The New Class*, New York: Frederick A. Praeger, 1957.

Dolgoff, S., ed., *The Anarchist Collectives*, Montreal: Black Rose Books, 1974.

Drache, D., ed., *Quebec—Only the Beginning*, Toronto: New Press, 1972.

Dwyer, David, "Plant Shutdown: An Examination of the Human Consequences," M.A. Thesis, University of Western Ontario, 1984.

Easton, L.D. and K.H. Guddat, eds., *Writings of the Young Marx on Philosophy and Society*, New York: Doubleday and Company, 1967.

Edwards, P.K. and H. Scullion, *The Social Organization of Industrial Conflict: Control and Resistance in the Workplace*, Oxford: Basil Blackwell, 1982.

Edwards, R., *Contested Terrain: The Transformation of the Workplace in the Twentieth Century*, New York: Basic Books, 1979.

Edwards, R.C., M. Reich, T.E. Weiskopf, eds., *The Capitalist System*, Englewood Cliffs: Prentice-Hall, 1972.

Employment Injuries and Occupational Illnesses 1972-1981, Ottawa: Labour Canada, 1984.

Faber, S., "Working Class Organization," *Our Generation*, 11, Summer, 1976, pp. 13-26.

Faunce, W.A., *Problems of an Industrial Society*, Second Edition, New York: McGraw-Hill, 1981.

Flood, M., "The Growth of the Non-Institutional Response in the Canadian Industrial Sector," *Industrial Relations*, 27, 1972, pp. 603-615.

Flood, M., *Wildcat Strike in Lake City*, Ottawa: Information Canada, 1970.

Ford, H., "Mass Production," in *Technology, Industry and Man*, edited by C.R. Walker, New York: McGraw-Hill, 1968, pp. 51-55.

Ford, R., *Motivation Through the Work Itself*, New York: American Management Association, 1969.

Foreign Direct Investment in Canada, Ottawa: Information Canada, 1972.

Forsyth, C., "The Technician," in *Work: Twenty Personal Accounts*, Vol. I, edited by R. Fraser, Harmondsworth: Penguin Books, 1968, pp. 219-231.

Foster, J. Bellamy, "On the Waterfront: Longshoring in Canada," in *On the Job: Confronting the Labour Process in Canada*, edited by C. Heron and R. Storey, Montreal: McGill-Queen's University Press, 1978, pp. 281-308.

Fox, B., *Hidden in the Household: Women's Domestic Labour Under Capitalism*, Toronto: The Women's Press, 1980.

Gagan, D. and H. Mays, "Historical Demography and Canadian Social History: Families and Land in Peel County, Ontario," *Canadian Historical Review*, 14, 1973, pp. 27-47.

Galbraith, J.K., *The New Industrial State*, New York: Signet Books, 1967.

Gannagé, C., *Double Day, Double Bind: Women Garment Workers*, Toronto: Women's Press, 1986.

Garson, B., *All the Livelong Day: The Meaning and Demeaning of Routine Work*, New York: Penguin, 1977.

Georgopolous, B.S. and F.C. Mann, "Supervisory and Administrative Behavior," in *People and Productivity*, 2nd edition, edited by R.A. Sutermeister, New York: McGraw-Hill, 1969, pp. 359-363.

Glaberman, M., *Theory and Practice*, Detroit: Facing Reality, 1969.

Glazebrook, G.P. de T., *Life in Ontario*, Toronto: University of Toronto Press, 1968.

Gold, C., *Labor-Management Committees: Confrontation, Cooptation or Cooperation?*, Ithaca, NY: New York State School of Industrial and Labor Relations, Cornell University, 1986.

Goldthorpe, J.H., D. Lockwood, F. Bechhofer, J. Platt, *The Affluent Worker in the Class Structure*, Cambridge: The University Press, 1969.

Gonick, C., *Out of Work*, Toronto: James Lorimer, 1978.

Gonick, C., "The Twisted Mind of Donald MacDonald and Co.," *Canadian Dimension*, January-February, 1986, pp. 19-23.

Gooding, J., "The Fraying White Collar," *Fortune*, 82, 1970, pp. 78-81, 108-109.

Goodrich, C.L., *The Frontier of Control: A Study in British Workshop Politics*, London: Pluto Press, 1975 (first published 1920).

Gorz, A., "Workers' Control is More Than Just That," in *Participatory Democracy in Canada*, edited by G. Hunnius, Montreal: Black Rose Books, 1971, pp. 325-343.

Gouldner, A.W., *The Future of Intellectuals and the Rise of the New Class*, New York: Continuum, 1979.

Grayson, J.P., *Corporate Strategies and Plant Closures: The SKF Experience*, Toronto: Our Times, 1986.

Grayson, L.M. and M. Bliss, eds., *The Wretched of Canada*, Toronto: University of Toronto Press, 1971.

Greenberg, E.S., "Context and Cooperation: Systematic Variation in the Political Effects of Workplace Democracy," *Economic and Industrial Democracy*, 4, 2, 1983, pp. 191-223.

Guillet, E.C., *Pioneer Days in Upper Canada*, Toronto: University of Toronto Press, 1964.

Gunn, C. Eaton, *Workers' Self-Management in the United States*, Ithaca, NY: Cornell University Press, 1984.

Gutman, H.G., "Work, Culture, and Society in Industrializing America, 1815-1919," *American Historical Review*, 78, 1973, pp. 531-587.

Halpern, N., "Sociotechnical Systems Design: The Shell Sarnia Experience," in *Quality of Working Life: Contemporary Cases*, edited by J.B. Cunningham and T.H. White, Ottawa: Labour Canada, 1984, pp. 31-69.

Hann, R.G., G.S. Kealey, L. Kealey, P. Warrian, *Primary Sources in Canadian Working Class History, 1860-1930*, Kitchener: Dumont Press, 1973.

Harris, R.C., *The Seigneurial System in Early Canada*, Madison: University of Wisconsin Press, 1966.

Harris, R.C. and J. Warkenton, *Canada Before Confederation: A Study of Historical Geography*, Toronto: Oxford University Press, 1974.

Harvey, E., *Educational Systems and the Labour Market*, Don Mills: Longman Canada, 1974.

Harvey, E. and J. Blakely, "Education, Social Mobility and the Challenge of Technological Change," in *Transitions to Work*, University of Manitoba: Institute for Social and Economic Research, 1985, pp. 46-65.

Hébert, G., "Public Sector Bargaining in Quebec: A Case of Hypercentralization," in *Conflict or Compromise: The Future of Public Sector Industrial Relations*, edited by M. Thompson and G. Swimmer, Montreal: Institute for Research on Public Policy, 1984, pp. 229-281.

Heilbronner, R., ed., *In the Name of Profit*, New York: Doubleday and Company, 1972.

Heilbronner, R., *The Limits of American Capitalism*, New York: Harper and Row, 1965.

Henshel, R. and A.M. Henshel, *Perspectives on Social Problems*, Second Edition, Don Mills: Academic Press, 1983.

Heron, C., "The Crisis of the Craftsman: Hamilton's Metal Workers in the Early Twentieth Century," *Labour/Le Travailleur*, 6, Autumn, 1980.

Heron, C. and B.D. Palmer, "Through the Prism of the Strike: Contours and Contexts of Industrial Unrest in Southern Ontario, 1901-1914," *Canadian Historical Review*, 8, 1977, pp. 423-458.

Heron, C. and R. Storey, "On the Job in Canada," in *On the Job: Confronting the Labour Process in Canada*, edited by C. Heron and R. Storey, Montreal: McGill-Queen's University, 1978, pp. 3-46.

Heron, C. and R. Storey, eds., *On the Job: Confronting the Labour Process in Canada*, Montreal: McGill-Queen's University, 1978.

Herzberg, F., *Work and the Nature of Man*, New York: Mentor Books, 1966.

Herzberg, F., B. Mausner, B. Snyderman, *The Motivation to Work*, New York: John Wiley and Sons, 1959.

Hill, S., *Competition and Control at Work*, London: Heinemann, 1981.

Hodgetts, J.E., *The Canadian Public Service: A Physiology of Government, 1867-1970*, Toronto: University of Toronto Press, 1973.

Howard, R., *Brave New Workplace*, New York: Viking, 1985.

Hoxie, R.F., *Scientific Management and Labor*, New York: Augustus M. Kelley Publishers, 1966.

Huxley, C., "Council Communism," *Labour/Le Travailleur*, 12, Autumn, 1983.

Hyman, R., *Industrial Relations: A Marxist Introduction*, London: Macmillan, 1975.

Hyman, R., *Strikes*, London: Fontana/Collins, 1972.

Hyman, R., "Workers' Control and Revolutionary Theory," *Socialist Register*, 1974, pp. 241-278.

Isbester, F., "Asbestos 1949," in *On Strike*, edited by I. Abella, Toronto: James Lewis and Samuel, 1974, pp. 163-196.

Jamieson, S., *Times of Trouble: Labour Unrest and Industrial Conflict in Canada, 1900-66*, Ottawa: Information Canada, 1971.

Johnson, L., "The Political Economy of Ontario Women in the Nineteenth Century," in *Women at Work: Ontario, 1850-1930*, edited by J. Acton, P. Goldsmith, and B. Shepard, Toronto: Canadian Women's Educational Press, 1974, pp. 13-31.

Johnson, L.A., "Land Policy, Population Growth and Social Structure in the Home District, 1793-1851," *Ontario History*, 63, 1971, pp. 41-60.

Kadt, M. de, "Insurance: A Clerical Work Factory," in *Case Studies on the Labor Process*, edited by A. Zimbalist, New York: Monthly Review Press, 1979, pp. 242–256.

Kahn, R.L., "The Meaning of Work: Interpretation and Proposals for Measurement," in *The Human Meaning of Social Change*, edited by A. Campbell and P.E. Converse, New York: Russell Sage Foundation, 1972, pp. 159–203.

Karl Marx and Frederick Engels: Selected Works, Moscow: Progress Publishers, 1970.

Katz, M., "The People of a Canadian City: 1851-2," *Canadian Historical Review*, 53, 1972, pp. 402–426.

Kealey, G.S., *Canada Investigates Industrialism*, Toronto: University of Toronto Press, 1973.

Kealey, G.S., "The 'Honest Workingman' and Workers' Control: The Experiences of Toronto Skilled Workers, 1860–1892," *Labour/Le Travailleur*, 1, 1976, pp. 32–68.

Kealey, G.S., *Toronto Workers Respond to Industrial Capitalism, 1867–1892*, Toronto: University of Toronto Press, 1980.

Kealey, G.S., *Working Class Toronto at the Turn of the Century*, Toronto: New Hogtown Press, 1973.

Kealey, G.S., "1919: The Canadian Labour Revolt," *Labour/Le Travail*, 13, Spring, 1984, pp. 11–44.

Kealey, G.S. and B.D. Palmer, *Dreaming of What Might Be: The Knights of Labor in Ontario, 1880–1900*, New York: Cambridge University Press, 1982.

Kelly, J., *Scientific Management, Job Redesign and Work Performance*, New York: Academic Press, 1982.

Kelly, J. and D. Bilek, "White Collar Unions: Does Middle Management Want Them," *Canadian Business*, 46, 1973, pp. 56–58.

Kennedy, D.R., *The Knights of Labor in Canada*, London: University of Western Ontario, 1956.

Kerr, C., J.T. Dunlop, F.H. Harbison, C.A. Myers, *Industrialism and Industrial Man*, New York: Oxford University Press, 1969.

Kliman, M., "L'Affair Lip," *Canadian Forum*, 1974, pp. 4–8.

Kohn, M.L., *Class and Conformity*, Homewood: Dorsey Press, 1969.

Kornhauser, W., *Scientists in Industry: Conflict and Accommodation*, Berkeley: University of California Press, 1962.

Kraft, P., *Programmers and Managers: The Routinization of Computer Programming in the United States*, New York: Springer-Verlag, 1977.

Kraft, P., "The Industrialization of Computer Programming: From Programming to Software Production," in *Case Studies on the Labor Process*, edited by A. Zimbalist, New York: Monthly Review Press, 1979, pp. 1–17.

Kusterer, K.C., *Know-How on the Job: The Important Working Knowledge of "Unskilled" Workers*, Boulder, CO: Westview Press, 1978.

Kuyek, J. Newman, *The Phone Book: Working at the Bell*, Kitchener: Between the Lines, 1979.

Labour Canada Task Force on Micro-Electronics and Employment, *In the Chips*, Ottawa: Labour Canada, 1982.

Landes, D., *The Unbound Prometheus*, Cambridge: University Press, 1969.

Langdon, S., "The Emergence of the Canadian Working Class Movement, 1845-75," *Journal of Canadian Studies*, 8, 1973, pp. 3–13.

Langer, E., "The Women of the Telephone Company," *New York Review of Books*, March 12, 1970.

Leschohier, D.D., *The Knights of St. Crispin, 1867–1874*, Madison: Bulletin of the University of Wisconsin, 1910.

Likert, R., *New Patterns of Management*, New York: McGraw-Hill, 1961.

Lipton, C., *The Trade Union Movement of Canada 1827–1959*, Montreal: Canadian Social Publications, 1968.

Livingstone, D., "Job Skills and Schooling: A Class Analysis of Entry Requirements and Underemployment," in *Transitions to Work*, University of Manitoba: Institute for Social and Economic Research, 1985.

Lockwood, D., *The Blackcoated Worker*, London: Unwin, 1958.

Logan, H.A., *Trade Unions in Canada*, Toronto: The Macmillan Company, 1948.

Logan, H.A. and C. Thomas, *Mondragon: An Economic Analysis*, London: George Allen and Unwin, 1982.

Lombard, G., *Behavior in a Selling Group*, Boston: Harvard University Press, 1955.

Long, M.H., *A History of the Canadian People*, Vol. I, Toronto: Ryerson Press, 1942.

Lowe, G., "Class, Job and Gender in the Canadian Office," *Labour/Le Travailleur*, 10, Autumn, 1982.

Lowe, G., "Mechanization, Feminization, and Managerial Control in the Early Twentieth-Century Canadian Office," in *On the Job: Confronting the Labour Process in Canada*, edited by C. Heron and R. Storey, Montreal: McGill-Queen's University Press, 1978, pp. 112-209.

Lowe, G., "The Administrative Revolution in the Canadian Office: An Overview," in *Essays in Canadian Business*, edited by T. Traves, Toronto: McClelland and Stewart, 1984.

Lowe, G., "The Rise of Modern Management in Canada," *Canadian Dimension*, 14, 3, December, 1979, pp. 32-38.

Lowe, G., *Under Pressure: A Study of Job Stress*, Toronto: Garamond Press, 1986.

Lower, A.R.M., *Canadians in the Making*, Toronto: Longman Canada, 1958.

Luxton, M., *More Than a Labour of Love*, Toronto: The Women's Press, 1980.

Mackenzie, G., *The Aristocracy of Labor*, London: Cambridge University Press, 1973.

MacKinnon, M.H., "The Industrial Worker and the Job: Alienated or Instrumentalized?", in *Working in the Canadian Context*, edited by K. Lundy and B. Warme, Toronto: Butterworths, 1981, pp. 255-275.

"Management and Control of the Civil Service," in *Canadian Public Administration*, edited by J.E. Hodgetts and D.C. Corbett, Toronto: Macmillan Company of Canada, 1960, pp. 250-264.

Manga, P., R. Broyles, and G. Reschenthaler, *Occupational Health and Safety: Issues and Alternatives*, Ottawa: Economic Council of Canada, 1981.

Mansell, J., *An Inventory of Innovative Work Arrangements in Ontario*, Toronto: Ontario Ministry of Labour, 1978.

Mantoux, P., *The Industrial Revolution in the Eighteenth Century*, London: Jonathan Cape, 1961.

Marchak, P., "Women Workers and White Collar Unions," *Canadian Review of Sociology and Anthropology*, 10, 1973, pp. 134-147.

Marcson, S., *The Scientist in American Industry*, New York: Princeton University, Industrial Relations Section, 1960.

Marcuse, H., *Reason and Revolution*, Boston: Beacon Press, 1968.

Marglin, S.A., "What Do Bosses Do? The Origins and Functions of Hierarchy in Capitalist Production," *Review of Radical Political Economics*, 6, Summer, 1974.

Martijn, C.A., "Canadian Eskimo Carving in Historical Perspective," *Anthropos*, 59, 1964, pp. 546-596.

Martin, W.S., PSSRB (Public Service Staff Relations Board), Adjudication Report, 1969.

Marx, K., *Capital*, Vol. I, London: Lawrence and Wishart, 1974.

Marx, K., *Economic and Philosophic Manuscripts of 1844*, Moscow: Foreign Languages Publishing House, 1961.

Marx, K., "Wage Labour and Capital," in *Karl Marx and Frederick Engels: Selected Works*, Moscow: Progress Publishers, 1970, pp. 71-93.

Mathewson, S., *Restriction of Output Among Unorganized Workers*, Carbondale: Southern Illinois University Press, 1969.

Mayo, E., *The Human Problems of an Industrial Civilization*, Cambridge: The MacMillan Company, 1933.

McCormack, R., "The Industrial Workers of the World in Canada: 1905-1914," Canadian Historical Association, *Historical Papers*, pp. 167-190.

McDermott, P., "The New Demeaning of Work," *Canadian Dimension*, 15, December, 1981, pp. 34-37.

McDonald, J.C., *Impact and Implications of Office Automation*, Ottawa: Department of Labour, 1964.

McGregor, D., *The Human Side of Enterprise*, New York: McGraw-Hill, 1960.

Meiksins, P.F., "Science in the Labor Process: Engineers as Workers," in *Professionals as Workers: Mental Labor in Advanced Capitalism*, edited by C. Derber, Boston: G.K. Hall, 1982, pp. 121-140.

Meissner, M., "The Long Arm of the Job: Social Participation and the Constraints of

Industrial Work," in *Canada: A Sociological Profile*, 2nd edition, edited by W.E. Mann, Toronto: Copp Clark, 1971, pp. 362-377.

Melman, S., "Industrial Efficiency Under Managerial Versus Cooperative Enterprises in Israel," *The Review of Radical Political Economics*, 2, 1970, pp. 7-34.

Meltz, N.M., *Manpower in Canada 1931 to 1961: Historical Statistics of the Canadian Labour Force*, Ottawa: Department of Manpower and Immigration, 1969.

Menzies, H., *Women and the Chip: Case Studies of the Effects of Informatics on Employment in Canada*, Montreal: Institute for Research on Public Policy, 1981.

Mészáros, István, *Marx's Theory of Alienation*, New York: Harper Torchbooks, 1972.

Michels, R., *Political Parties*, New York: The Free Press, 1962 (first published in 1915).

Miliband, R., *The State in Capitalist Society*, London: Weidenfeld and Nicolson, 1969.

Miller, D.C. and W.H. Form, *Industrial Sociology*, 2nd edition, New York: Harper and Row, 1964.

Mills, C. Wright, *The New Men of Power*, New York: Harcourt, Brace, 1948.

Mills, C. Wright, *White Collar*, New York: Oxford University Press, 1956.

Moberg, D., "No More Junk: Lordstown Workers and the Demand for Quality," *Insurgent Sociologist*, 7, 1978, pp. 63-69.

Monk, J., "Working on the Assembly Line," in *Working in Canada*, Revised Second Edition, edited by W. Johnson, Montreal: Black Rose Books, 1983, pp. 49-56.

Morse, N.C. and R.S. Weiss, "The Function and Meaning of Work and the Job," *American Sociological Review*, 20, 1955, pp. 191-198.

Muir, J.D., "Collective Bargaining by Canadian Teachers: Experience and Direction," *Education Canada*, 10, 1970, pp. 40-50.

Mumford, L., *Technics and Civilization*, New York: Harcourt, Brace, 1934.

Mundy, K., "Lip Workers Win," *Canadian Dimension*, 10, 1974, pp. 13-14.

Myers, G., *A History of Canadian Wealth*, Toronto: James Lewis and Samuel, 1972.

Myers, M. Scott, "Overcoming Union Opposition to Job Enrichment," *Harvard Business Review*, 17, 1971.

Nader, R., P. Petkas, and K. Blackwell, *Whistle Blowing*, New York: Grossman, 1972.

National Council of Welfare, *The Working Poor: People and Programs*, Ottawa, 1981.

National Council of Welfare, *1984 Poverty Lines: Estimates by the National Council of Welfare*, Ottawa, March 1984, Table 2.

Nelson, D., *Managers and Workers*, Madison: University of Wisconsin Press, 1975.

Newton, K., "Employment Effects of Technological Change," Ottawa: Economic Council of Canada, 1985.

Nichols, T. and H. Beynon, *Living with Capitalism: Class Relations and the Modern Factory*, London: Routledge and Kegan Paul, 1977.

Nicolaus, M., "The Unknown Marx," in *The New Left Reader*, edited by Carl Oglesby, New York: Grove Press, 1969, pp. 84-110.

Nightingale, D.V., *Workplace Democracy: An Inquiry into Employee Participation in Canadian Work Organizations*, Toronto: University of Toronto Press, 1982.

Niosi, J., *Canadian Multinationals*, Toronto: Garamond Press, 1985.

Niosi, J., "Continental Nationalism: The Strategy of the Canadian Bourgeoisie," in *The Structure of the Canadian Capitalist Class*, edited by R. Brym, Toronto: Garamond Press, 1985, pp. 53-65.

Niosi, J., *The Economy of Canada: A Study of Ownership and Control*, Montreal: Black Rose Books, 1978.

Noble, D.F., *Forces of Production: A Social History of Industrial Automation*, New York: Alfred A. Knopf, 1984.

Oakeshott, R., *The Case for Workers' Co-ops*, London: Routledge and Kegan Paul, 1978.

Ollman, B., *Alienation: Marx's Conception of Man in Capitalist Society*, Cambridge: University Press, 1971.

Olsen, D., *The State Elite*, Toronto: McClelland and Stewart, 1980.

"One More Time: How Do You Motivate Employees?", *Harvard Business Review*, September-October, 1968, pp. 53-62.

Ornstein, M., "Canadian Capital and the Canadian State: Ideology in an Era of Crisis," in *The Structure of the Canadian Capitalist Class*, edited by R. Brym, Toronto: Garamond Press, 1985, pp. 129-161.

Orwell, G., *Homage to Catalonia*, New York: Harcourt, Brace, and World, 1952.

Palmer, B.D., *A Culture in Conflict: Skilled Workers and Industrial Capitalism in Hamilton, Ontario, 1860–1914*, Montreal: McGill-Queen's University Press, 1979.

Palmer, B.D., "Industrial Capitalism and the Emergence of a Local Proletariat: The Case of London, Ontario," University of Western Ontario, unpublished manuscript, 1973.

Palmer, B.D., "The Rise and Fall of British Columbia's Solidarity," in *The Character of Class Struggle: Essays in Canadian Working-Class History, 1850–1985*, edited by B.D. Palmer, Toronto: McClelland and Stewart, 1986, pp. 176–200.

Palmer, B.D., *Working Class Experience: The Rise and Reconstitution of Canadian Labour, 1800–1980*, Toronto: Butterworths, 1983.

Panitch, L. and D. Swartz, *From Consent to Coercion: The Assault on Trade Union Freedoms*, Toronto: Garamond Press, 1985.

Panitch, L. and D. Swartz, "Towards Permanent Exceptionalism: Coercion and Consensus in Canadian Industrial Relations," *Labour/Le Travail*, 13, 1984, pp. 133–157.

Parker, M., *Inside the Circle: A Union Guide to QWL*, Boston: South End Press, 1985.

Peitchinis, S., *Canadian Labour Economics*, Toronto: McGraw-Hill of Canada, 1970.

Pelletier, W., "Childhood in an Indian Village," in *Making it: The Canadian Dream*, edited by B. Finnigan and C. Gonick, Toronto: McClelland and Stewart, 1972, pp. 12–21.

Pentland, H.C., "The Development of a Capitalistic Labour Market in Canada," *Canadian Journal of Economics and Political Science*, 25, 1959, pp. 450–461.

(The) People's History of Cape Breton, Halifax: Opportunities for Youth, 1971.

Pierson, R.R., *"They're Still Women After All": The Second World War and Canadian Womanhood*, Toronto: McClelland and Stewart, 1986.

Phillips, P. and E. Phillips, *Women and Work: Inequality in the Labour Market*, Toronto: James Lorimer, 1983.

Phillips, P. and S. Watson, "From Mobilization to Continentalism: The Canadian Economy in the Post-Depression Period," in *Modern Canada 1930–1980's*, edited by M. Cross and G.S. Kealey, Toronto: McGraw-Hill of Canada, 1970, pp. 20–45.

Polanyi, K., *The Great Transformation*, Boston: Beacon Press, 1957.

Porter, J., *The Vertical Mosaic*, Toronto: University of Toronto Press, 1965.

Quine, T., *How Operation Solidarity Became Operation Soldout*, Toronto: International Socialists, 1985.

Ramsey, H. and N. Haworth, "Worker Capitalists? Profit-Sharing, Capital-Sharing and Juridical Forms of Socialism," *Economic and Industrial Democracy*, 5, 3, 1984, pp. 295–324.

Rankin, D.L., "The Mobilization and Demobilization of Canadian Women in the Work Force During the Second World War," M.A. Thesis, University of Western Ontario, 1986.

Reasons, C., L. Ross, and C. Patterson, *Assault on the Worker: Occupational Health and Safety in Canada*, Toronto: Butterworths, 1981.

Reiter, E., "Life in a Fast Food Factory," in *On the Job: Confronting the Labour Process in Canada*, edited by C. Heron and R. Storey, Montreal: McGill-Queen's University Press, 1978, pp. 309–326.

Reiter, E., "Out of the Frying Pan Into the Fryer—The Organization of Work in a Fast Food Outlet," Ph.D. Thesis, University of Toronto Press, 1985.

(The) Report of the Peoples' Commission on Unemployment in Newfoundland and Labrador, St. Johns: Newfoundland and Labrador Federations of Labour, 1978.

Report of the Royal Commission on the Status of Women in Canada, Ottawa: Information Canada, 1970.

Rinehart, J., "Appropriating Workers' Knowledge: Quality Control Circles at a General Motors Plant," *Studies in Political Economy*, 5, 1981, pp. 55–78.

Rinehart, J., "Contradictions of Work-Related Attitudes and Behaviour: An Interpretation," *The Canadian Review of Sociology and Anthropology*, 13, 1978, pp. 1–15.

Rinehart, J., "Improving the Quality of Working Life Through Job Redesign: Work Humanization or Work Rationalization?", *The Canadian Review of Sociology and Anthropology*, Vol. 23, no. 4, 1986, pp. 507–530.

Roberts, M., "A Labor Perspective on Technological Change," in *American Jobs and the Changing Industrial Base*, edited by E. Collins and L. Dewey Tanner, Cambridge: Ballinger, 1984, pp. 183–205.

Roberts, W., *Honest Womenhood: Feminism, Femininity and Class Consciousness Among Toronto Working Women, 1893 to 1914*, Toronto: New Hogtown Press, 1976.

Roberts, W. and J. Bullen, "A Heritage of Hope and Struggle: Workers, Unions, and Politics in Canada, 1930–1982," in *Modern Canada 1930–1980's*, edited by M. Cross and G.S. Kealey, Toronto: McClelland and Stewart, 1984, pp. 105–140.

Rocher, G., "Research on Occupations and Social Stratification," in *French Canadian Society*, Vol. I, edited by M. Rioux and Y. Martin, Toronto: McClelland and Stewart, 1970, pp. 328–341.

Roethlisberger, F.J., *The Elusive Phenomenon*, Boston: Harvard University Graduate School of Business Administration, 1977.

Roethlisberger, F.J., and W.J. Dickson, *Management and the Worker*, Cambridge: Harvard University Press, 1939.

Romano, P. and R. Stone, *The American Worker*, Detroit: Bewick Editions, 1972.

Rose, J.B., "Growth Patterns of Public Sector Unions," in *Conflict or Compromise: The Future of Public Sector Industrial Relations*, edited by M. Thompson and G. Swimmer, Montreal: Institute for Research on Public Policy, 1984, pp. 83–119.

Rosenbluth, G., "Concentration and Monopoly in the Canadian Economy," in *Social Purpose for Canada*, edited by M. Oliver, Toronto: University of Toronto Press, 1961, pp. 199–248.

Ross, D.P., *The Working Poor: Wage Earners and the Failure of Income Security Policies*, Toronto: James Lorimer, 1981.

Roy, D.F., "Banana Time: Job Satisfaction and Informal Interaction," *Human Organization*, 18, 1960, pp. 158–168.

Roy, D.F., "Making Out: A Counter-System of Workers' Control of Work Situation and Relationships," in *Industrial Man*, edited by T. Burns, Harmondsworth: Penguin Books, 1969, pp. 359–379.

Roy, D., "Quota Restriction and Goldbricking in a Machine Shop," in *Readings in Industrial Sociology*, edited by W.A. Faunce, New York: Appleton–Century–Crofts, 1967, pp. 311–334.

Roy, D.F., "Work Satisfaction and Social Reward in Quota Achievement: An Analysis of Piecework Incentive," *American Sociological Review*, 18, 1953, pp. 507–514.

Royal Commission on the Economic Union and Development Prospects for Canada, Ottawa: Ministry of Supply and Services Canada, 1985.

Ryan, W., *Blaming the Victim*, New York: Vintage Books, 1972.

Ryerson, S.B., *Unequal Union*, Toronto: Progress Books, 1973.

Sable, C.F., *Work and Politics: The Division of Labour in Industry*, New York: Cambridge University Press, 1982.

Sahlins, M., *Stone Age Economics*, New York: Aldine–Atherton, 1972.

Salzman, H. and P. Mirvis, "The Work Force Transition to New Computer Technologies: Changes in Skills and Quality of Work Life," in *Transitions to Work*, edited by E.B. Harvey and J. Blakely, University of Manitoba: Institute for Social and Economic Research, 1985, pp. 66–87.

Schacht, J., "Toward Industrial Unionism: Bell Telephone Workers and Company Unions, 1919–1937," *Labor History*, 16, 1, 1975, pp. 5–36.

Scott, B., "'A Place in the Sun': The Industrial Council at Massey-Harris, 1919–1929," *Labour/Le Travailleur*, 1, 1976, pp. 158–192.

Sennett, R. and J. Cobb, *The Hidden Injuries of Class*, New York: Alfred A. Knopf, 1973.

Sexton, P.C. and B. Sexton, *Blue Collars and Hard Hats*, New York: Vintage Books, 1971.

Shaiken, H., *Work Transformed: Automation and Labor in the Computer Age*, New York: Holt, Rinehart and Winston, 1984.

Shapiro, M., *Getting Doctored: Reflections on Becoming a Physician*, Kitchener: Between the Lines, 1978.

Sheppard, H.L. and N.Q. Herrick, *Where Have All the Robots Gone?: Worker Dissatisfaction in the 70s*, New York: The Free Press, 1973.

Simon, H., "Authority," in *Research in Industrial Human Relations—A Critical Appraisal*, New York: Praeger, 1957.

Simpson, R.L. and I.H. Simpson, "Women and Bureaucracy in the Semi-Professions," in *The Semi-Professions and Their Organization: Teachers, Nurses, Social Workers*, edited by A. Etzioni, New York: The Free Press, 1969, pp. 196–265.

Smith, D.A., "Strikes in the Canadian Public Sector," in *Conflict or Compromise: The*

Future of Public Sector Industrial Relations, edited M. Thompson and G. Swimmer, Montreal: Institute for Research on Public Policy, 1984, pp. 197-228.

Social Planning Council of Metropolitan Toronto, *Guides for Family Planning*, 1981.

Spelt, J., *The Urban Development in South-Central Ontario*, Assen: Koninkeyke Van Gorcum, 1955.

Statistics Canada, *Employment Earnings and Hours*, Ottawa, May 1981.

Stirling, R. and D. Kouri, "Unemployment Indexes—The Canadian Context," in *Economy, Class and Social Reality: Issues in Contemporary Canadian Society*, edited by J. Fry, Toronto: Butterworths, 1979, pp. 169-205.

Storey, R., "Unionism, Politics and Culture: Steel Workers and the Hamilton Working Class 1935-1948," Ph.D. Thesis, University of Toronto, 1981.

Sugiman, P.H., "The Sales Clerks: Worker Discontent and Obstacles to its Collective Expression," *Atlantis*, 8, 1982, pp. 13-33.

Susman, G.I., "Process Design, Automation, and Worker Alienation," *Industrial Relations*, 11, 1972, pp. 34-45.

Swimmer, G., "Militancy in Public Sector Unions," in *Conflict or Compromise: The Future of Public Sector Industrial Relations*, edited by M. Thompson and G. Swimmer, Montreal: Institute for Research on Public Policy, 1984, pp. 147-195.

Tanzer, M., *The Sick Society*, New York: Holt, Rinehart, and Winston, 1968.

Tataryn, L., "A Tragically Repeating Pattern: Issues of Industrial Safety," in *Work in the Canadian Context*, edited by K. Lundy and B. Warme, Toronto: Butterworths, 1981.

Taylor, F.W., *The Principles of Scientific Management*, New York: Harper and Brothers, 1919.

Taylor, F.W., *Scientific Management*, New York: Harper and Brothers, 1947.

Taylor, L., *Occupational Sociology*, New York: Oxford University Press, 1968.

Taylor, L. and P. Walton, "Industrial Sabotage: Motives and Meanings," in *Images of Deviance*, edited by S. Cohen, Harmondsworth: Penguin Books, 1971, pp. 219-244.

Teeple, G., "Land, Labour, and Capital in Pre-Confederation Canada," in *Capitalism and the National Question in Canada*, edited by G. Teeple, Toronto: University of Toronto Press, 1972, pp. 43-66.

Terkel, S., *Working*, New York: Pantheon Books, 1974.

Thomas, K., "Work and Leisure in Pre-Industrial Society," *Past and Present*, December, 1964, pp. 50-62.

Thompson, E.P., "Time, Work-Discipline, and Industrial Capitalism," *Past and Present*, December, 1967, pp. 56-97.

Thompson, M., "Collective Bargaining by Professionals," in *Union-Management Relations in Canada*, edited by J. Anderson and M. Gunderson, Don Mills: Addison-Wesley, 1982, pp. 379-397.

Thompson, M. and G. Swimmer, "Summary," in *Conflict or Compromise: The Future of Public Sector Industrial Relations*, edited by M. Thompson and G. Swimmer, Montreal: Institute for Research on Public Policy, 1984, pp. xiii-xliv.

Thompson, P., *The Nature of Work: An Introduction to Debates on the Labour Process*, London: Macmillan, 1983.

Thornley, J., "Workers' Co-operatives and Trade Unions: The Italian Experience," *Economic and Industrial Democracy*, 4, 3, 1983, pp. 321-344.

Todd, R., "Notes on Corporate Man," *The Atlantic*, 228, 1971, pp. 83-88, 91-94.

Touraine, A., *The Post-Industrial Society*, New York: Random House, 1971.

Traves, T., "Security Without Regulation," in *The Consolidation of Capitalism, 1896-1929*, edited by M. Cross and G. Kealey, Toronto: McClelland and Stewart, 1983.

Trist, E., *The Evolution of Socio-Technical Systems*, Toronto: Ontario Quality of Working Life Centre, 1981.

Trist, E., G. Higgin, H. Murray, and A. Pollock, *Organizational Choice*, London: Tavistock, 1963.

Trofimenkoff, S., "One Hundred and Two Muffled Voices: Canada's Industrial Women in the 1880's," in *Canada's Age of Industry: 1849-1896*, edited by M. Cross and G. Kealey, Toronto: McClelland and Stewart, 1982.

Trower, C., "Collective Bargaining and Industrial Democracy," in *Workers' Control*, edited by G. Hunnius, G.D. Garson, and J. Case, New York: Vintage Books, 1973, pp. 136-144.

"Unemployment: A New Analysis," *Our Generation*, 8, 1972, pp. 6–26.

U.S. Department of Health, Education & Welfare, *Work in America: Report of a Special Task Force to the Secretary of Health, Education & Welfare*, Cambridge: MIT Press, 1972.

U.S. Department of Labor, *Characteristics of Company Unions 1935*, Bulletin no. 634, June 1937.

"Up Against the State: Experiences of a Railworkers' Group," *The Newsletter*, April, 1974.

Ure, A., *The Philosophy of Manufacturers*, London: Charles Knight, 1835.

Urquhart, M.C. and K.A.H. Buckley, eds., *Historical Statistics of Canada*, Toronto: MacMillan Company of Canada, 1965.

Váli, F., *Rift and Revolt in Hungary*, Cambridge: Harvard University Press, 1961.

Wallace, J., "Building Up Office Efficiency," *Canadian Business*, 43, 1970, pp. 46–55.

Wallot, J., "Le Régime Seigneurial et Son Abolition Au Canada," *Canadian Historical Review*, 50, 1969, pp. 367–393.

Warrian, P., "The Challenge of the One Big Union Movement in Canada 1919-1921," M.A. Thesis, University of Waterloo, 1971.

Watson, B., *Counterplanning on the Shop Floor*, Boston: New England Free Press, 1972.

Weber, M., *The Protestant Ethic and the Spirit of Capitalism*, New York: Charles Scribner's Sons, 1930.

Wei Djao, A., "The Welfare State and Its Ideology," in *Economy, Class and Social Reality: Issues in Contemporary Canadian Society*, edited by John Fry, Toronto: Butterworths, 1979, pp. 300–315.

Wells, D., "Autoworkers on the Firing Line," in *On the Job: Confronting the Labour Process in Canada*, edited by C. Heron and R. Storey, Montreal: McGill–Queen's University Press, 1978.

Wells, D., *Soft Sell: "Quality of Working Life" Programs and the Productivity Race*, Ottawa: The Canadian Centre for Policy Alternatives, 1986.

Whitaker, R., "The Liberal Corporatist Ideas of Mackenzie King," *Labour/Le Travailleur*, 2, 1977, pp. 137–169.

White, J., *Women and Part-Time Work*, Ottawa: The Canadian Advisory Council on the Status of Women, 1983.

White, T., *Human Resource Management—Changing Times in Alberta*, Edmonton: Alberta Labour, 1979.

Whitehead, T.N., *Leadership in a Free Society*, Cambridge: Harvard University Press, 1936.

Whyte, W.F., *Money and Motivation*, New York: Harper and Brothers, 1955.

Whyte, W.H., *The Organization Man*, New York: Doubleday Anchor Books, 1957.

Wilensky, J. and H. Wilensky, "Personal Counselling: The Hawthorne Case," *American Journal of Sociology*, 57, 1951/1952, pp. 265–280.

Williams, G., *Not for Export: Towards a Political Economy of Canada's Arrested Industrialization*, Toronto: McClelland and Stewart, 1983.

Wilson, G.W., S. Gordon, and S. Judek, *Canada: An Appraisal of its Needs and Resources*, Toronto: University of Toronto Press, 1965.

Wolfe, D.A., "The Rise and Demise of the Keynesian Era in Canada: Economic Policy 1930-1982," in *Modern Canada 1930-1980's*, edited by M. Cross and G.S. Kealey, Toronto: McClelland and Stewart, 1984, pp. 46–78.

Women at Work in Nova Scotia, Halifax: Halifax Women's Bureau, 1973.

Wood, S., ed., *The Degradation of Work? Skill, Deskilling and the Labour Process*, London: Hutchinson, 1983.

Zeitlin, M., "Corporate Ownership and Control: The Large Corporation and the Capitalist Class," *American Sociological Review*, 79, 1974, pp. 1073–1119.

Zeitlin, M., *Revolutionary Politics and the Cuban Working Class*, New York: Harper Torchbooks, 1970.

Zimbalist, A., ed., *Case Studies on the Labor Process*, New York: Monthly Review Press, 1979.

Zinner, P.E., *Revolution in Hungary*, New York: Columbia University Press, 1962.

Zwerdling, D., *Workplace Democracy*, New York: Harper and Row, 1980.

INDEX